THE LIFE OF EKNĀTH

THE LIFE OF EKNĀTH

ŚRĪ EKNĀTH CHARITA

Translated from the Bhaktalīlāmṛta

JUSTIN E. ABBOTT

with the Introduction by
G.V. TAGARE

MOTILAL BANARSIDASS PUBLISHERS
PRIVATE LIMITED • DELHI

First Edition: Poona, 1927
Reprint: Delhi, 1981, 1983, 1997

ISBN: 81-208-1360-x (Cloth)
ISBN: 81-208-1361-8 (Paper)

Also available at:

MOTILAL BANARSIDASS
41 U.A. Bungalow Road, Jawahar Nagar, Delhi 110 007
8, Mahalaxmi Chamber, Warden Road, Mumbai 400 026
120 Royapettah High Road, Mylapore, Madras 600 004
Sanas Plaza, Subhash Nagar, Pune 411 002
16 St. Mark's Road, Bangalore 560 001
8 Camac Street, Calcutta 700 017
Ashok Rajpath, Patna 800 004
Chowk, Varanasi 221 001

PRINTED IN INDIA
BY JAINENDRA PRAKASH JAIN AT SHRI JAINENDRA PRESS,
A-45 NARAINA, PHASE I, NEW DELHI 110 028
AND PUBLISHED BY NARENDRA PRAKASH JAIN FOR
MOTILAL BANARSIDASS PUBLISHERS PRIVATE LIMITED,
BUNGALOW ROAD, DELHI 110 007

DEDICATED

TO THE MEMORY OF MY BELOVED WIFE,

CAMILLA,

who died at Miraj June 26th, 1921 who shared with me interest in the Poet-saints of Mahārāshṭra; who visited with me the shrines of Dnyāneśvara, Nāmdeva, Janārdan, Eknāth, Tukārām and Rāmdās, at Ālandi, Paṇdharpur, Devagiri, Paiṭhan Dehu, Parali, and other places dear to the Indian heart; who, wherever she went, left a kindly memory; whose last conscious words were

"We must do more to make this a better and a happier world."

PREFACE

In my volume on Bhānudās, the first in the *Poet-saints of Mahārāshṭra* Series, I Indulged in a rather lengthy Preface, covering the whole ground of my purpose and plans regarding the Series. A resumé of that Preface is all that seems necessary here.

In that Preface I called attention to the fact that I felt there was moral value in the stories of the Marāṭhā Saints, and that that fact had influenced me to make these translations. For these translations I had chosen the oldest original sources, or at least those that were the best expression of tradition. I paid my respects to Mahīpati, who collected the old stories, and rewrote them in his own graphic style. I briefly discussed the question of the historic character of these stories, and the confused subject of chronology. I confessed to difficulties in the path of these translations, and of their production in India. But I expressed my confidence in the generosity and courtesy of my Indian readers, to whom I was offering these flowers, if I may be permitted so to call them. I made my *namaskār* to those Marāṭhī scholars who have done so much for the old Marāṭhī literature, and expressed my thanks to Dr. Nicol Macnicol for his extreme kindness in seeing these translations through the press.

As a special preface to this volume on Eknāth the following points may be referred to.

The reader may ask why I translated Mahīpati's account in the Bhaktalīlāmṛita, when that account is but the same story as that told by Keśavaswāmi, only rewritten in Mahīpati's own words. The truthful answer is that I had already translated it before I was properly aware of Keśavaswāmi's version, and the relation of Mahīpati's Bhaktalīlāmṛta to it. However, Mahīpati's version has this advantage that the story of Eknāth is more interestingly told. And moreover the slight differences between his account and that of Keśava may possibly be accounted for; because of access to other traditions, such as he used when twelve years before he wrote the short and incomplete account of Eknāth in his Bhaktavijaya. To this may be added the advantage of using Mahīpati's Bhaktalīlāmṛta account as it is the popular version for all modern references to Eknāth. The two modern *Eknāth charitras* by Sahasrabuddhe and Pāṅgārkar and Ajgaonkar in Marāṭhī are but resumés of this Bhaktalīlāmṛta account.

A few words regarding Mahīpati, the author of the Bhaktalīlāmṛita will not be out of place. He was born at Tāharābād in the Rāhuri Tālukā of the Ahmednagar District in the year 1715. He was early inclined to the religious life, but the death of his father necessitated his engaging in secular affairs. He was for a time a Government servant, but finding his worldly duties interfering with his religious inclinations he gave up the former. His interest centered on the lives of the Marāṭhā Saints, and his writings are nearly all on that subject. He is the author of many works, but the two for which he is especially known are the Bhaktavijaya, completed in 1762, and the Bhaktalīlāmṛta completed in 1774. (See Mahārāshṭra Sārasvata by Mr. V. E. Bhave, first edition, page 372, on Mahīpati.)

It would have been possible to add to my translation any number of references and footnotes. They would have interested scholars, but would be a burden to the ordinary reader and certainly a burden to the writer, who feels his time and strength can be better employed.

I am aware of many defects connected with these translations and accompanying notes. The reader will, however, bear in mind that hitherto little has been done to give to English readers a knowledge of the lives of the Marāṭhā saints. A pioneer has always difficulties that do not beset the path of those who follow. Edwards' *Life of Tukārām*, and the *Poems of Tukārām*, translated by Fraser and Marāṭhe, are the only attempts hitherto made that give a full account of a Marāṭhā saint, and his works. Short resumés of the lives of the most prominent of the Marāṭhā saints appear in many works, and in many histories of the Marāṭhā people. *Tales of the Saints of Pandharpur* by C. A. Kincaid is a condensation of stories from the Bhaktavijaya (the story of Eknāth is strangely omitted.) Dr. Nicol Macnicol has very effectively put into English verse many of the lines of the Marāṭhā poets. But so far as I am aware no English writer has taken up an exhaustive study of the whole field of the Marāṭhā saints. In therefore leading the way by means of translations of the original sources I have met with difficulties of many kinds, and I am only too well aware of the imperfections of my work. But, if my efforts bring about a better acquaintance with the Marāṭhā saints, my real object will have been accomplished, and the path will be easier for those who follow me.

My own feeling regarding Eknāth is that, although he does not enjoy the popularity of Tukārām as to his writings, in character, in ideals, in learning, in the consistency and nobleness of his life, he is the greatest of the Marāṭhā poet-saints. I have already expressed the opinion that these traditional stories, told by Mahīpati and others, are not necessarily exact history, but rather history plus the variations that have come about as they were handed down from mouth to mouth, and yet that are in keeping with the impression which the man made on his generation. That impression is after all the mportant thing, and there Eknāth excels.

JUSTIN E. ABBOT,
Summit, N. J.,
U. S. A.
April 1926

CONTENTS

INTRODUCTION
(Eknāth and his works)

Eknāth (A.D. 1533 ?—1599), the great scholar-philosopher-saint-poet *cum* social reformer occupies a unique place among the saints of Maharashtra. "He surpassed all saints (of Maharashtra) in accomplishing a high degree of reconciliation between worldly and spiritual life" (R. D. Ranade—*Indian Mysticism* p. 256). He did not write for personal fame but for the uplift of the masses by spreading the gospel of Lord Kṛṣṇa among the down-trodden voice-less millions to whose service he devoted his life. Naturally, a cycle of legends enveloped the historical Eknāth as can be seen from the following. J. E. Abbot's translation of Mahipati's works which were based on Keśava's "Life of Eknāth" written at Devagad in A.D. 1720 (Śaka 1642). It must be conceded that many of the stories must have some historical basis in the actual life of that saint. I, however, write on the evidence given by Eknāth himself and his earliest biographer Kṛṣṇadāsa Jagadānanda. The latter wrote his *Pratiṣṭhāna-caritra* (P.C.) in 1698 (Śaka 1620)—within hundred years after Eknāth and shows some historical sense. It seems that it was not available to Mahipati and due to its publication in 1948 (Trinity Publications, Bombay), modern biographers of Eknāth of the last generation (e.g. Pangarkar, Ajgaonkar and others) were not aware of it.

The following appear to be the facts regarding the life of Eknāth :

Eknāth was the great-grandson of Saint Bhānudāsa of Paiṭhaṇa, a holy place on the Godāvarī, a traditional centre of Sanskrit learning possibly from the days of the ancient

Sātavāhanas who ruled over the Deccan from this place. Bhānudāsa was the leader of the deputation of saints of Maharashtra who visited the king of Vijayanagar and brought back the idol of Śrī Viṭṭhala and re-installed it at Pandharpur. His son Cakrapāṇi who brought up orphan Eknāth, was also a wellknown scholar-saint. We are told that when Eknāth went to Janārdana for his education, the latter asked him why on earth Eknāth took the trouble of coming to him when Cakrapāṇi himself was "a great saint and scholar who had realized the Brahman" (PC.2.30-40)

Eknāth lost his mother Rukmiṇī Bāī when he was hardly one year old and his father Sūrya-nārāyaṇa when he was about three years of age (PC.1.20). Sūrya-nārāyaṇa is called "a warrior" (PC.1.19) by profession (?). The birth-date of Eknāth is yet to be firmly established but as the tradition goes, he accepted voluntary death (*Samādhi*) at the age of 66 in A.D. 1599, hence 1533 is presumed as his birth-date. Cakrapāṇi brought up Eknāth, the only scion of his family. Noting the bright intelligence of his grand-son and his own advanced age, Cakrapāṇi entrusted Eknāth to his junior friend Janārdana Swamy (A.D. 1504—1575) who was a famous scholar-saint of that period. PC. states that he was at "Amadāvatī" (Mod. Ahmednagar ?) and not at Daulatabad or Devagiri as in Mahipati. The name of Janārdana's spiritual preceptor is given as Candraśekhara (PC.1.28) and is called the "incarnation of Dattātreya". Janārdana was transferred to Daulatabad after completion of Eknāth's education (in *circa* 1547) (PC.4.101—104). Janārdana accepted Eknāth after convincing himself that Eknāth was deputed to him for further education by Cakrapāṇi and Eknāth did not run away to Janārdana. Eknāth had to be convinced by Cakrapāṇi that he and Janārdana were one and that he should accept Janārdana as his parents and *guru* (PC. 1.62-75). This version appears more reasonable than the current story of Eknāth's secretly running-away from his affectionate aged grand-father and not communicating to him for 12 years and Cakrapāṇi's total ignorance about the whereabouts of Eknāth who was at Devagiri—not far-off from Paiṭhaṇa.

Not much information about the course of studies of that period is available. From PC. Ch. 3, we learn that Janārdana made Eknāth undergo spiritual exercise early at dawn (*Brāhma Muhūrta*), then trained him in vocal music which was (and still is) necessary for performance of *Kirtana*. Eknāth helped his *guru* in office-work which included Accountancy. He attended the office along with his *guru*. From Eknāth's writing it is clear that Janārdana taught him Śaṅkara Vedānta and all the accessories like Grammar, Mīmāṁsā and others. Janārdana elucidated the (Sk.) *Bhāgavata Purāṇa* (Bh.P.) and the *Bhagvad Gitā* (as interpreted by Jñānadeva). Eknāth quotes Jñānadeva so profusely and shows his mastery of that work in his commentary on the Bh.P. Skandha XI that he must have learnt that text under his *guru*. His edition of *Jñāneśvarī* and renovation of the Samādhi of Jñānadeva at Ālandī in later life, show how deeply he was devoted to Jñāneśvara.

Janārdana did not make Eknāth do laborious work or any menial work for him. On the contrary, when Eknāth voluntarily tried to render such service, Janārdana ran to him and washed him clean with his own hands (PC.4.40-44). It appears that by the age of 14, Eknāth completed his education. Janārdana, of his own accord, found a bride for Eknāth —the daughter of Trivikrama Śāstrī of Daulatabad. Cakrapāṇi and his wife—the grand-parents of Eknāth were duly invited. Janārdana paid his respects to his elderly friend Cakrapāṇi, and requested him to take with him his newly-married grandson. The marriage was celebrated with great *eclat*. Janārdana urged Cakrapāṇi to stay with him for one month, after which he gifted ornaments to Eknāth and asked him to keep his grand-father in happiness. At the insistence of Eknāth, Janārdana gave his *Pādukās* (wooden sandals) to Eknāth (PC.4.50-100) for worship.

It was after Eknāth's departure to Paiṭhaṇa that Janārdana was transferred to Daulatabad (PC. 4.101-102)

The above version differs from the current legends according to which Eknāth went to Janārdana at Daulatabad and performed the pilgrimage of northern India and stopped at the very place in Paiṭhaṇa where he got his *guru's* letter to discontinue his pilgrimage forthwith. Traditionally it is believed that Eknāth's bride Girajābāī hailed from Bījapur (Karnatak).

Eknāth belonged to a well-to-do family. As there was no need for him to earn money to maintain his family, Eknāth spent the rest of his life in writing books and preaching (both by elucidating the Purāṇas especially the Bh.P. and by *Kīrtana*). The daily routine of his life described in Ch. 5 of the PC shows how he was strictly regular in performing his duties as a Brāhmaṇa house-holder and a preacher and saint setting up a model for others to follow. When he was summoned to Varanasi, he spent three years (A.D. 1570-73) there, where he completed his commentary of the Bh.P. XI and wrote a spiritual romance *Rukmiṇī-Svayaṁvara*. In A.D. 1583 he went to Āḷandī and got the *Samādhi* of Jñāneśvara renovated and the next year (A.D. 1584) he completed his (the-then type of) critical edition of the *Jñāneśvarī*. He began to write the voluminous *Bhāvārtha Rāmāyaṇa*, but left it incomplete and took *Samādhi* in A.D. 1599 on the 6th day in the dark half of Phālguna—a date of crucial importance in the life of Janārdana and Eknāth.

WORKS OF EKNĀTH

Eknāth was a prolific writer. He contributed profusely

to all the forms of literature in vogue in his times. But he was a saint, a preacher and a philosopher first. Being a gifted poet, he utilised his literary capacities for the uplift and spiritual education of the masses. Fortunately, he met an equally competent *guru* (spiritual preceptor) who synthesized the spiritual and the temporal or rather spiritualized the temporal life. He brought up his pupil not only in the rigorous dicipline of Yoga and Bhakti but taught him the basic texts of the Śāṅkara (*Advaita*) Vedānta, Śrīmad Bhāgavata and elements of Sanskrit Grammar, lexicons, Pūrva Mīmāṁsā and such other disciplines necessary for the proper understanding and propagation of Vedānta and Bhakti. Eknāth's mastery over Jñānadeva's Commentary on the *Bhagavadgitā* shows his close study of the text in his student days. His *guru* Janārdana encouraged him to write commentaries on Vedāntic texts in Marathi and there is some ground to believe that at least the first few chapters of his *magnum opus*, his commentary on the eleventh Skandha of the *Bhāgavata Purāṇa* (Bh.P.)was seen and blessed by Janārdana.

CATUḤŚLOKĪ BHĀGAVATA

The first contribution worth the name is Eknāth's commentary on the *Catuḥ-śloki Bhāgavata*. This title is applied to Bh.P.II.9.32-35. These are regarded as being addressed by Lord Nārāyaṇa to god Brahmā when he was at a loss to know how to create the world and as such are regarded as the essence of the Bh.P.—in fact the whole of the 9th Chapter of the II Skandha is the elucidation of that essence and Eknāth commented practically on that complete chapter. As to the *genesis* of the work the legend goes that while Janārdana along with Eknāth was going for the pilgrimage of Nasik and Tryambakeśvara, they happened to halt in the evening in the house of a Brāhmaṇa called Candra Bhaṭa at Cāndavaḍa in Nasik district. As was his usual, Candra Bhaṭa delivered his sermon on *Catuḥ-śloki Bhāgavata*. That appealed to Janārdana so deeply that he asked his pupil Eknāth to write a lucid interpretation of those verses.* Under the guidance of his *guru*, Eknāth completed his commentary on *Catuḥ-śloki Bhāgavata* during that pilgrimage.

As this was his first work, he thought it audacious on his part to translate an important Sk. work like the Bh.P the translation of which, according to his knowledge, was not attempted by anyone. Hence, Eknāth gratefully acknowledges the debt of his *guru*: "It is Janārdana who made me speak whatever has been stated in this book".*

In this short treatise of 1036 *Ovis verses*, we find the making of a future great commentator of the Bh.P.

MISCELLANEOUS TREATISES

Eknāth shows more philosophic maturity in his interpretation of Śaṅkara's *Hastāmalaka* and *Śukāṣṭaka* and his small but independent treatises like *Ānanda-lahari* (Surges of spiritual delight) and *Svātma-sukha* (Bliss of the Self). In these he advocates what may be called 'Karma Yoga' in modern parlance. He advocates the one-ness of God and Man :

Jana toci Janārdana / Jana Janārdana abhinna.

According to him, equanimity and sense of equality to all living beings is *Samādhi* and not the wooden-log like motionless state of the body. (*Svātma-sukha* 1060-1061)

These smaller treatises show that a full-fledged competent interpreter of the philosophy of the Bh.P. was now prepared to undertake the elucidation of the eleventh Skandha of the Bh.P.

०तेणे स्वानंदे गर्जोन । श्रीमुखें स्वयें जनार्दन । बोलिला अति सुखावून । हें वर्णी गुह्यज्ञान देशभाषा ।।

Catuś śloki Bhāgavata Ovi : 102

THE BHĀGAVATA PURĀṆA

The *Bhagavadgītā* (BG) and the *Bhāgavata Purāṇa* (Bh.P.) are regarded as the basic texts of Vaiṣṇavism in Maharashtra. The influence of the latter is so great that Vaiṣṇavism in this region is called *Bhāgavata Sampradāya*. As Eknāth explicitly states, it was Janārdana who created in him such absorbing interest in the Bh.P. (EB.-*Eknāthi Bhāgavata* 15.21-23). It was Janārdana who completed him to expound (the Bh.P.) (EB. 9.454 -456). "Just as a father holds the hand of a child for copy-writing, Janārdana made me elucidate the inner significance of XI Skandha (of the Bh.P.). It is under my name that Janārdana himself became the author (i.e. he wrote this under my name) (EB.31.497-560).

There is possibly another reason for the selection of the Bh.P. XI. Although written some three centuries back, there was a good Marathi commentary on the BG. Dāsopant, a contemporary of Eknāth was writing a bulky commentary on the same. The Bh.P. XI like the BG., is a discourse between Lord Kṛṣṇa and another of his dearest friend and devotee Uddhava, the philosophic import of which is similar to the BG., though the object was different. And no commentary worth the name was available in non-Mahānubhava sects on this Skandha. This is probably the consideration which might have led Janārdana to the selection of the Bh.P. But Eknāth was such a great author that his exposition of the Bh.P.XI is "so simple, so lucid, and so popular that nobody before his time or nobody after him has ever been equally successful in presenting philosophy in such a popular manner" (R.D. Ranade—*Indian Mysticism*, pp. 256-57)

---

*He states elsewhere that his *guru's* order was so powerful that he could visualize the inner significance of the work while doing the usual worldly duties, even during sleep. Hence Janārdana is the real expounder of the inner meaning of the work (*Catuḥ ślokī Bhāgavata* 1002-1006

Eknāth began his commentary on the Bh.P. XI. at Paiṭhaṇa in A.D. 1570 (Śaka 1492). He completed the first five chapters of the work at Paiṭhaṇa. Though Eknāth is silent about the reasons of his migration to Varanasi to write the remaining 26 chapters there, the legend goes that while a Brāhmaṇa disciple of Eknāth was reading these preliminary chapters on the bank of the Gaṅgā at Varanasi, the Pandits thereof became infuriated that the holy teaching of Vyāsa was being "polluted in the vernacular spoken by Śūdras" and Eknāth was summoned to Varanasi where he convinced the Pandits that his was the correct interpretation and that translation of a holy work in a modern language does not pollute it. And when the work was completed (as the traditional legend goes) the presiding deity of Varanasi vouchsafed for the correctness of translation after which it was led in a procession—a sort of a victory-parade on behalf of the upholders of the cause of modern Indo-Aryan languages.

The colophon of this Commentary (*Ekākāra-ṭīkā*) on the Bh.P. XI shows that this big commentary of 18,800 *Ovi* verses was completed at Varanasi in A.D. 1573 (Śaka 1495, Vikrama Samvat 1630). Eknāth mentions both the eras current in Maharashtra and at Varanasi.*

Anyone who peeps through my translation of the Bh.P.

वाराणसी महामुक्ति क्षेत्र । विक्रमशक वृष संवत्सर ।
शके सोकाशे तिसोत्तर । टीका एकाकार जनार्दनकृपा ॥५५२॥
महामंगल कार्तिकमासी । शुक्लपक्ष पूर्णमेसीं ।
सोमवार शिवयोगेसी । टीका एकादशी समाप्त जाहली ॥५५३॥
स्वदेशीचा शक संवत्सर । दंडकारण्य श्रीराम क्षेत्र ।
प्रतिष्ठान गोदावरी तीर । तेथील उच्चार तो ऐका ॥५५४॥
शालिवाहन शक वैभव । संख्या चौदाशे पंचाणव ।
श्रीमुख संवत्सराचे नोव । टीका अपूर्व तैं जाहली ॥५५५॥

(Pub. Motilal Banarsidass, Delhi) will find that commentators belonging to different schools of the Vedānta try to show painstakingly that the Bh.P. supports their metaphysical stance. Eknāth shows a distinct influence of Śaṅkara's Monism.

He acknowledges the debt of Śrīdhara, the oldest and one of the ablest annotators of the Bh.P. in glowing terms (EB. 1.119), but he differs from him in some respects e.g. exposition of *Karma*, *Akarma* and *Vikarma* in Bh.P.X17.8.

As stated above, Eknāth advocates the idealistic spiritual Monism of Śaṅkara, which accepts the Brahman as the only Real and the world as the manifestation of Nescience or Māyā and is unreal like mirage or misconception of a rope as a serpent. To explain the plurality of the world, Eknāth accepts Śaṅkara's hypothesis of Māyā—a modified Śāṅkhya concept of Avidyā. After stating the traditional meanings of *Vidyā*, *Avidyā* and *Māyā*, Eknātha holds that *Vidyā* and *Avidyā* are the powers of Māyā which being neither real nor unreal is called "Indescribable", but on closer scrutiny is found to be Self's own idea. (EB.11.98-106). To him the discussion about the nature of the Māyā is futile like that of the birth of a son to the daughter-in-law of a barren woman, horns of a horse and such other unrealities (EB.3.33-40, 52-73). For explaining to the ignorant, he gives a number of instances to show that there is no room for the world either in the Self or in the body.

Eknāth shows the essential identity between the Individual Soul and the Universal Soul—the Jīva and Śiva, the famous Upaniṣadic bird-friends occupying the same branch of a tree. He explains that the reflection of God in the soiled mirror of *Avidyā* is Jīva, while the same in the clear mirror of *Vidyā* is Śiva—the duality between them is apparent and not real (EB.11.164-205, 22.111-113). The Ātman is a detached witness in all states of body and mind and as such is neither born nor dead. (EB. 13.481-491; 28.258-59).

The all-pervading soul is the only Reality and it is ever free as the so-called bondage of the soul is nothing but an illusion (EB.11.29-32.)

EB. is an excellent guide to the path of God-realization. Eknāth emphasizes the cultivation of the following virtues in a spiritual aspirant :

1. Purity—not merely of the body but the internal one of the heart as well as the external one of good actions (EB.3.380-399).
2. Penance or constant meditation on God and not fasting or torturing the body. (EB.19.451-454).
3. Retirement from worldly affairs to lead a life of silent meditation in solitude. (EB.9.87-115).
4. Calm endurance of the weak points of others and slander of one's self without feeling anger as the *Ātman* is the same (non-dual) in all. (EB.19.574-79, 23, 778-81).
5. Strict celibacy (EB.23.305-307; 26.241-244). Avoidance of the company of lewd men and women. In order to exercise control over the cravings of the flesh, the Veda enjoined marriage-system and performance of sacrifices. But the real remedy is the transcendance of body-consciousness. (EB.5.208-239)
6. Discharge of one's duties. (18.380-87)
7. Performance of Bhakti at first of the *Saguṇa* type culminating into the *Nirguṇa* type. (11.1100-1109). (25. 251-352)

   The ideal is the Esoteric Bhakti when the devotee realizes the presence of God everywhere. Such a stage is possible through His Grace. (29.275-84)

When a *Bhakta* practises these virtues and abides by the precepts of his Spiritual *guru*, the aspirant attains the Brāhmī stage and real Samādhi. According to Eknāth *Samādhi* is not the loss of consciousness or stiff motionless condition of the body, but establishment in the Brāhmī state in which one enjoys constant divine experience. (2.423-432)*

RUKMIṆĪ SVAYAṀVARA

While Eknāth was staying at Varanasi commenting on the Bh.P., he wrote what may be called "a romantic novel" on the marriage of Kṛṣṇa and Rukmiṇī. The theme has caught the imagination of poets in Maharashtra since the thirteenth Century. But it was Eknāth who transformed the abduction of a Vidarbha princess by Kṛṣṇa into a sustained allegory of the union of Jīva and Śiva—the proverbial Upaniṣadic couple of birds perching on the same branch of a tree.

Traditionally we are told that Lord Kṛṣṇa served as a servant in the house of Eknāth under the pseudonym "Śrī khaṇḍyā". Eknāth wanted to celebrate the marriage of this faithful servant. But due to the "disappearance" of Śrīkhaṇḍyā, Eknāth became disappointed. Lord Kṛṣṇa then bade him to write *Rukmiṇi Svayaṁvara* (RS) and derive thereby the credit of celebrating his marriage as he himself was Śrīkhaṇḍyā.

Apart from the claim of modern researchers of tracing the modern descendants of Śrīkhaṇḍyā implying thereby that Śrīkhaṇḍyā was a human being who worked for some days as a servant in the house of Eknāth, Eknātha himself does not support this legend. He plainly states that it was of his own accord and without being requested or suggested by anyone else that he composed this work (RS.18.69). He completed this work at Varanasi on the Rāma Jayantī in Śaka 1493 (A.D. 1571).

*As it is not possible to summarise the whole of the EB. in a brief Introduction, readers are recommended to read R. D. Ranade's Indian Mysticism (Both its Preface and section on Eknātha). The present writer proposes to deal with different aspects of the EB. in the Introduction of his (English) translation of the EB.

Eknāth explicitly states that the RS. is a marriage-union between Jīva and Śiva and should be understood as such. It leads to the attainment of the self or self-realization.

This work is divided in 18 chapters called *Prasaṅgas*. Out of them, Chapters 8-12 describe the battle between Yādavas and the allies of Rukmī (Rukmiṇī's brother). It is a picture of traditional fighting as Eknāth, though trained in the use of weapons, was not a military expert. Chapters 14-18 describe the marriage of Kṛṣṇa with Rukmiṇī. These chapters are sociologically very interesting as they depict the then-prevalent customs and manners in the marriage-ceremonies of well-to-do Brāhmaṇa families of Maharashtra. There is no basis for them either in the *Bhāgavata Purāṇa* or in the *Harivaṁśa*, the works on which Eknāth based this story in Marathi. To stretch the word *vidhivat* (according to proper formalities) in the Bh.P. to cover what is called in Marathi "Telvaṇ", "Dheṇḍā-nṛtya", "Talī-nartana", etc. is strictly speaking anachronic. But Eknāth was not writing history. He was writing an interesting novel to invite the attention of the public of his times to the spiritual union of Jīva and Śiva.

We are however amused to find that though Kṛṣṇa and Rukmiṇī were Kṣattriyas, the menu of the marriage-feast was strictly vegetarian and the articles prepared were Maharashtrian. More funny is the advice of Balarāma's queen Revatī to the newly married princess Rukmiṇī to perform menial household work as if there were no servants in the palace of the king of Dvārakā. But Eknāth was writing for the ordinary public of his times and such sane advice was used to be given to newly married girls in our houses. And it did appeal to masses as can be seen from its immense popularity for the last 400 years.

The outline of the remaining chapters is as follows : A Brāhmaṇa called Kīrti describes the personal charms of Kṛṣṇa in Bhīṣmaka's court. Rukmiṇī who is present, is deeply attracted with love for Kṛṣṇa and falls in a swoon. Her parents are willing to give her in marriage to Kṛṣṇa but her brother Rukmī staunchly opposes the plan and proposes the name of Śiśupāla in stead. Rukmiṇī sends a letter to Kṛṣṇa through a Brāhmaṇa named Sudeva. Kṛṣṇa instantly starts alone for Kuṇḍinapura (Rukmiṇī's native town). Balarāma wisely follows him with Yādava army. Rukmiṇī is anxiously waiting as her marriage-day is approaching. But like a true *Sadguru* bringing about the union of Jīva with Śiva, Sudeva reports the success of his mission. (Hence the propriety of the long eulogy of *Sadguru* here). To avoid unnecessary conflict with Śiśupāla and his allies, Kṛṣṇa expressed his desire to camp at Ambāpura near the shrine of the guardian deity of the royal family. Citizens of Kuṇḍinapura who saw Kṛṣṇa, felt him to be the proper consort to their princess.

Rukmiṇī goes to pay her respects to their family deity Ambā and prays her to grant Kṛṣṇa as husband. To show her grace, the goddess drops her garland in the folded hands of Rukmiṇī. In the meanwhile, Rukmī who quarrelled with his father on the point of Rukmiṇī's marriage, advises Śiśupāla and his allies to deploy their forces for the protection of Rukmiṇī. In spite of these precautions, Kṛṣṇa abducts her as soon as she comes out of the temple. A bloody battle ensues. Rukmī is totally discomfited. King Bhīṣmaka offers Rukmiṇī to Kṛṣṇa at Prabhāsa and the marriage takes place near Dvārakā according to the Brāhma type of marriage current then in Maharashtra.

RS. is full of poetic imagery, romantic episodes, description of Rukmiṇī's personal charms etc. which cannot be quoted for lack of space. The RS has still such a powerful hold on Maharashtrians that many girls of marriagable age read (and are advised by the elders to read) the RS for getting a good husband !

BHĀVĀRTHA RĀMĀYAṆA

This voluminous, amplified version of the Rāmāyaṇa is the last work of Eknāth. After his return from Varanasi, Eknāth found that the kingdom of Vijayanagar, the last bastion of Hinduism in the Deccan, had fallen and something had to be done to overcome the spreading gloom in society. and Rāma was the sole deliverer of gods and men from the slavery and tyranny of the demon Rāvaṇa. Eknāth's junior contemporary, Tulasī Dās, later on, turned to Rāmāyaṇa to give solace to the masses suffering under an alien rule. The *Bhāvārtha Rāmāyaṇa* (BR) is mainly based on the Vālmīki Rāmāyaṇa but has been supplemented by materials culled from the *Adhyātma Rāmāyaṇa*, *Krauñca Rāmāyaṇa*, *Śiva Rāmāyaṇa*, *Yoga Vāsiṣṭha*, *Kālikā Khaṇḍa*, and a number of verses from the Bh.P. and *Subhāṣitas* handed down from olden times. But the literary artist has amalgamated all these materials in the Rāma story so finely that one is not aware of its diversity while reading. The BR. consists of 297 chapters out of which Eknāth is said to have written 172 (i.e. the first five *Kāṇḍas* and 44 chapters of the Yuddha Kāṇḍa and Gāvabā, one of his disciples, is credited with the remaining 48 chapters of the Yuddha Kāṇḍa and the whole of Uttara Kāṇḍa. As we find at least three *Uttara Kāṇḍas* —attempts to complete Eknāth's *Bhāvārtha Rāmāyaṇa*—and as the style of the Uttara-Kāṇḍa is different from the genuine BR. of Eknāth it can be definitely said that the present Uttara Kāṇḍa is not from the pen of Eknāth. But the Yuddha Kāṇḍa appears to be homogeneous and Eknāth must have completed the Yuddha Kāṇḍa before he accepted voluntary death (*Samādhi*) in 1599. In this context the spuriousness of the Uttara Kāṇḍa in Vālmīki might have been one of the reasons of Eknāth's decision to stop after Yuddha-Kāṇḍa. The social conditions depicted in the BR and the equation of the alien rulers with "Rākṣasas" in it and the efficacy of Rāma's name as a panacea against all evils and ills are significant. At the same time Eknāth did not forget his mission—spread of God's devotion among the masses. Eknāth was eminently successful in both the objects in the BR.

ABHAṄGAS

Eknātha is not merely a saint and an expounder of the Vedānta. He was a poet of a very high order. Be it the depiction of the love sentiment, the heroic spirit, pathos or even terror, Eknāth is a past-master in its graphic presentation. Not only did he sing of his mystical experiences and propagated Bhakti and the importance of the name of God, in his so-called *Bhāruḍas*, the spiritual allegories, he gives us a clear picture of the different divisions in the society and professions-cum-vocations of his times that no student of literary and social history of Maharashtra can ignore him. Next to Jñaneśvara, Eknāth is the greatest writer of Maharashtra and as such deserves to be translated for non-Marathi readers.

G. V. Tagare.

ŚRI EKNATH CHARITRA.

THE LIFE OF EKNĀTH.

As told by the poet Mahīpati in his Bhaktalīlāmṛita, Chapters thirteen to twentyfour.

CHAPTER 13.

MAHĪPATI'S INVOCATION.

1. Obesiance to Śrī Gaṇeśa! Victory, Victory to the Brother-of-the-Helpless, Husband-of-Rukmiṇi, Tender-lover-of-Bhaktas, Ocean-of-Mercy, Sea-of-Compassion, Deliverer-of-the-lowly, Lord of-All, Pāṇḍuraṅg. 2. All-Auspicious, Supreme-lord-of-the-Auspicious, Beyond-all-Evil, Lord-of-the-Senses, Saviour-of-the-Universe, Lord-all-Supreme, Indivisible One, Guru-of-the-World. 3. Victory to Thee, Thou, who-makest-the-intellect-to act, Pure-Intelligence, Internal-Light, Slayer-of-Madhu, Thou, who-art-beyond-Māyā, Thou, in-whom-the-*guṇas*-exist. Thou, both-*nirguṇa*-and *saguṇa*, Ocean-of-Joy, 4. Thou takest great delight in the deeds of the *bhaktas*. In their distresses Thou comest in person to their relief. Thou doest miraculous deeds in the sight of men. And these deeds become beautiful subjects of thy praise. 5 Placing therefore, the trust of my heart in Thee, I have begun

this Bhaktalilāmṛita. Do thou carry the whole work to completion, enabling it to escape the many possible disasters. 6. I indeed lack intellect, I am dull of understanding; I do not know the right meaning of words, and their grammatical relations. I am ignorant of how to use proper language for a book. 7. But if the Almighty takes one by the hand, who will show him slight. Just as when the iron is touched by the touchstone (*parisa*) its value becomes great. 8. So by Thy favour, O Husband-of-Rukmiṇi, my uncouth language will become acceptable, for I, a humble man, am dull of understanding, as all men know. 9. Thou, in reality, art the holder of the guiding string, as I know most certainly in my heart. So now giving me the assurance that I need not fear, cause me to relate the life of thy *bhaktas*.

THE CHILDHOOD OF EKNĀTH.

10. In the last chapter there was related the delightful story of the discussion which took place between Kabir, a worshipper of Rām, and Rohidās, a worshipper of Krishna. 11. Now, you good people, reverently listen to the delectable tale of Eknāth of Partishṭhāna, who appeared among men as an *avatāra* of Vishṇu.

12. Śri Bhānudas, chief jewel of *bhaktas*, who brought back the image of Pāṇḍuranga, had a son of noble character. His name was Chakrapāṇi. 13. Chakrapāṇi's son was Suryanārāyaṇa, lustrous through the brilliancy of his knowledge. His wife, of noble character, had the name of Rukmiṇi. 14. To Rukmiṇi was born in the Kali Yuga, for the good of the Universe, Eknāth, image of the supreme

Brahma, the Guru-of-the-World in visible form, 15. While Eknāth was still a child, both his father and his mother died, and he was cared for by his grandfather Chakrapāṇi. 16. And they being grandfather and grandmother, they fondled him and seeing that the child had many noble qualities they were both very happy.

17. Eknāth did not enjoy the ordinary games of children. Instead, he would so arrange his marbles as to represent gods, and would offer them flowers. 18. He would place on his shoulder a ladle, and pretend it was a lute. Then in his lisping words he would invoke the King-of-Heaven. 19. Sometimes the Haridās would come, performing *kīrtans*. Eknāth would listen attentively, then repeating the same words, he would dance in ecstasy. 20. And God, seeing his simple faith, would reveal himself in the marbles. The Husband-of-Ramā, hungry for the worship of men, took his abode in the marbles. 21. He was always repeating the names of God "Rām, Kṛishṇa, Hari, Govinda, Achyūta, Ananta, Āanadakanda, Śrī Govinda, Guru-of-the-World." 22. He used to take a little stick in his hand, and with an old rag make it into a banner. He would then carry it on his shoulder, saying, "I am off for Paṇḍhari." 23. Seeing these signs of piety while in his childhood, his grandparents took great comfort in him. He was always repeating the names "Rām, Rām," never ceasing for a moment. 24. Eknāth was not at all like other children, who were always complaining, even when there was no reason for doing so. 25. He was ever happily content with whatever sweetmeat was given him. Thus those signs appeared in him now, which were to be characteristic of him in the future. 26. Chakrapāṇi

once said to his wife, "My father, Bhānudās, was once worshipping before the image of Pāṇḍuraṅg, and the Glorious-lord showed him his favor. 27. Viṭhobā said to him, "Bhānudās, ask some boon of me." Bhānudās replied, "Become an *avatāra* in my family. I have no other desire." 28. The Husband-of-Rukmiṇi, hearing this request, said, "It shall be so." And now it seems to me, that it is really He who has become an *avatāra* in Eknāth, 29. His wife replied, "Your surmise is true. This child, of such noble character, is not a mere human being. If his father and mother were but living, they would look upon him with contended eyes." 30. And as she thus spoke, the memory of her own son came back to her. She became choked with emotion, and tears flowed from her eyes. 31. But at the same time the grandmother took courage, and exclaimed, "If only this remnant of our family line lives, he will be the saviour of our family, and bring us safely to the Hereafter." 32. Thus comforting herself, she tenderly cared for her grandson. When he was six years of age they lovingly invested him with the sacred thread. 33. Eknāth conducted himself exactly as the family Guru instructed him. He regularly performed the thrice-a-day devotions, with the prescribed ceremonies. 34. He attended regularly to his morning toilet, to the use of the clay, and the washing of his feet. Before bathing he would not so much as drink water. While eating he would not utter a single word. 35. If his Brāhmaṇa guru told him to commit something to memory, he would quietly take up the Pavamāna *stotra*. It was no painful effort for him to commit it to memory. 36. His grandfather taught him at home the cursive handwriting (*pishācha lipi*, *modi.*) He acquired that knowledge also without any difficulty. 37. In all his conduct Eknāth was remarkable. He had no liking for the ordinary worldly life. He acted as one would, when born in a Vaishṇava family. 38. One of noble character is born only in a noble family. All praise such. All honor such. The times are propitious to such an honoured one. Such an one has no restlessness of soul even in his dreams. 39. And he who is free from restlessness of soul is one to be recognized as a *bhakta* of Vishṇu. It is to such that *Bhakti* comes to serve, and all the *Siddhis* become his slaves. 40. Well, enough of such general remarks. Eknāth's life was beyond compare. He loved the worship of Śrī Rām. People wondered at him. 41. They would exclaim. "In years he is so young, and yet his heart seems always indifferent to the things of this world. He will not listen to funny stories and jests. He would rather listen to the reading of the *Purāṇas.* 42. In repeating *ślokas,* and in explaining their meaning, he never makes the least mistake. And as he eagerly repeats them, even the distinguished Twice-born listen to him with delight. 43. They say he is a *yogabhrashta.* He has thorough knowledge of the Vedanta philosophy. He has become an *avatāra* in human form, to bring full salvation to the world." 44. Whenever Eknāth had an opportunity of being alone with his pandit he would ask questions. And as the Brāhmaṇa pandit listened to the questions he became dumbfounded, and would exclaim "Our knowledge has been taught us. 45. By study we have acquired our conversancy with the contents of the Purāṇas, for the purpose of gaining a livelihood. His expressions do not come within our experience. Eknāth, your questions are most extraordinary. 46. A little pond looks like a great lake, so long as the ocean is not seen. So our knowledge, in fact, is insignificant before yours, Eknāth. 47. As the light of the fire fly at once and naturally vanishes before the glare of a lamp, so I listen to your questions, but cannot comprehend their full meaning. 48. The stars are beautiful only so long as the Husband-of-Rohiṇi (the moon) has not arisen. So in the presence of your questions my mental activities cease. 49. So long as one has not seen the nectar of the gods, one places the marvels of medical remedies first. So, as I listen to your questions I am too confused to reply. 50. Or as when the sun rises, the moon looks as pale as a cloud. So my words pale before your knowledge." 51. When thus lauded by the *Purāṇik*, Eknāth would make a namaskār and say, "My words are but those of a child. Do not be angry with me." 52. The *Purāṇik* would then eagerly arise, and tenderly caress his face, saying, "One should wave the salted *nimb* leaves over your noble character. 53. You look like the statue of the Supreme Brahma, and yet you manifest the acts of a child. It is my good fortune to see you with my own eyes, and my worldly existence has thereby become a fruitful one." 54. Eknāth replied, "If I should have doubts in my mind, to whom should I go for an answer? Tell me at once now." 55. The Puṇdit answered, "In this life below one should have the intimacy of a *Sadguru*. Only thus can the snare of this life be truly broken, and the coming and going through birth and death be avoided." 56. No sooner did Eknāth hear these words, than his heart was pierced by them, and he exclaimed, "With undivided devotion I must go to the feet of a *sadguru*. 57. The Sadguru pervades the entire Universe. No space is seen empty of him. Yet one should seek for him in a visible *sagun̩* form, and serve him day and night." 58. With this fixed purpose in mind Eknāth was ever thinking, "When will such a *Svāmi* greet my sight!" And this was his great concern day and night. He now cared for nothing else.

EKNĀTH MEETS JANĀRDANPANT.

59. Now it happened one day that Eknāth had gone into the temple of Śiva. It was during one of the watches of the night, and there all alone he was lovingly worshipping. 60. In his heart was the great longing that a *Sadguru* might appear to his sight. When suddenly he heard a divine voice, saying to him, 61. "In Fort Devagiri there is one named Janārdanpant, who has received the favor of discipleship from Śrī Datta. Go and see him." 62. When Eknāth heard this heavenly voice, he was filled with joy, and at once started off alone, and without even taking the leave of his grandparents. 63. As one in the heat of Summer, overcome with thirst, goes searching for water, and plunges in it, so Eknāth longed to meet his *Sadguru.* He no longer had the least bodily consciousness. 64. Or as a hungry child goes searching for its mother, so Eknāth longed; saying, "I must meet Janārdanpant."

EKNĀTH HEARS A HEAVENLY VOICE.

65. Devagiri was five *yojanas* from Paiṭhaṇ. Walking that distance eagerly, he arrived at the home of the *Sadguru.* 66. The door keeper stopped him, and would not allow him to enter. but going within said to Janārdan,

"Some one has come, who claims to be a disciple of yours. 67. He wishes to see you. His name is Ekobā." Janārdan now bethought himself of certain signs, and said to himself, "To day's omens have been very good. 68. My right eyelid has been drooping to-day. My arm twitches every now and then. Some good man must have come here to see me." With this he at once arose. 69. And hurrying to the door saw the heroic Vaishṇava. Janārdan embraced him and his eyes filled with tears. 70. Eknāth seeing the *Sadguru,* made him a *sāshṭāṅg namaskār,* and said, "Let me ever remain here in your service, and give me the assuring blessing that I need not fear." 71. Then putting palm to palm, he added, "O Sadguru, you who are pure Intelligence, care for the honour of your *bhaktas,* receive me into your care. I have come as one who has no other refuge. 72. Desires, longings, troublesome thoughts grow excessively within me. The six foes of the soul are tormenting me greatly. Oh save my soul." 73. As the Sadguru recognized these evidences of penitence, he deeply rejoiced, and drawing Eknāth closely to his heart, lovingly embraced him, 74. Exclaiming, "By association with you my own life will attain its true purpose." This exclamation made Eknāth rejoice. He felt the kind of happiness that accompanies love. 75. As the child Dhruva, who had sulked, and was wandering alone in the forest, rejoiced when the Muni Nārada met him, 76. So it happened to Eknāth when he met Janārdana. He lost thought of body, home, and self, in the happiness of his soul. 77. The *Sadguru,* then taking Eknāth by the hand led him inside the house, and immediately gave him something to eat. 78. Janārdan said to himself, "This Eknāth is truly a divine *avatāra,* not a human being. My good fortune is most extraordinary."

EKNĀTH SERVES JANĀRDAN.

79. Eknāth, intent on serving his *sadguru* ministered to him in every kind of service, high and low. He allowed himself to fail in nothing whatever. 80. He became one who looked upon all the animate and inanimate creation from the standpoint of being *Ātma.* This being his state of mind, hear now in detail how Eknāth served his *sadguru.* 81. He used to arise while the night still lacked four *ghatikas,* for his morning's repetition of the names of God. After performing his toilet, and rinsing out his mouth, he began the house-worship. 82. He took the broom eagerly in his hands, and with his own hands swept the house. Gathering the sweepings in a basket he would throw them far away, all the while most happy. 83. While the men servants and maid servants were fast asleep he would be smearing the floors, bringing out the vessels used in worship, and polishing them with his own hands. 84. When Janārdan awoke, Eknāth would bring him the water for his toilet, and place the bath board for the washing of his feet. 85. He never failed in having ready the clay, the tooth stick, the warm water for his bath, and the cold water for rinsing out his mouth. 86. He would also place in readiness the materials used in the worship of God, the flowers and the *tulsi.* After doing this Eknāth would take his own bath, and plait his guru's *dhotar.* 87. Eknāth would then hand to Janārdan the water for his

bath, and stand ready at hand with *dhotar* and scarf. 88. He would wring out the wet cloth, used for wiping, and eagerly place his shoes before him. All this he did in the fulness of his love. 89. The *Sadguru* had an abundance of servants, but Eknāth thought of himself as Janārdan's one and only servant. He wanted to do all there was to be done, and he did it with a joy that was accompanied with love. 90. When the *Svāmi* sat down for his Vishṇu worship, Eknāth would lovingly prepare the fragrant pigments, and place near at hand the offerings to be made, the incense, the lights, the five-light platter. 91. When Eknāth saw his *sadguru* sitting in the act of meditation, what did this good disciple do, but go and sweep his Guru's bedroom and deftly arrange his bed. 92. He would spread out the bedding carefully. He prepared the *Vida* and placed it on the tray. Lovingly he washed out Janārdan's spitoon, and placed it near him. 93. While the *Sadguru* sat at his meals, Eknāth would drive away the flies. He would then eat with supreme happiness what his *Guru* had left on his plate, 94. Remarking, "If I eat a great deal I shall become lazy, and so fail in my duties to my *Svāmi.*" He therefore ate very sparingly. 95. He would himself pass the *Vida* to his *Svāmi,* and stand before him with palm joined to palm. If the *Svāmi* went to his bed for rest, Eknāth would massage his feet. 96. He was ready on every occasion. He failed in nothing. In this service months and years went by, but he never wearied. 97. In his great joy of service Eknāth felt that the authority to serve his *Guru* was his alone, and that so long as he lived he should have no partner in that service. 98.

He kept all the domestic accounts in an account book, and he never made an error. In years he was young, it is true, but in intelligence he was great. 99. In thus devoting himself with enthusiasm to his *Sadguru's* service he made worldly cares, and the Supreme purpose of life, one. The act of worship and himself as worshipper, he made one. All difference absolutely vanished. 100. When Janārdan once questioned Eknāth, saying, "You have left your mother and father, and are living here with me, but how are they faring?" 101. Eknāth replied, "My mother and father are both dead. My Grandfather and grandmother are living at Paiṭhaṇ. I left them to come here. 102. There is no duty more important than the service of a *Svāmi.*" Eknāth did not permit in his thought the memories of the past. In his loving emotions he was wholeheartedly his *Guru's.* 103. The service of a *Sadguru,* that is Japa. The service of a *Sadguru,* that is *tapa.* And increase of wrong conception here, one should feel to be sin. 104. Eknāth, the loving *bhakta,* so longed for his *Sadguru's* blessing that in his love he regularly drank the contents of Janārdan's spitoon. 105. He would rechew the *tāmbūl* that Janārdan had chewed, and he regarded the nectar of Brahma as inferior to it. But what his feelings were on these occasions he told no one. 106. While Janārdan would be reading aloud the Amṛitānubhava and the Dnyāneshvari, Eknāth would listen with delight and with fixed attention. 107. It was Janārdan's habit to complete his regular morning's duties and then to visit the king. After finishing his various official duties he would return home.

EKNĀTH SUBSTITUTES HIMSELF FOR JANĀRDAN.

108. Now it happened one day, when it was about the fourth *ghatika,* that a great invading army suddenly arrived to capture *Devagiri.* 109. Spies announced that a certain enemy of the king was approaching with an army. The king fell into a great fright. 110. The mace-bearers hurried to the house of Janārdan, to tell him that a great invading army had arrived, and that he should come at once. 111. Now Janārdan had just completed his ablutions and devotions, and was sitting in meditation. To convey to him the news at such a time would be overstepping the grounds of propriety. 112. Eknāth, an *avatār* able for miraculuos deeds, now performed a miracle. He assumed the form of Janārdan, but no one, other than himself, was aware of the fact. 113. He hurriedly put on the garments of his *Svāmi,* and changed his own form to that of his. He took his dagger in hand and sat in his *palanquin.* 114. In his talk and carriage he differed not in the least from his *guru.* He went to the king's council and learned all the news. 115. The royal patron was in great perplexity. "A great invading army has arrived," he said. "Now what plan shall we adopt?" Eknāth listened and replied. 116. "By the might of your good deeds I will conquer the enemy in no time." So saying he gave his command to the generals, "Be ready immediately." 117. And with this order he had the kettle-drums beaten. Instruments of music gave out their various sounds, and the army marched forward out of the city. 118. Eknāth, an avatār able for miraculous deeds, now showed to the enemy his wonderful power.

His own army was very small, but to the enemy it seemed very great. 119. The arrows now flew *saṇa saṇa*. The weapons clashed ***khaṇa khaṇa***. The spirit of heroism rose high. Slaughter raged violently. 120. The struggle lasted four *ghatikas*. The sky became clouded with dust, and still the Vaishṇava hero had not ended his assault. But now the whole invading army began to flee. 121. The foe was panic stricken. "We see no good before us," they exclaimed. And in their dire straits they sent a superior officer to the Commander of the army, who said, "I have come for an interview." 122. When the messenger of the enemy proposed a parley, Eknāth, ***bhakta*** of the *Sadguru*, felt pity for him. He did not show him harshness but met him in a playful manner. 123. He brought this enemy into the city, introduced him to his royal patron, gave him garments and ornaments, and said, "Now return to your place." 124. Having thus gained the victory, Eknāth returned to his home. He changed his form back again, and stood ready to serve.

JANĀRDAN DISCOVERS EKNĀTH'S MIRACULOUS DEED.

125. During all this while Janārdan had been alone in the god-room in meditation. Finally completing his mind-worship he came back to bodily consciousness. 126. He had not heard the news of what had occurred outside. So as usual he made his offering to the idol, and to the fire, and finished his meal. 127. He then took his four *ghatikas* of sleep, after which he called for his *palanquin*

and quickly went to the Hall of Administration. 128. When his royal patron saw him coming he affectionately arose to receive him. He gave him a seat by his side, and thus addressed him, 129. "The invading army that came to-day was very great. Yet you went against them, conquered the enemy, gaining a notable victory." 130. After the royal patron had thus lauded him, the chief members of the Council did the same, and ordered fresh garments to be brought immediately. 131. The royal patron then presented these to Janārdan, saying, "You took but a small army with you, you brought back victory." 132. The crowd around then shouted, "Victory, Victory (to Janārdan)" and the minstrels began to sing aloud of his distinguished deeds. Janārdan was utterly confused by all this, thinking it most strange. 133. "I was at home in meditation," he said to himself. "How could all these things have happened?" Then suddenly he understood it all and exclaimed, "It must have been Eknāth, an avatār able for miraculous deeds. 134. He must surely have taken my form, and accomplished this deed. Yet I had better not reveal this fact, or it will become notorious." 135. Settling the matter thus in his mind Janārdan returned to his home, and taking Eknāth aside lovingly embraced him. 136. Caressingly patting him on the back, he exclaimed, "Blessed are you, *bhakta* of the *Sadguru*. You have performed a most marvellous deed. I divined it in my own mind." 137. Hearing these nectar-words Eknāth fell at his feet in sincere devotion, saying, "You, *Svāmi,* you are the holder of the guiding string. The deed was not mine."

JANĀRDAN TESTS EKNĀTH.

138. The days thus passing it happened once that Janārdan said to Eknāth, "You have written up the accounts in your book, bring them now to me." 139. "I will do so," responded the *bhakta* of the *sadguru*, and went off by himself to balance the account. He found in it an error of one *adhelā.* This greatly diṣtressed his mind. 140. He added oil to the lamp, and went over the account again and again. Two and a half watches of the night thus passed, he conquering his drowsiness and keeping awake. 141. Not willing that his *Guru* should suffer any loss, he kept up his search for the missing *adhelā.* Suddenly the account balanced to his great joy. 142. He burst out laughing and slapped his thigh. Just then Janārdan happened to come and watch him from behind. "What good thing have you found," said he. 143. "What are you so happy about that you should be now laughing?" Hearing his Sadguru's voice Eknāth touched his forehead to the feet of his *Guru.* 144. "In looking over the account," he replied, "there was an error of one *adhelā.* I have just discovered it and am feeling very happy." 145. "Now," said Janārdan, "I want you to concentrate your mind in the same way on Krishṇa. Only by so doing can you attain your highest well being in this life below." This is all the comment Janārdan made. 146. Eknāth then placed his pen at his *sadguru's* feet and cried, "What you have said is what I have been longing for, and now that you have told me what to do, your word will not go in vain." 147. So saying he broke out into an Abhaṅg. Listen to it, ye pious *bhaktas.* They are

sweet words of his experience. I gladly quote them in this book.

1. Janārdan is the Lord of the three worlds.
   He opened an account with me.

2. The account was for large amounts.
   And always in the name of Rām.

3. He gave me " I am He " as his bond.
   I reverently accepted it.

4. He gave me garments of love.
   I received from him the leaves of Salvation.

5. I quickly built the city of Absorption-into-Brahma.
   I went and sat in the bastion of Chaitanya.

6. I will collect the revenue of Self-knowledge and I will send it to my *Svāmi.*

7. By the hands of the saints will I send the balance of accounts.
   Bhakti will be the beautiful receipt.

8. Such are the business relations I acquired through *puṇya* in a former birth.
   I am fully satisfied in Janārdan.

148. After repeating this *Abhang,* he put the *Modi* account book aside. Now hear how he served his Guru with true devotion.

EKNĀTH'S SPECIAL ACTS OF SERVICE.

149. He cleaned with his own hands the place where Janārdan performed his toilet. He smeared the place with cow dung and decorated it with coloured powders. 150. After some days had passed the *Sadguru* questioned him. " Who is it that sweeps out the privy, tell me. 151. I see the place smeared with cowdung, and always decorated with the coloured powders. The Halālkhor surely does not do this. I am wondering who does it." 152. Eknāth replied, " Am I an ungrateful wretch? I have offered my whole body to my Svāmi to serve him in every way." 153. When Janārdan heard this reply, he was deeply moved, and said to himself, "I should not let him serve me. Eknāth is not a mere man. 154. I must see to it that he has a visible manifestation of Śrī Dattātreya, Guru-of-the-world. And what an intellect Dattātreya will see," thought he.

JANĀRDAN'S WORSHIP OF DATTĀTREYA.

155. Janārdan's royal patron, the king, issued an order to his secretaries, that none need come to visit him on Fridays. 156. In accordance with this order of the king, instead of going to the Council Hall on that day, Janārdan made it his habit to devote the day to his own most important private duties. 157. There was a very extensive lake on the plateau of the near by mountain, the water of which was very pure. There was no passing by of people there. 158. There was also a dense forest, beautiful with flowers and fruit. Simply viewing the scene brought rest to the mind. It seemed as though one

could not leave the spot. 159. If one searched over all that country one could not find so charming a spot. One had only to look at that clear and pure water to experience a sense of peaceful rest. 160. Srī Dattātreya was accustomed to come to that spot, and any good man who performed *anushṭhāna* here could have a visible manifestation of him. 161. So Janārdan every Friday used to climb the mountain, take his bath in the lake and perform his accustomed rites. 162. He would then make a thousand *lingas* of clay, and worship them with proper ceremony. At the completion of his worship Śrī Datta would give him a visible manifestation of himself. 163. As each met the other, each was filled with joy. They would converse together on the Happiness of the soul. They experienced a shower of joy. 164. Janārdan was one day thinking to himself, " Eknāth is a *Sadguru Bhakta*. He very faithfully serves me. 165. I must now arrange for him a visible manifestation of Śrī Dattātreya. He will recognize Eknāth's intellect and in mercy will give him a special boon."

JANĀRDAN TAKES EKNĀTH TO MEET DATTĀTREYA.

166. With this idea in mind, on a Friday, as he was about to go to the mountain, he asked Eknāth to go up with him. 167. Filled with joy at this request, Eknāth worshipped the lotus feet of his *Guru*, and started with him at once carrying the prayer-mat and the idol-bag. 168. As when a father prepares to go to a feast, and calls his child to go

with him, the child feels overjoyed, so it was in this case. 169. Śrī Janārdan took Eknāth by the hand and led him up the mountain. There alone by themselves he told Eknāth how Śrī Datta was accustomed to manifest himself at that place. 170. "In a *Māyā* body he lovingly manifests himself in any odd form. So when you see him let no suspicious doubt fill your mind. 171. Aside from him no human being will come to this mountain spot." Such were his words of instruction. 172. Janārdanpant then bathed in the water of the lake, said his usual prayers, made his offerings, and began the *linga* worship. 173. Eknāth collected the clay, and brought it to Janārdan, who made of it a thousand *lingas,* and worshipped them with appropriate rites. 174. Having finished all his worship he began his meditation of the Guru-of-the-World. Suddenly the Son-of-Anusuyā appeared, but in the guise of a Muhammadan. 175. His body was clothed in a leather garment. His eyes looked large and blood-red. Counting prayers on a rosary, he sat contemplating the Being-without-Qualities. 176. He had brought with him a Wish-cow, but to one's sight she appeared a bitch. Janārdan recognized him through his inner sight, and reverently made him a *namaskār.* 177. Just as there is no recognizable difference between the *Saguṇ* and the *Nirguṇ,* so Dattātreya and Janārdan lovingly embraced one another, as one. 178. Or indeed as light and the sun are conjoined to one another, or as the flower and its honey do not differ, so was the love of the two. 179. Or again just as there is no difference whatever between a musical instrument and its sound, or as nectar and its sweetness are alike. 180. Or as the body and the soul are united in love, so Janārdan and *Avadhūta* appeared as one.

181. Sitting close together they conversed on Soul-happiness. Eknāth listened attentively with great joy of heart. 182. Dattātreya now drew out an earthen bowl from under his folds and asked Janārdan to go at once and milk the bitch, sitting near by. 183. Instantly obeying, Janārdan took the bowl in his hands and quickly milked the bitch, filling the vessel full of milk. 184. He fetched it back to where Avadhūta was sitting and placed it before him, who taking out some dry pieces of bread, crumbled them into the milk. 185. This was in reality divine food, but to one's sight it seemed like stale bread, such as the begging student gathers as he wanders from house to house. 186. It was to test the faith of his *bhakta* that Dattātreya performed in their sight this strange act. Eknāth understood it, yet not without a suspicious doubt in his mind. 187. *Avadhūta* now said to Janārdan, " Sit down now beside me and let us eat together." At this invitation Janārdan overflowed with joy. 188. Janārdan and Dattātreya, in his visible form, ate together out of the one vessel. When their appetite was satisfied by this nectar of joy, they prepared to wash their hands. 189. They washed their hands in the earthen bowl, rinsed out their mouths, and to purify their mouths they took the *Viḍa,* and each withdrew to his seat. 190. Then Eknāth was told to go to the lake, wash the vessel and bring it back. " I will do so surely," he said. 191. Sitting at the edge of the lake, he thought to himself, "This great loving gift has come to me. Let me lovingly drink it." 192. This food left in it by the Sadguru is Gaṅgā *Bhāgirathi* itself. All the many means of acquiring what I need are to be found right here in this. This will be the way of salvation for my soul. 193. With this thought in mind, he put the

earthen bowl to his lips saying to himself, "There can be no one in the whole universe as fortunate as I am." 194. When Janārdan saw this act of Eknāth's he made this request to Dattātreya, "Call to your side this servant of mine, and give him a vision of yourself, O *Svāmi*. 195. He did not make obeisance to you because you have assumed the form of a Muhammadan. So reveal to him your own true form." With these words Janārdan touched his feet. 196. Dattātreya replied, "One should not call Eknāth a lad. He is an *avatār* of Viṭṭhal, in order to save the Universe. 197. Men will listen to his Kīrtans, and very many will turn to *Bhakti*. Through his eloquence, his poetic power he will speak inspired words. 198. Vyāsa having churned the Vedas produced the cream of Śrī Bhāgavat, and Eknāth in his own words will make its meaning very clear. 199. Of the Ramāyaṇa of Vālmiki he will make a Prākrit version. Whoever shall read all his poetic works, his soul will have a direct revelation from God. 200. In his *Kīrtans* he will compose many *padas* and other poems. His fame will endure as long as the moon and the sun endure." 201. While thus speaking these words of blessing, his form now changed and the bitch that was lying beside him now appeared to the eye as the Wish-cow. 202. Casting aside his Muhammadan guise, he assumed the beautiful *Saguṇ* form six armed, of elongated eyes, his face the ornament of the universe. 203. Revealing himself in this form, he called Eknāth to him. Eknāth touched his feet with his forehead, and then lovingly embraced them. 204. Dattātreya stretching out his six arms embraced Eknāth and caressed his face. He then became invisible. 205. Thus through the favor of

Janārdan Eknāth had the visible manifestation of Śrī Datta. Then taking Eknāth by the hand the two returned to their home.

206. And now, pious folk, listen to the interesting story to follow. And just as a miser's thought does not wander even for a moment while counting his money, so let not your minds wander. 207. It is the Husband-of-Rukmiṇi merciful to the humble, who is recalling the story to my memory, for know that otherwise Mahīpati is one dull of understanding. Mahīpati and Dullness are equivalent terms. 208. *Swasti.* This book, is the Śrī Bhaktalīlāmṛita. By merely listening to it one's desires are fulfilled. Listen then to it, ye loving pious *bhaktas.* This is the thirteenth interesting chapter. *Verses 208.*

CHAPTER 14.

MAHĪPATI'S INVOCATION.

Obeisance to Ganeśa.

1. Men who seek the highest attainment desire to acquire God. What is the supreme method of acquiring God? It is by associating oneself with the good. 2. All the *tirthas,* small and great, formed in the Purāṇas, the well known and honored, these all are in the possession of the saints, along with the regularly occurring holy times and seasons. 3. In the *Kali Yuga* the *Yoga* exercises, rites, and ceremonies are not means for acquiring God. By their means one cannot meditate on the Supreme Vishṇu. One cannot by them hold in restraint the fickle mind. 4. In order, therefore, that one may easily cross over the Sea-of-life,

God has prepared a ship, namely, His Name. The wise Vaishṇava knows that there is no other supreme way. 5. Śrī Krishṇa has said in the Bhāgavata that the acquirement of man's highest state is assuredly through the Name. So also is the saying of the Vedas in the Vishṇusukta. 6. If one therefore feels the desire in his heart that his faith should rest on the Name, he should seek association with the Good, for thereby the mind becomes easily enlightened. 7. Association with *Sādhus* naturally leads to hearing. Hearing leads to thinking, and thinking leads at once to tense contemplation of God. 8. In the last chapter we had the beautiful story of how Janārdan looked upon Eknāth with the eye of deep interest, and brought about the meeting with Śrī Datta, revealing that wonder to his sight.

JANĀRDAN INSTRUCTS EKNĀTH.

9. The Sadguru, feeling deep love for Eknāth led him by the hand until they reached their home. And now what further happened, listen. 10. Through the favor of the *Svāmi,* Eknāth's mind by full enlightenment attained peace, and even though he was the recipient of the boon by Datta, yet in his service to Janārdan he failed in no point whatever. 11. More punctilious than before, with special love for ministering to his *Svāmi,* and freed from the seductions of all temptations, he worshipped Śrī Purushottama. 12. Just as the wind pervades the Universe and yet does not lose its mobility, or as the Ganges while mingling with the ocean, yet upstream its flow does not cease. 13. Or again as the *bhakta,* when

worshipping Śrī Hari, is changed into His very form, and yet does not overstep the proper duties of a *Bhakta,* just so was it with Eknāth. 14. Through the enlightenment of his soul he had perfect peace within, and in addition had received the boon from the *Sadguru,* yet for all that he was always standing ready for service, with never the least bit of laziness. 15. The thought now came to Janārdan, " Truly, truly in all the three worlds there is no *Bhakta* of the *Sadguru* like him. His love is simply marvellous. 16. In order to save the world Śrī Pāṇḍuraṅg has become an *avatār.* If I hold him longer in my service, I shall not at all be keeping within my bounds of duty towards him." 17. As he thus thought within himself he went into the house in search of Eknāth. He found him sitting alone, singing the praises of Śrī Datta. 18. When Eknāth saw Janārdan he arose and reverently bowed to him. The Sadguru then sat in his accustomed place, and thus instructed Eknāth, 19. "Through the favor of the *Sadguru* you have acquired *ātma*-knowledge. Nevertheless, keep in mind not to do away with *saguṇ* Bhakti. 20. *Yogīs,* by restraining their organs of sense, forget sensual objects, but without *bhakti* they cannot have the visual manifestation of the *saguṇ* God. 21. By the power of *yoga* they exhibit marvellous deeds and powers, but unless there is *bhakti* with love there can be no meeting with Śrī Pati. 22. He may regard all humanity as himself. He may even forget himself in bodily unconsciousness, and yet with all this he may not have the visual manifestation of the *saguṇ* God. This manifestation, Eknāth, is difficult to obtain. 23. So long, indeed, as one has life, one should love the *saguṇ* God. And now I will tell you the right thing to do. Listen to it with attention."

JANĀRDAN SENDS EKNĀTH TO MOUNT SULABHA.

24. " In the region back of Devagiri there is a mountain called Sulabha and there is a *tirtha* called Sūryakuṇḍa. It is a beautiful quiet spot. 25. *Sādhakas* are accustomed to go to this place and perform their rites. Here God appears to them in fully bodily form. The place is holy and purifying. 26. Therefore, now listen, you who are so dear to my heart. Go at once to that spot, bathe in the Sūryakuṇḍa, repeating the name of Śrī Pāṇḍuraṅgarāya. 27. Concentrating your mind, contemplate the Supreme Vishṇu. Do not talk with anyone. My command is your authority. 28. Whatever you may obtain by chance, that be content to eat. Do not have anxious thought about me, for I am near you. 29. That was once the abode of the Ṛishi Mārkaṇḍeya, so the Purāṇa clearly states. So with loving heart fix your mind on Śrī Kṛishṇa. 30. If you should there see any thing strange, come back here to tell me." As Eknāth listened to these words of his *sadguru,* he was moved within with joy. 31. To begin with, Eknāth was a true and loving discipline, and farthermore his *guru* had prescribed a definite act of worship. He felt, therefore, supremely happy, and worshipping the feet of his *guru* he started off. 32. Other gurus instruct in knowledge, but neglect to teach the *bhakti* of the *saguṇ* God. Janārdan was never such an one. 33. Knowledge, without *bhakti,* is like the babbling of a babbler. Listen, good people, to one of Eknāth Svāmi's own sayings.

1. Knowledge was born from the womb of *Bhakti*.
   The glory of Knowledge is through *Bhakti*.

2. *Bhakti* has given Knowledge its glory.
   Bhakti is the root of Knowledge and Vairāgya.

3. Without *Bhakti* one is seized by Darkness.
   If there is no root, how can there be any fruit?

4. He who does deeds that are united to *Bhakti* for Janādan only, Brahma-knowledge falls at his feet.

34. Therefore listen, good people; he who, discarding *Bhakti*, preaches the doctrine of knowledge, or he who argues against the communion of God and his *bhakta*, there is no one as vile as he. 35. Blessed is this noble *sadguru*, Janārdan! It appears to me he is Janārdan Himself become *saguṇ* in order to save the world. 36. But let me now pass on, and let not the listener grow weary, because while relating the story of the guru and his bhakta, I interrupted it by a digression. Only for a moment have I thus spoken by way of illustration.

EKNĀTH'S WORSHIP ON MOUNT SULABHA.

37. As soon, then, as the sadguru gave his command, Eknāth made a *namaskār*. I now turn to what the Vaishṇava hero did on reaching Mount Sulabha. 38. As he viewed the beautiful spot, he felt a sense of supreme rest. He

bathed in the Sūryakuṇḍa and completed the prescribed rites. 39. He then sat down, looking to the East, and concentrated his mind, bringing to his imagination the image of Pāṇḍuraṅg, accompanied with a feeling of love. 40. While thus repeating his name, and while in this act of contemplation the Husband-of-Indirā revealed Himself to him. Eknāth's *vritti* (soul) assumed His form, and he lost all bodily consciousness. 41. Now on that mountain there lived a great serpent, and as it saw Eknāth sitting in contemplation it ran to bite him. 42. But as it began to coil itself around Eknāth its evil nature left its body, and now full of affection, he protected him, and how, let us see. 43. Lest Eknāth suffer from cold or heat it coiled all around him, with the end of its tail at Eknāth's navel, and its wide spread hood over Eknāth's head. 44. The serpent had lost his evil nature, and gained a good nature. The moment it touched the saint this complete change of disposition took place. 45. As Eknāth came back to consciousness, and his body slightly moved, the serpent glided away and was no longer in sight. 46. Because Eknāth's soul was united with the Name and Form, (*saguṇ* God) he had therefore been without bodily consciousness, and did not know of the serpents's coiling around him.

THE PIOUS FARMER ON MOUNT SULABHA AND HIS WIFE.

47. Now at the foot of the mountain there was a miserable hamlet. In it a Vaishṇava lived, a pious farmer. 48. In a former birth his austerities had been

interrupted (*yoga bhrashṭa*), he was therefore one of pure conduct. At his door was the *tulsi* altar, and he performed regularly his ablutions and worship. 49. He kept his clothes and dishes clean. He never ate without first bathing. While carrying on his daily occupation, he was always repeating the names of God. 50. His wife also was supremely dutiful and lived as he did. She knew to what her lord's mind inclined, and so reverenced *Sādhus* and Saints. 51. She fed the hungry, she gave water to the thirsty. She had a heart for doing good to others. She never told a lie. 52. If she ever saw an ascetic performing his rite on Mount Sulabha she would bring him milk to drink with expressions of love. 53. Near by on a level spot on the mountain side the farmer had sown a field of grain. While the rich crop was ripening he was accustomed to stay there for its protection. 54. So when Eknāth went by to perform his rites the farmer saw him, and taking fresh milk, heated at his house, he went to where Eknāth was. 55. Eknāth had finished his love-accompanied contemplation, and was just sitting about, when the farmer prostrated himself before him and made the following request. 56. "I have brought this heated milk. The Svāmi must please drink it." Eknāth granted the man's request and thanked him. 57. "The enjoyer of this milk is Śrī Krishṇa." So saying, Eknāth put the vessel to his lips. The farmer felt great satisfacion and returned to his place. 58. His wife, as instructed by him, brought milk every day to the field. They first gave of this to Eknāth, and then took their own food. 59. Only if there is a store of good deeds laid up in a previous birth does there come about such an opportunity of serving a saint. This places obligation on God, and He then delivers the server of the saint from the ocean-of-this-life. 60. The Life-of-the-world is pleased with him who serves a Saint, and there is no higher way to please Him. 61. This farmer was fortunate, and so there was born in him a good heart. While carrying on his wordly pursuits, he at the same time acquired the supreme purpose of life. His goodness had no limit. 62. One day his wife arose at midnight to grind. She sang verses in praise of God, and quickly her grinding was finished. 63. The moon was then shining so brightly that she thought it was dawn. So she milked the cow and put the milk in separate vessels. 64. Although it was not time for so large a yield, she milked a very large amount. She heated the milk in brass vessels carefully, and placed a dung-cake over it. 65. Then performing her toilet, bathing with cold water, and completing her cooking well, just then the sun arose. 66. She said to herself, "I must have arisen very early to do my grinding, when it was still long before daylight. If I delay going up to the field the food will surely become cold. 67. Thus talking to herself, the beautiful one tock the bread basket on her head, and the milk vessel in her hand and hurried along. 68. As the beloved wife came to the hedge of the field her husband saw her, relieved her of the milk vessel, and went to perform his bath. 69. After performing his usual rites and repetition of God's names he said to his wife, "You have brought the food very early this morning. What is the reason? Tell me. 70. I am not yet hungry, it is not a festival day, nor the twelfth of the month. The ascetic is now sitting performing his rites. We cannot eat until he has eaten." 71. The wife replied,

"I became awake while it was still very early, and so lest the food should become cold I have come thus early. 72. But," said she, "go up the mountain side and give the milk to the Brāhmaṇa, and then eat your breakfast." 73. So taking the vessel he climbed up the mountain side, when to his vision a most remarkable sight appeared. Listen, ye wise ones, with reverence.

THE FARMER SEES A SERPENT COILED AROUND EKNĀTH.

74. Eknāth had finished his ablution and prayers, and the performing of his rites, and his mind was now in contemplation on Śrī Krishṇa. He was now absolutely without bodily consciousness. 75. A serpent had come and coiled itself around Eknāth's body, with the end of its tail at his navel, and its hood over his head. 76. When the farmer saw this, great terror was aroused in his mind, exclaiming, "The Brāhmaṇa is performing his rites, and the serpent is holding him in its coil. 77. O Lord Paṇḍhari, hasten quickly. Do thou save him. I can render no help at all. My strength and mind are both in vain. 78. The ascetic's body is not moving. The serpent has probably bitten him. All the results of my service have now become fruitless." The farmer became violently agitated. 79. He shouted, he loudly called for help, but the serpent would not move away. "The Brāhmaṇa is dead, is dead," he exclaimed. 80. The spot was a lonely one on the mountain. Men did not pass by there. Who then could there

be there to listen to his cry? Still he made the attempt to save Eknāth's life. 81. At last he knew he must do something at the moment. So from his mouth went out a loud piercing cry. "O Chakrapāṇi, Lord-of-the-Helpless, hasten and come to the rescue." 82. While the farmer was making this great outcry Eknāth became gradually conscious of the noise, and as his body began to move, the serpent glided quickly away. 83. When he became fully conscious, he applied water to his eyes, and said to the farmer, "What has happened. Tell me quickly." 84. The farmer was all in a tremor of body because of the sight of the serpent, but gradually coming to his senses, he approached Eknāth. 85. With reverence he made his *namaskār*, and replied, saying, "A great serpent had just now coiled itself around your body." 86. And as I saw this sight a great terror seized me, and I made a loud outcry, at which the serpent fled. 87. The *Svāmi's* confidence is at the feet of God, therefore your life has been saved at this time. Death came, but it was not the time for him, so it appears to me." 88. Hearing this explanation of the farmer Eknāth replied in an *Abhaṅg*. I quote it in this book with affection. So listen to it, ye pious folk.

ABHANG.

1. Death came to sting me.
   But he changed to a Merciful one.
2. Now I know him well.
   For heart has met heart.

3. Though in the body, my bodily consciousness disappeared;

So Death himself lost his power.

4. Ekā Janārdan now dances on his feet.

To the tune of, "No flavor to life or death."

89. With these verses recited in love, Eknāth closed his eyes, and in his mind contemplated the image of Pāṇḍuraṅg, his heart being full of love.

EKNĀTH HAS A VISION OF GOD.

90. And exlaimed, "Dweller-in-the-Ocean-of-Milk, O Thou-who-dost-rest-on-the-serpent, O Husband-of-Indirā, Enchanter-of-the-heart, Internal witness, Mass-of-Intelligence, Life-of-the-World, Śrī Hari. 91. Victory, Victory, Lord of-Vaikuṇṭh; infinite and boundless is Thy fame. In describing Thy glory even the *Śrutis* have exhausted themselves. The minds of all reach their limit here. 92. Thou the Unborn, the unconquered, the Unchangeable, Unaffected by Māyā, Tranquil, when reason seeks to comprehend Thee it cannot reach Thy depths. 93. Thus art Thou the Supreme-God-of-Gods. Śiva, in repeating Thy names became calmed. Thou dost pervade the whole Universe, yet there is no way of comprehending Thy depths. 94. Still, in order to come to the assistance of thy *Bhaktas,* Thou becamest the Four-armed *avatār*. My eyes are hungry to see Thee in that form." 95. Hearing these words of praise, the Husband-of-Rukmiṇi revealed Himself in that form, four-armed, dark of complexion, and adorned with the conch-shell and the disk in his hands.

96. His glorious, adorned face, enchanted the heart. In his ears were earrings in the form of crocodiles. On his neck the beautiful *Kaustubh* jewel sparkled. His divine yellow garment was translucent. 97. The brilliant Vaijayanti necklace, and the *trivali* sparkled on his breast. The little bells on his feet tinkled. The sight brings rest to the soul. 98. His whole body was smeared with sandal-wood paste. A saffron *tilak* well marked his forehead. He wore a garland of the tender *Tulsi* stems. On his breast was the *Śrī vatsa* mark. 99. So bright was his appearance, that the light of the sun's orb seemed inferior. As Śrī Eknāth opened his eyes there stood before him the Supreme Brahma, in his beauty. 100. With feelings of love in his heart, and with reverence Eknāth embraced his feet. The Supreme-lord-of-the-universe then embraced Eknāth drawing him close to his heart. 101. Having seated God beside him he worshipped Him in mental adoration, exclaiming, " He has placed over me the shadow of his mercy, and fulfilled the desire of my heart. 102. This meeting together of God and *Bhakta* was clearly seen by the farmer, and feeling a sense of supreme joy he exclaimed, " I am the special child of Fortune." 103. And so exclaiming he again and again made Eknāth a *namaskār*. Suddenly Śrī Hari took leave of Eknāth and vanished from sight. 104. The farmer recognizing that The-lord-of-life had made, as his happy resting place, the heart of his *bhakta,* he bowed to Eknāth with reverence. 105. And said to him, " By my being in company with the *Svāmi* I have seen with my own eyes the lord-of-heaven. Otherwise I should not have done so, for I am of inferior caste and dull of mind. 106. To save the world He has become an *avatār* in this saint.

This miracle has come into my experience this day." Again and again he repeated words of praise. 107. He then took up the vessel of milk and offered it to Śrī Eknāth earnestly pleading, "It is my earnest desire that you partake of this, O Sadguru, in bodily form." 108. Recognizing the sincerity of the farmer's feelings Eknāth drank the milk, and by a motion of the eye signified to him that he should now return to his home. 109. The farmer made a *pradakshiṇā,* prostrated himself on the ground before him, and went back to his home with joy in his heart. 110. He was pierced with the conviction that Śrī Eknāth was the Supreme Brahma in bodily form. Returning to his home he related to his wife all the events that had occurred.

EKNĀTH RETURNS TO TELL JANĀRDAN.

111. Now as to Eknāth. The sun had reached noontide, and the heat had become fierce. So he withdrew to the shade of a banyan tree, and there rested for a few hours. 112. And here while being relieved from the intense heat he suddenly remembered Janārdan's command, that if he saw anything very unusual, he was to return back to him. 113. It was truly by the *Sadguru's* favor that he had seen the visible appearance of the *Sagun̦* God. There could be nothing more marvellous than this. A great blessing had come to him. 114. Thus thinking to himself he worshipped, and returning to Devagiri he met the Sadgurumurti. 115. He bowed prostrate before him, and lovingly embraced him. Janārdan recognized by his appearance that something had happened, and said to himself, "I see

signs of a changed appearance." 116. The *Sadguru* asked what had happened. Eknāth in reply, told him of all the mysterious occurrences, and exclaimed. "It is truly by the *Svāmi's* favor that the otherwise unattainable had been attained."

JANĀRDAN AND EKNĀTH GO ON PILGRIMAGE.

117. It happened one day that Janārdan said to Eknāth, " A great desire has come to me to bathe in the Gaṅgā, [Godavari] 118. I want to see with my own eyes Nāsik, Panchavaṭi, and Śrī Trimbakrāj." Hearing this intention of the *Sadguru,* Eknāth was overjoyed. 119. Choosing an auspicious day Janārdan prepared to start on his pilgrimage to the *Tirthas.* He assigned to Eknāth a mare to ride on. 120. A horse for their things, and one for himself. He appointed a Brāhmaṇa cook, and all promptly started. 121. Whenever they found a beautiful spot there they rested for the night. Here they would discuss between themselves in happy mood of questions about the soul. 122. They especially loved those places where *sādhus* and saints congregated. There they would spend the night very happily, saying, " A blessed, happy day is this ! "

* THE PILGRIMS MEET CHANDRABHAT.

123. As they thus journeyed far they came to a large town. At this place there lived a Brāhmaṇa, named Chandrabhat, a distinguished Vaishṇava. 124. Hearing of his good fame, the *Guru* and his disciple were delighted,

*Compare Chatuśloki Bhāgavata 1028—1035; Keśavasvāmi Kṛit Eknāth Charitra 5, 1—57.

and as the sun was setting they put up for the night at his house. 125. Chandrabhat, seeing his distinguished Vaishnava guest, welcomed him with respect. Bowing to one another they mutually embraced. 126. Chandrabhat was an ascetic Brāhmaṇa. Though he had a family his mind was free from desires. Living on what came to him unasked, he maintained himself without hindrance. 127. He was ever performing austerities of body, speech and mind. The defilement from the filth of an untruth never so much as touched his lips. 128. In his ablutions and prayers, in his worship of God, and in good deeds to others, he spent his life. He looked on all men as himself, and was all kindliness to every creature. 129. In order to break the snares of *saṅsār*, he always sought association with the good, saying to himself, "When will these entanglement of *saṅsār* cease!" The ascetic idea had entered his heart like an arrow. 130. It was such a Chandrabhat, a Brāhmaṇa free from desires, indifferent to worldly things, and of an ascetic mind, whom Eknāth and Janārdan lovingly met. 131. After performing their evening devotions, they partook of their simple meal. As soon as it was finished the Brāhmaṇa withdrew by himself and unwrapped a book. 132. He turned to that portion of the Chatuśloki Bhāgavata, where Śrī Hari discoursed to Brahmadeva. Chandrabhat began to comment on it, and unfold its meaning in detail. 133. Eknāth and Janārdan then came and sat near him, exclaiming, "Blessed is this happy day in which we have met this saint." 134. As he thus found listeners loving, all-wise and expert, his heart rejoiced. And as he explained the meaning of the text, the minds of the listeners were deeply pierced. 135. As he related things out of his own experience, his voice was choked with emotion. Tears of love flowed from the eyes of all, and all three reached the state of bodily unconsciousness. 136. It truly seems to me as though the three Gods, Brahmā, Vishṇu and Maheśvara had come together. This thought impresses me. 137. If not that figure, then one might say, that as the three rivers Gaṅgā, Yamunā, and Sarasvati join together and flow on as one, so the love of the three united. And thus they spent the night. 138. When the reading of the book was finished they honored the night a little (with sleep). Both felt the desire that they might always be in Chandrabhat's company. 139. Eknāth and Janārdan said to one another, " Chandrabhat is deeply versed in the three Śāstras, *Karma, Upāsanā* and *Dyāna*." 140. Thus the night was spent. They arose in the morning and were about to start, when Chandrabhat made an earnest plea. " Hear my request," he cried. 141. " After you finish your ablutions and devotions please sanctify my *āśrama*." " I will do so," replied Janārdan, as he recognized his sincerity. 142. Food was cooked in the house, all the appointed rites were performed, offerings were made to the idols and to the fire, and they then sat down to eat. 143. Eknāth, Janārdan and the host, Chandrabhat sat in one line. After them the food was passed to others. 144. After the rinsing out of the mouth, and the passing of the *pān supāri*, Chandrabhat made another request. Said he, " A desire has arisen in my heart to be with you night and day." 145. To this Janārdan replied, " That is exactly what is in our mind. Without any hesitation come along with us." 146.

Chandrabhat, happy at heart, exclaimed, "Happily have I fallen into the company of the good, living the peaceful and the ascetic life."

THE PILGRIMS CONTINUE THEIR JOURNEY.

147. With worshipful spirit full of love, and of his own accord, he began the journey with them. He continued to interpret the Chatuśloka (Bhāgavat) and was full of joy. 148. Whenever he met on the way *sādhu, sant* or *yogī* he felt great love for them, and conversed with them on questions concerning the soul. 149. As they journeyed along in this manner they soon arrived at Panchavaṭi, and bathed in the Rāmakuṇḍa with penitent hearts. 150. After the due performance of the tirtha rites they went to their place of lodging, and later went to obtain the sight of Śrī Rāmchandra, with undivided love. 151. They worshipped with due ceremonials; they sang many songs of praise. They gave a feast and made the Brahmaṇs happy.

JANĀRDAN URGES EKNĀTH TO COMPOSE MARATHI BOOKS.

152. Janārdan then said to Eknāth, "I am going to tell you something, listen. On your head is the boon of Śrī Datta, which by your good fortune you unexpectedly received. 153. Chandrabhat has brought with him the Chatuśloki Bhāgavata. Prepare a commentary on it in Prakrit, (Marathi) in an extensive form." 154. Hearing his Sadguru's words, Eknāth became supremely happy, and began to

write the book and continued to do so with love. 155. He first wrote the (Sanskrit) Śloka and then gave its meaning. When the work was completed he showed it to his Śrī Guru. 156. Chandrabhat, Janārdan, and the learned Brahmaṇs of that holy place listened to the reading of the book and were greatly pleased. 157. As his first book Eknāth produced this Prakrit Commentary on the Chaṭu-śloki Bhāgavata. The *Sadguru* then said to him, 158. "Let your lips produce a Prakrit version of the Śrī Ekādaśa *skandha* (of the Bhāgavata Purāṇa). Śrī Krishṇa will be your helper, and cause you to express its complete meaning." 159. When Janārdan had thus spoken Eknāth bowed. Chandrabhat now took Eknāth's commentary on the Chatuśloki (Bhagavata) and gave readings from it. 160. Chandrabhat was versed in the *Karma, Bhakti* and *Dyāna Śastras;* still he adopted the practice of reading aloud the *Prākrit* [Marathi] version made by Eknāth. 161. The reverential feelings of Chandrabhat were great. Said he, "This *guru* and his disciple are *avatāras* of Hari and Śaṅkar for the salvation of the world. 162. Janārdan is Lord-of-Kailas, Eknāth is Vishṇu in visible form." With this feeling of reverence in his heart, he continually sang their praise. 163. And as the Brāhmaṇs of that sacred place heard it, all exclaimed, "Blessed, Blessed!" The three now journeyed on to Tryambakeśvara, and bathed in the Kuśavarta. 164. Keeping Brahmagiri on the right they visited Tripurāri. Here they performed their *tirtha* rites, and remained there for three nights. 165. With this visit they completed their pilgrimage and returned to Devagiri. The mind of Chandrabhata, indifferent to worldly things, had abandoned the desire of home. 166. His mind had already wearied of wife, son, home and wealth, therefore he could not leave the company of Janārdan and Eknāth, and so came with them to Devagiri. 167. After Janārdan reached his home, the very next day he fed Brahmans. His tongue revelled in the repetition of the names of God, and his heart was full of love. 168. Chandrabhat with feelings of sincere reverence would exclaim, "Eknāth is an avatāra in human form. In age and stature he is little, but his intellect is great in its power of expressing thought. 169. I must not leave his company as long as I live." With this strong determination he continued to remain there. 170. After he had passed many days there he attained bodily unconsciousness. The whole universe including himself appeared to him in the form of Janārdan. 171. He lost all consciousness of the concept. "I [God] and my body." He performed good deeds automatically. He viewed the whole world as his own soul. 172. He became fully enlightened, and so his name became changed. Everywhere people began to call him Chānd Bodhalā.

CHANDRABHAT DESIRES TO BE ENTOMBED ALIVE.

173. After some days were passed in this way he approached Janārdan in person and said, "The desire has arisen in me to be entombed alive." 174. Janārdan appreciated the desire of his heart, and arranged for his being entombed alive, while in his state of bodily unconsciouness. But lest the Mahomedans should cause trouble they devised a special plan. 175. They built a structure just like a Mahomedan tomb, and thus both Hindus and

Mahomedans were satisfied. 176. *That structure is still there to-day on Devagiri mountain, and many miracles take place there, seen and recognized universally.

JANĀRDAN SENDS EKNĀTH ON DISTANT PILGRIMAGES.

177. It now happened one day that Janārdan thought to himself, "I must send Ekobā on a pilgrimage to the sacred watering places. This earth will be made holy thereby." 178. Calling Eknāth aside he said to him, "Listen to my proposal." Eknāth humbly placed his head at his *guru's* feet, and with his lips uttered words of praise. 179. "Victory, Victory to Thee, Janārdan. Thou who art untouched by Māyā, Spotless-one, *Nirgun*. I am merely your darling, your infant. What can I know of Thy marvellous glory! 180. The *Srutis* and *Śāstras* praise Thee, but their power of expression fails them. All the *Purāṇas* and all knowledge are insufficient to declare Thy full praise. 181. When the serpent attempted to praise Thee, O God of Gods, he became confounded. His tongue was split in two. Of what value then is my desire to praise. 182. The Lord-of-serpents, who forms

---

*Note—The *samādhi,* or tomb of Chandrabhat, or Chand Bodhala as he is also called, is still to be seen at Daulatābād, formerly called Devagiri. It is situated to the East of the fort, and is worshipped both by Hindus and Muhammadans. A fair in his honor takes place on the 5th of the lunar half of the Hindus month of Chaitra (April). The *samādhi* is near the Hammam Khana, or Hammam Bada as it is called. The place was recently visited Mr. N. R. Godbole of Poona, from whom I have this information.

Thy couch, causing thee to lie upon him, enjoys love accompanied by happiness. 183. The Creator-of-the-world, the Four-faced-one, even He did not comprehend Thy power. When he stole away the calves, Thou, didst show a wonderful miracle. 184. Thou didst in fact create other cows and calves. Then with his four mouths, the Brahma, praised Thee, and came as a suppliant to Thee. 185. By Thy power the senses perform their regular functions in the body. How am I to compensate Thee! I who possess nothing at all. 186. In the animate and the inanimate, which appear to my sight, I see only Thee in all. And through this my mind has truly reached abiding rest." 187. With these words of praise, Eknāth, with sincere reverence touched his head to Janārdan's feet, and exclaimed, "Whatever you now command me, I will, in every particular, take it to heart." 188. Hearing Eknāth's nectar words, Janārdan replied with a satisfied mind. "Go and visit at least once all the sacred watering places that this earth possesses. 189. Make a three nights' rest in some places, a five nights' rest in others. Whenever you meet with what is related to God you should make a *namaskāra*. 190. Though you go for the purpose of a pilgrimage, you will at the same time meet with Saints. Śrī Krishna Himself will provide for all your daily needs. 191. Go as far as Badrināth, and view that northern lake, Mānas, with your eyes. To the south, visit Rāmeśvara, and then return to me here." 192. As Eknāth heard these words of his Sadguru, there came to him both joy and sorrow. If you ask how this could come about, listen to the reason. 193. His heart was happy, because he would meet with Saints. He was sad, because he would lose the sight of his *Sadguru*. 194. Food was cooked in the house and the two ate together sitting in a line. They rinsed out their mouths, they took the *pān supāri,* and were happy together.

EKNĀTH STARTS ON HIS LONG PILGRIMAGE.

195. When Śrī Nāth started on his pilgrimage, Janārdan saw him on his way. Just as it happens when a woman is going back to her father-in-law these two were choked with emotion. 196. The way first led through a forest, and Eknāth placed his head on his Sadguru's breast exclaiming, "Now let your favor rest upon me. I place myself in your affection." 197. He was choked with emotion and tears of love flowed. The same happened to the *Sadguru,* who could not at all restrain the expression of his love. 198. Janārdan now said to him, "I shall always be in your heart. Hold this thought in your remembrance, that you and I are not separated. 199. You are as dear to me as my own life, and I am your very soul. Now let go the delusion of duality, and be not sad over this separation,. 200. With this, Janārdan placed on Eknāth's head his own turban. And as this great blessing so wonderfully came to him, Eknāth overflowed with love-acompanied joy. 201. Śrī Eknāth then made a request, "Again give me a *darśan* of yourself." The Sadguru understood the inner mystic meaning of this request and replied, "I will do so." 202. Eknāth made a *pradakshiṇā* around Janārdan, making *namaskārs* with expressions of love, and so carrying in his mind the visible form of Janārdan, he started on his way. 203. He walked away quickly, but every few paces he turned back to look at his *Guru,* and so long as he could see Janārdan again and

again prostrated himself on the ground towards him. 204. Exclaiming, "Victory, Victory to Thee, Janārdan," he went on his way in haste. The *Sadguru,* having thus seen Eknāth on his way, returned to his abode. 205. But very often there would come to his mind the noble character of Eknāth, and the *Sadguru* felt very sad, and his mind was not at rest.

206. Saints are in fact Pāṇḍuraṅg in human form. Who then can adequately describe them? I, dull of mind, can only babble, and this seems like a sin. 207. But because they are dear to me, I speak of them, though in foolish uncouth words. The real author of this book is the Husband-of-Śrī Rukmiṇi, He who abides on the bank of the Bhimā river. 208. That Pāṇḍuraṅg, performer of wonderful things through Māyā, is the one who is relating His own deeds. He is making me, Mahīpati, only a pretext. I am neither a poet nor an author. 209. Swasti. This is the Śrī Bhaktalilāmṛita. By merely listening to it one's desires are fulfilled. Listen then to it, ye, loving pious Bhaktas. This is the fourteenth delightful chapter.

CHAPTER 15.

MAHĪPATI'S INVOCATION.

1. Obeisance to Śrī Gaṇeśa. In singing the infinite praise of the Limitless-One the power of expression of even the greatest minds has failed, how then can my commonplace mind be equal to the task? 2. To use a simile, over the immense store of sea water ships sail across the sea, but how can my little broken checkerboard raft cross to the opposite shore? 3. The moon, together with all the

constellations, disappear as the sun arises. So it is impossible to think that before the rising sun the light of the firefly can be great. 4. There is no balance so immense that with it one can readily weigh this world. It is evident that one cannot cover the etherial space with one's hand. 5. Where is the light so brilliant that with it one can see the entire disk of the sun? So in attempting to describe the attributes of the Supreme Vishṇu the mind with its intellect goes insane. 6. But just as when a little infant sees its mother it prattles all kinds of meaningless words, and she through the power of her love laughingly supplies its little desires. 7. So the Saits should accept my foolish words, considering me, Mahipati, but an ignorant child.

THE DISTRESS OF EKNĀTH'S GRANDPARENTS.

8. The last chapter contained the noteworthy story of Eknāth's starting on his pilgrimage, and of Janārdan's feeling sad at heart, as there constantly came to his mind Eknāth's noble character.

9. Let us now turn back to Pratishṭhana, where Eknāth's grandfather and grandmother lived. Eknāth (it will be remembered) had slipped away to Devagiri without asking their permission. 10. Busy in the service of his *sadguru* he had not returned to them. Thereby the aged couple were in distress of mind, and they began to search for him from house to house. 11. Now of this one, now of that one they began to enquire, " Have you seen our Eknāth?" When they replied, "We do not know where he is," they both would weep. 12. Both wandered about the sacred city enquiring from house to

house. They had no rest of mind day or night. Eknāth filled their hearts. 13. Food and drink tasted good no longer. Their nights seemed as long as years, as there came to their minds the goodness of the boy. And no one was able to help them in their search. 14. They used to say to themselves in their distress, " His father and mother died when he was an infant. Only this family twig has survived. With his support we had hoped to drag out our days. 15. On what island has this blind folk's staff got caught? When shall we ever see him again?" And so saying they deeply sorrowed. 16. Of the three kinds of people in the city there were some with evil surmisings. Some remarked, " Perhaps the grandparents had spoken harshly to the boy, so that he ran away. 17. The grandfather and grandmother are attached to him, but they cannot have feelings similar to those of a mother or father. He whose the child is will accept the burden. To others he is a trouble." 18. Others said, "That is a false idea. They have coddled and pampered him too much. Boys are boys, cruel by nature. He simply left them and ran away. 19. We have been watching coincidences connected with him from his infancy. First his mother and father died, then poverty came quickly. 20. His grandfather and grandmother remain, but he has brought them distress, and now in their old age there is no one even to give them water to drink." 21. Well, to continue, these three classes of people had their various says, but the aged couple could find no rest of mind. They made many efforts. 22. Pilgrims to sacred places, travelling merchants, and cloth peddlers were approached with the question, "Have you seen our Eknāth?" 23. They asked even crows, and *sālonkis,* and parrots "Have you seen our Eknāth?" They went to the river sand bed, and prostrated themselves to the Gaṅgā [Godavari] river, 24. Exclaiming, "Our eyes do not behold our child. Perhaps you have drowned him in your water. Tell us truly and quickly." Thus they were accustomed to plead with the Gaṅgā river. 25. Through Eknāth's going to meet with his *Sadguru* the aged couple were sunk in the sea of distress, and as they mourned day and night their eyes were weakened by their weeping. 26. Kindred, near relations, even the slanderers, close friends and other good people used to come to their home and seek to comfort them. 27. They would say, "He is young in years, but in character he is noble. His mind was always in the attitude of worshipping God. He was always listening to the reading of the *Purāṇs.* 28. He was strongly attached to *sādhus* and *sants,* and distinguished Vaishṇavas. On his lips there was unceasingly the worshipful praise of Śrī Rām. 29. As we with pleasure watched his mental ability, we used to feel supreme wonder. The Lord-of-Vaikuṇṭha is surely his protector. Mourn no longer. 30. He had a strong attraction to listening to philosophical books. We certainly think that he must have attached himself somewhere to some good man." 31. One suggested that as Eknāth was accustomed to sit with the Pandit listening to his reading of the *Purāṇs,* the Pandit may have enticed the boy away, and taken him away with him to the army. 32. This suggestion, made by one of them, was approved by all, that the *Purāṇik* had made the child his disciple, and enticed him away. 33. Thinking of this possibility the aged couple were moved with both joy and sorrow. They proceeded to the Paṇdit's house and there enquired. How they enquired, listen. 34.

"The *Purāṇik* has gone away to the army. He has deceived the child and enticed him away. We are in great sorrow, and are mourning night and day." 35. The people of the house replied to this, "The master of the house has gone to the army, it is true, but whether he took the child with him we do not know." 36. The people of the city, however, continued to suspect that Eknāth did go away with him, and the sorrowing grandfather and grandmother watched for his return. 37. They expected the *Purāṇik* would soon return from the army, and would bring the child back with him, so they kept watching day and night. Four years thus passed. 38. Suddenly the army returned, and the couple went again to the*Purāṇik's* house, and said, "The *Purānik* has seduced our boy and taken him away. The *Purāṇik* is a vallain hero indeed! 39. He has deceived our child in some way, made him his disciple, and taken him far away. If he does not bring him back safely, we shall commit suicide here at his door." 40. The people of the house hearing this threat were alarmed and sent a letter to the *Purāṇik,* saying, "Have you deceived Ekā and enticed him away, or has a false charge come upon you?" 41. When the Brāhmaṇ received the letter from his home folk he was greatly distressed, and exclaimed, "I have truly committed no wrong, and yet this false charge has come upon me." 42. The Paṇdit acquainted his employer with the matter, took his pay, and started home, saying to himself, "I wonder where Eknāth has gone to. Suspicion has fallen on me. 43. Eknāth did give me an intimation of his intense desire to go to Devagiri to meet with the Śrī Guru Janārdan." 44. As this recollection suddenly came to him he said to himself, "I will go there in search of Eknāth, and if he is there, I will bring him back with me." 45. With this thought in mind, the Purāṇik came to Devagiri, and meeting Janārdanpant related the whole matter to him. 46. The Sadguru replied, "Eknāth was here up to the present. By his faithful service he gratified me. 47. And now at my command indeed he has gone on a distant pilgrimage." Janārdan then sent a letter by the *Purāṇik* to the grandparents that they should not be in the least concerned about Eknāth. 48. The *Purāṇik* on his return to Pratishṭhāna went to Eknāth's home where he found the aged couple sitting and told them the news. 49. "Your Eknāth went to Devagiri to visit Janārdan. Here is a letter in Janārdan's own handwriting." And he showed it to them. 50. Hearing the news of the finding of their lost son, they were overjoyed, exclaiming, "We were dying, but life has returned. We had no one to care for us." 51. When they were certain that the news was true they could hardly believe their ears. They brought sugar and put it into the *Purāṇik's* mouth. 52. The *Purāṇik* further added, "If you do not believe me, go yourselves to Devagiri and enquire of Janārdan." 53. And with this remark the Brāhmaṇ returned to his home. The aged couple, however, were greatly troubled in their minds as to what to do. 54. "If we should send a man to Devagiri," they said to one another, "we have no money to give him. So let us go ourselves to that place and see Janārdan."

THE GRANDPARENTS VISIT JANĀRDAN.

55. And so deciding, and slowly, slowly trudging along the path, they came to Devagiri, and met Janārdan. 56. They related to him their story from beginning to

end, with eyes filled with tears. "Nāth has cast us off, and has not returned home." 57. Janārdan arose to receive them, welcomed them with affection, and told them in loving words of the noble character of Eknāth. 58. "In order to save the Universe, Śrī Vishṇu has become in him an *avatār*. Blessed is your holy family line. Salvation has come to your whole lineage. 59. He seems to your minds to be merely a child, but in reality he is Pāṇḍuraṅg in human form. You will in the future observe the course of his life, and then your doubts will vanish." 60. With these assurances of Janārdan they were comforted, and said, "Full six months must pass, and then Nāth will return." 61. Janārdan made them stay in his home for a month, and with affection he gave them to eat always fresh and daintily cooked food. 62. He gave them clothes, adornments, ornaments and an abundance of money to spend, and finally with his own hand he wrote a letter to be given to Eknāth. 63. The substance of the letter was this, "As soon as you see this letter cease your wanderings to sacred places, and make your abode there at Pratishṭhāna." 64. The *Sadguru* wrote this letter with His own hand, and gave it to them. He provided horses and men to accompany them, and he personally saw them on their way. 65. Janārdan also further said to them, "After visiting the sacred watering places on the North and the Mānas Lake, Eknāth will on his return pass through Paiṭhaṇ, and you must be on the watch to recognize him. 66. After you show him my letter he will not go on any further. Do not be troubled any longer in your minds." Such were his assurances. 67. The couple were made happy by these words of Janārdan, and returning to Paiṭhaṇ related their whole story. 68. To every one they praised the nobleness of Janārdan. The letter they preserved very carefully, and told every one about it, 69. saying, "If Eknāth should suddenly arrive, perhaps in the next six months, and you should recognize him, so plan that he remain."

EKNĀTH'S WANDERINGS.

70. To turn now to Eknāth. By the command of his *Sadguru* he had gone on this pilgrimage. His thought and mind were filled with Janārdan. He saw only him in all the animate and the inanimate of the three worlds. 71. He visited many sacred watering places and shrines to set an example to the people. Wherever he found a restful place he tarried a three-night. 72. In some places finding a company of saints he would remain a five-night. He would worship and bathe at such places, and leave whenever it so pleased him. 73. He visited the great river watering places, the Pūrṇā, Payoshṇi, Tapati, Narmadā. The sight of Mahākāleśvara at Avanti brought peace to his mind. 74. He visited also Mathura, Gokul and Vrindāvana with great delight, where loving Vaishṇavas wag their heads as they sing the praises of God. 75. At such places he found pious *Bhaktas*. He saw their cermonious worship of Vishṇu. He looked upon them with great delight. His heart was charmed with that place. 76. It made him exclaim, "Blessed, blessed is this holy place. Here Chakrapāṇi performed his miraculous deeds." In meeting the Vaishṇavas who lived at the place he was very happy. 77. The performance of *rās*, the *Hari-kītans*, the people all intent on worship, Krishṇa being in their thoughts

and minds, all this deeply impressed him. 78. Śrī Eknāth spent many days at this Vishṇu holy place. Then making his *namaskāra* to God he started on his further journey. 79. He soon arrived at Banares (Vārāṇasi,) the supreme holy place. He bathed in the Maṇikarṇikā, and worshipped before Viśveśvara. 80. He remained there a five-night, and then hastened on with the idea that through the power of Śrī Janārdan he might visit that place again. 81. He continued his way to Prayāg, and bathed at the junction of the three rivers. The sight of Mādhava brought peace to his soul. 82. He journeyed on to Gayā, where with love he bowed before the feet of Śrī Vishṇu, and as he worshipped in reverence he experienced joy. 83. Those who with an undivided devotional spirit place body, speech and mind at the feet of Vishṇu, by that very fact perform the ceremonies at Gayā. Who can count their uncountable good deeds that give them this opportunity? 84. Those who are wholly devoted to the feet of Śrī Hari, are by that very fact performers of all good deeds. And as their feet touch the *tirthas* these watering places become purified. 85. The rivers Yamunā, Godāvari, Bhāgirthi, Krishṇā, Venyā, Sarasvati, Narmadā, Tāpi, Bhimarathi, all long for the coming of the saints. 86. Janārdan had known of their desire and had compassion on them. He therefore had commanded Eknāth to visit all the sacred watering places. 87. And Śrī Nāth, filled completely with the thought that Janārdan pervaded mankind, wandered from *tirtha* to *tirtha,* the principal ones of which I have already mentioned. 88. After visiting Gayā, Prayāg and Kāśi, he journeyed on to Ayodhyā. The people living at this *Kshetra* (holy place) are devoted to the name of Rām. 89. He worshipped before the images of Rām, Sitā, Lakshmaṇa, Bharata and

Śatrughna, which brought a feeling of peace to his mind. 90. To Eknāth all Vishṇu *kshetras* were especially attractive, for, there, loving Vaishṇavas live, and in their love wag their heads in singing Vishṇu's praise. 91. After seeing Ayodhyā, he went to Badrināth, visited the *tirtha* of Adipushkara, bathing in its water. 92. At the mere sight of Pushkara all filth of the *Kali yuga* is immediately destroyed. This place also was purified by the coming there of Eknāth. 93. Then he went into the Himālayas, to where the water of the Bhāgirathi starts to flow, where there is a very profound gorge, which the eye can hardly bear look down into. 94. He had to sit in the sling (of the rope bridge) in order to cross to the other side, but Eknāth did not experience the slightest fear. 95. With superlative delight he viewed that spot, and seeing Badri Nārāyaṇa he made his *sashṭāṅga namaskār* before him. 96. Just as in Nar-Nārāyaṇa there is no idea of difference between them, so God and a *Bhakta,* one in nature, mutually increase the glory of one another. 97. All the dwellers at that *Kshetra,* with loving devotion praise the miraculous deeds of Śrī Hari. Because Udhava had been sent to this hermitage of Badrika, he there inaugurated this custom. 98. Whatever examples the saints set, the pious follow accordingly, and all doubts vanishing they become *Jivanmuktas* (liberated though alive) 99. Taking leave of Badrināth, Eknāth came to Dvārkā. And seeing a lonely place in a forest he began there to worship Śrī Hari. 100. His mind became absorbed in his name and form and in this contemplation he lost all bodily consciousness. The whole universe seemed to be Janārdan, including himself. 101. With that thought in mind he went to Dvārakāpuri, and as he bathed on the banks of the Gomati he felt joy in his heart. 102. He then proceeded to the temple, and with love made a *sāshtāṅg namaskār*. Seeing the image of Śrī Krishṇa he was made happy. 103. Eknāth remained here a whole month, observing the morning, noon and evening offerings and worship, and listening to the praise services. 104. And now to see with his own eyes the southern sacred watering places, he turned southward from there. Journeying, the first place to greet his sight was Junāgad, the place where Narsi Mehta had lived. 105. Eknāth also visited the place where the ancient idol of Dvārakā seeing the devotion of his *bhakta* came to Ḍākur in love. 106. Thus having visited the northern *tirthas* thoroughly, and having seen the twelve chief Śiva shrines, and the seven chief cities, he danced in the fulness of his joy.

EKNĀTH RETURNS TO PRATISHṬHĀNA.

107. Then gradually making his way he arrived at the holy city of Pratishṭhana. He bathed by the bank of the Godā river, and made his *namaskār* to Pimpaleśvar. 108. Lest any of the people of the town should recognize him, and so embarrass him here, he kept himself hidden in the temple from early morning on. 109. But as he needed food, at noon time he had to wander into the town, and whenever and whatever he received of food he contentedly ate. 110. He had conquered his appetite in restraining his senses. He was no longer conscious of what was sweet to the taste. Whether he was honored or dishonored was alike to him, for enemy or friend seemed to be Janārdan himself. 111. It was with this thought that Eknāth had visited the *tirthas* and now had arrived here at Pratishṭhāna.

As he one day entered the town his grandparents suddenly saw him. 112. Śrī Nāth recognized them at once, and made a mental *namaskār* to them. "If I should make myself known to them," he thought, "they will entangle me in the worldly life. 113. The worldly life is a difficult position to be in. I shall fail in obedience to the command of my *Sadguru*. The southern sacred watering places are still to be visited, and I must hasten away." 114. With this thought in mind he did not make himself known to them, but his grandfather and grandmother looking intently at him suddenly recognized the marks of his identity. 115. "It is a long time," they said, "since as a child he left us and went away. His body has reached adulthood. We are in doubt." 116. Reasoning thus they both said to him on a chance, "Bapa, you cast us off. How could you have made your heart so cruel," and with this their eyes were filled with tears. 117. While the grandparents were thus talking to him a crowd of men and women collected, and they declared, "He is surely Nāth." 118. While one, however, said, "He is he most certainly," another remarked, "I have my doubts. The Fates are against the aged couple. One cannot understand the ways of Fate." 119. But Eknāth would not reply, either by saying he was or was not Eknāth, and as he arose to go away his grandparents seized hold of him. 120. And bringing out the letter of command which they had already procured from Śrī Janārdan, in his own handwriting, they showed it to him. 121. Śrī Nāth recognized it at once, and affectionately touched his forehead to it in worship. And taking in its meaning he sat down on the very spot where he then was. 122. Just as the Vindhya range of mountains fell to the earth as it bowed its head worshipfully to the command of the rishi Agasti, so as soon as Eknāth had read the letter of Janārdan he sat down on the ground on the very spot where he then was. 123. The people said to him, "There is no habitation here. Come along to your home." But this *Videhi* would listen to none of them. He kept dumb. He would not utter a word. 124. The animate and the inanimate world seemed to him as *Māyā*. It appeared to him as Janārdan. His body therefore knew neither cold nor heat. Though possessing a body he was unconscious of a body. 125. There were present pious people who suggested that food should be brought and served to him at once, and at that very spot. 126. What these all-wise suggested was listened to as an acceptable plan by the grandparents. They served him food at that place and Śrī Nāth ate it lovingly. 127. For three days he did not rise at all from that spot. His Grandfather and grandmother had to come there, seeing how determined he was. 128. He had no protection from the cold, heat or wind, and so some of the pious people of the town built a thatched roof over him. 129. Here Eknāth adorned with *sātvik* signs performed his *Bhajans* with enthusiasm, and the people hearing him were astonished. 130. And exclaimed, "He is still in his youth, and yet possesses complete *vairāgya*. One should not call him a human being. He seems a divine avatār."

EKNĀTH PERFORMS KIRTANS.

131. Thus praising him, people began to come to see him morning, noon, and night, and seeing their loving *bhakti*, he would perform services of praise. 132. Without any previous study he would by inspiration expound them,

and compose with ease verses in which he described the wonderful deeds of Śrī Hari. 133. He had no one to take the leading part in the chorus, and so God Pāṇḍuraṅg felt concern and himself took the form of a Brāhmaṇ and aided him in his *kirtans*. 134. As the words flowed from Eknāth's lips the Brāhmaṇ would reutter them with ease and thus with the cymbals in his hand he would accompany Eknāth in the flow of sweet music. 135. The Divinity of every form of song, the God-of-Gods, the Husband-of-Rukmiṇi, dwelling within Eknāth's soul brought to his recollection the words of his song. 136. And at the same time outwardly Śrī Hari took the leading part in the chorus (*dhruvapad*). Yet no one knew this, even though they were looking at him directly with their eyes.

EKNĀTH'S INFLUENCE FOR GOOD.

137. Hearers, as they listened to Eknāth's *kirtans* lost all bodily consciousness. And if his words fell on the ears of evil minded men they were changed into good men. 138. The dwellers in that sacred city, both men and women, discussed him among themselves, saying, " Śrī Eknāth has become an *avatār* to save the world. 139. No one can sing such loving songs and give such *kīrtans*, as he can. In the mere listening to them the minds of all are deeply impressed. Thus people praised him. 140. As he continued giving these *kīrtans*, the influential and wealthy citizens of the town took notice of them, and finally erected for him a building on which they spent much money. 141. They also gave to Eknāth a piece of land, a house, and a little open square. They held a house warming, and

offerings of food were made to Brāhmans, to their entire satisfaction. 142. His grandfather and grandmother comforted at last, brought their household gods with them and lived with him in this house. 143. Pious people gave them food and raiment of their free will. The goddess-of-plenty is always found serving him who is a friend to the Lord-of-Vaikuṇṭha. 144. On the Eleventh of the months Eknāth began to hold watch-night *kirtans* in praise of Hari that lasted all night long. Crowds of people attended to listen and to repeat in chorus the names and attributes of God.

EKNĀTH CELEBRATES KRISHṆA'S BIRTHDAY.

145. One day Śrī Eknāth suddenly announced that on Krishṇa's birthday in the month of Śrāvaṇa, a festival of love would be held. The idea was approved by all. 146. Rich merchants brought the things needed for the celebration in great abundance. The temple was whitewashed and decorated and a light bamboo structure was erected for the idol. 147. Some Brāhmaṇs went to Devagiri and met Janārdan. They told him all about Eknāth. Janārdan heard their story with great joy. 148. Just as a father feels satisfaction when he hears of his son's success, or as a mother feels keen delight in her soul when she sees the cunning ways of her child. 149. Just so the soul of the *Sadguru* could not contain his supreme joy. And with all his retinue he started on his journey to visit Eknāth. 150. He had made many preparations for assisting at the Krishṇa festival, and taking them along the journey began. 151. With musical instruments, flags and numerous eagle banners the procession marched along the way with great enthusiasm

o the accompaniment of stirring music. 152. In order :o feed the Brāhmans he took provisions along with ıim, made into bundles and carried on pack bullocks, and vhich he sent on ahead of him. 153. When Janārdan ırrived at Pratishṭhāna he went to Eknāth's house. As he ıpproached it a marvel greeted his eyes. 154. At the nain door Śrī Dattātreya stood in the form of a door keeper. He had in his hands the trident, and looked just like Śīva (Tripurāri). 155. As Janādan's eyes fell upon him he recognized the Jagadguru at once, and making a *sāshṭāṅga namaskār* he embraced him affectionately. 156. Śrī Datta then explained to Janārdan, "Eknāth is in reality Pāṇḍuraṅg in human form; therefore out of love for him I have taken my abode here at his main door." 157. With this explanation, a marvel occurred. Datta suddenly took human form and went inside to announce to Eknāth Janārdan's arrival. 158. "Janārdan has come from Devagiri with all his retinue to meet you," he announced. Eknāth hearing this announcement was overjoyed. 159. And when he heard the coming of his *Sadguru,* he prostrated himself, affectionately embraced him, and clasped his feet. 160. Eknāth took Janārdan by the hand and led him within the house, he seated his *sadguru,* and washed his feet with his own hands. 161. And as he drank the water with which the feet had been washed, his soul felt supreme joy. He then brought forward the materials for worship and offered them to his *Sadguru.* 162. He smeared on his person the pulp of the Chandan wood. He placed a garland of flowers around his neck, and he waved over the *Sadguru* in human form the incense, the lights and the five-lamp-tray. 163. After Eknāth had thus worshipped him he told him all his story from beginning to end. Although Janārdan was possessed with inner sight, yet he listened, manifesting loving interest. 164. The festival of the birth of Krishṇa was held in Eknāth's house. Musical instruments gave out their sweet sounds. The anointing and worship of the idol was followed by its installation in the bamboo structure. 165. All the inhabitants of the sacred city came in an uninterrupted flow for a *darśana* of the idol. They brought with them varieties of daintily prepared food, and fed the Brāhmaṇs. 166. Śrī Janārdan sat on a seat facing the audience. Eknāth performed the *kīrtan* before him. To describe the greatness of joy that was felt all language fails. 167. Pāṇḍuraṅg, taking the form of a Brāhmaṇ, led the chorus. He danced with little bells on his feet. God has great love for his *Bhaktas.* 168. As words of inspiration fell from the lips of Eknāth the Brāhmaṇ took up the same in chorus, repeating them as if he already knew them by heart. 169. To this the men and women of the sacred city listened and marvelled, exclaiming "This distinguished Brāhmaṇ, leader of the chorus, is able to repeat the whole story. 170. The two (Eknāth and the Brāhmaṇ) are but one body. The debt of love they owe one another belongs to a former birth. Supreme good fortune has come to us. It is for this that the two have come together." 171. During the daytime offerings of food were made to the Brāhmaṇs. At night *Hari Kīrtans* were performed and by all this the minds of the pious folk of Paiṭhaṇ were deeply impressed. 172. On the ninth of the month, a great quantity of dainty food was prepared, and the partaking crowd was large. The distinguished Vaishṇavas, always of loving hearts, ended the fasting.

173. Then followed the relating of the childish pranks of the infant Krishṇa, and the ceremony of the Gopalkālā was begun. The parts of Vadaje, Vankude and Pendhe were taken. Many other characters were also assumed. 174. There was wrestling and the games of lāvi, hāmāmā, humbari lapanḍāva. Śrī Nāth played the part of Yaśodā in churning, and Hari ate the butter. 175. They performed with gesticulations the games of ball, of phugaḍi, piṅgā and other kinds of amusements. Indeed whatever sports were related in the Bhāgavata, they imitated here. 176. Eknāth went through a dramatic performance and appeared in many different guises. He repeated poems of inspiration. The occasion was one of unusual interest. 177. Chakrapāṇi, who had assumed the form of chorus leader, repeated his words after him. The hearers marvelled and laughed heartily. 178. The six varieties of *darśanas,* the thirty six special heresies, and the Siddhānta were explained by Eknāth according to established truths, and excellently uttered. 179. The surface meaning was made plain. The ignorant were thereby made joyous, and the wise realized the *Siddhānta.* They called his words inspired. 180. Thus dancing and singing, the idol of Śrī Krishṇa was placed finally on the swinging cot. Then an auspicious ārati was performed and sweetmeats were distributed. 181. Janārdan now asked Eknāth, "Who is the Brāhmaṇ who leads the chorus. Where is he from, and who is he? Ask him his name. 182. He leads the chorus in a most unusual way. In acting and supporting your acting and in various brilliant ways, you and he appear as if you were one body. It does not seem to me as though you were two persons. 183. You have laid up a store of good deeds, therefore

you have this association with him. He puts life into the *kīrtans*. Hearers find rest of soul in listening to him. 184. You and he should be joined together in this way for life. If this could be, the salvation of the world would be greatly promoted as men listen to the music of the *kīrtans*." 185. Eknāth then asked him, "You are a Brāhmaṇ, from what place, and who are you? Where is your home, what is your name. Tell us." 186. The Husband-of-Rukmiṇi listened and replied, "I have no fixed abode. Where I discover loving pious men, I spend my time in their company. 187. Viṭhobā is the name of this body of mine. I have not the snare of wife or son. In *kīrtans* I lead the chorus. I am expert only in this. 188. I have no other desire in my heart but to live always in your company, being content with a morsel of food." This is all he told them of what might identify him. 189. Janārdan listened to this reply, and was greatly delighted, but it did not suggest itself to him that he was in reality the Husband-of-Indirā. 190. For fourteen days there had continued this giving of food to Brāhmaṇs and when all these provisions were distributed, Janārdan said.

JANĀRDAN INSTRUCTS EKNĀTH TO MARRY.

191. "I am now going back to Devagiri." As he was taking leave of the aged couple, they touched their heads to his feet and said, "We have one request to make of you, your lordship. 192. Of the descendants of Bhānudās, Nāth is the only surviving member. By your command he has remained here, but his mind is unattached to things of this world. 193. He has no wish to become

a householder. So we plead at your feet that the *Svāmi* may give him a command to marry. 194. If you bring about his marriage we shall be comforted. The fasting of our eyes will cease, and the *Svāmi* will gain glory." 195. Janārdan was deeply moved, hearing this pitiful plea of the aged couple. He called Eknāth to him and spoke to him nectar words. 196. "If a bride comes to you of her own free choice, then without hesitation enter the marriage bond. There is no objection to your living the householder's life, and thus freeing yourself from the possibility of public scandal. 197. Of all the superior *Aśrams the Grihasthāśram* is the noblest. Here you can control the organs of sense, and can in happiness carry on all your special duties. 198. Such as kindness to all creatures, wearing away your body in deeds of benevolence to others, giving food to Brāhmaṇs, guests and the hungry, 199. The worship of Vishṇu with due ceremonials, *Kīrtans* performed in love, and the continued repeating of the names and attributes of God with the feeling of love." 200. Eknāth quietly accepted this command of his *Sadguru*. In silence he touched his forehead to Janārdan's feet, and then replied, "If this is in my fate, it will take place." 201. Leaving this command with Eknāth that he should give happiness to his grandparents by marrying, Janārdan returned to Devagiri with all his retinue. 202. Eknāth saw his *Sadguru* on his way. He kept the memory of him in the recesses of his heart. There was no separation from his *Guru* even for a moment, for all within him and without him was in the form of his *Guru*. 203. And Janārdan, having left his friendship, his affection and love with Eknāth, arrived at Devagiri with his retinue.

204. The narrator of the delightful story in the next chapter is Śrī Rukmiṇipati himself. I Mahipati, am merely the pretext. You wise people, realize this by experience. 205. This is the Śrī Bhaktalīlāmṛita. By merely listening to it one's desires are fulfilled. Listen then to it, ye loving pious *Bhaktas*. This is the fifteenth delightful chapter.

CHAPTER 16.

Of the Bhaktalīlāmṛita.

MAHIPATI'S INVOCATION.

1. Obeisance to Śrī Gaṇeśa. Victory to Thee Recumbent on the serpent, Immeasurable-One, Limitless, Without-name, Uncomposed-of-the-three-Guṇas, Adorable-deity of the-God-that-burned-the-God-of-Love, Protector-of-true-*bhaktas*. 2. Lord of the Serpent-Enemy (Garuda,) Destroyer-of-Sorrow, Thou-who-lovest-as-his-own-soul-the-daughter-of-the-Ocean. Dweller-in-the-Ocean, Recliner-on-the-Serpent, Saviour-of-the-Sinner, Ocean-of-mercy. 3. Dweller-in-Vaikuṇṭha, Infinitely-generous-One, Thou-whose-abode-is-the whole-of-the-universe. Brāhma is thy name, Supreme God, Thou art Brahma, everlastingly good. 4. Holder-up-of mount-Govardhan, Lord-of-the-cows, Beloved-of-Gopis, Madana-in-visible-form, Thou dwellest in the organs of beings, and hence thou art called Gosāvi. 5. Do thou now, who art constantly seated in my heart, give my mind power of recollection. Recite through me this Śrī Bhaktalilāmṛita, whereby the love of the hearers may well up and overflow.

6. At the close of the last chapter, the story was that of Janārdan instructing Eknāth to live as a householder, and preach the Bhakti mārga. 7. Having thus instructed him he prepared to return to Devagiri. And now good folk and pious, listen to the further recital full of deep meaning.

THE GRANDPARENTS SEARCH FOR A BRIDE.

8. The aged grandfather and grandmother now became worried night and day, thinking, "Oh if we could but find a bride for Eknāth, he might be married before our eyes." 9. As they thus conversed with one another, pious people remarked to them, "God is your helper in this matter. Let not your heart be in the least troubled. 10. Śrī Nāth's mind is entirely disattached from the world, it is true, and we are troubled as to whether he will be willing to marry or not, but Pāṇḍuraṅg has fulfilled our longings. 11. Eknāth will not at all transgress the command of Janārdan. When the season for marriages arrives, we shall make great effort." 12. Hearing these reassuring words of the pious folk, the grandparents were comforted. Time passed by, and now the season for marriages arrived.

HOW THE BRIDE WAS FOUND.

13. Now there was in a certain town a Brāhmaṇ, whose daughter had reached the marriagable age. He had been looking for a husband for her, but as yet the horoscope

would not agree with that of anyone. 14. While in this greatly troubled state of mind, he was asleep at night, and Pāṇḍuraṅg came to him in a dream, and told him in the vision as follows. 15. "At Pratishṭhāna, on the bank of the Gaṅgā, [Godavari] there is living a Vishṇu *bhakta,* named Eknāth, a man of beautiful character. Go and place your daughter in that family, well adorned." 16. This vision, given by the Husband-of-Rukmiṇi was by night. The Brāhmaṇ suddenly awoke, and marvelled in his mind over the vision. 17. He told his wife of this vision, and himself coming to Pratishṭhāna enquired of the people where Eknāth lived. 18. They pointed out his house, and the Brāhmaṇ went to see him, and related what the Husband-of-Rukmiṇi had told him in the vision. 19. He bowed in reverence to the grandfather and grandmother, and said, "I give my daughter to your grandson." 20. The offer made to them was acceptable to the grandparents. They called in the Joshi astrologers, and handed to them the astral birth records. 21. As the astrologer read the signs of the Zodiac and the constellations he found the combination that revealed the future relation of bride and bridegroom to be thirty-six. So the day for the marriage was determined to the satisfaction of both parties. 22. The Brāhmaṇ gave a promise to the father of the bridgroom, saying, "I will begin to make preparations, and will come to Pratishṭhāna with my daughter, wife and attendants. 23. To give my daughter, well adorned, into your family, will mean for me an especially good deed." And with this promise the father of the bride returned to his home, 24. saying to his wife, "I have found a most unusual husband for our daughter, a most pious, and most distinguished Vaishṇava. He seems to me to be a divine *avatāra.*"

25. Happy in mind they began preparing at their home things (needful for the marriage.) Now let us turn to the city of Pratishṭhāna. Listen to what took place there.

WEDDING PREPARATIONS.

26. The grandparents marvelled at the growing great fame of Eknāth, an *avatāra* in the family line of Chakrapāṇi, and light of that line. 27. Yet as they sat in their home, they expressed their thoughts to one another thus, "The ceremony is going to be performed at our house, but our relatives are far away. 28. The province of Vijāpur, is, as a matter of fact, seventeen *Yojanas* distant. Our relatives and dear friends are there. Let us send a letter of invitation to them." 29. There lived there a son of a brother, a most pious man, a Vaishṇava, named Uddhava. A letter, accordingly, was written to his address, inviting him to the wedding. 30. Other letters of invitation were also written to the address of other dear friends, relatives and connections, beautifully adorned with saffron figures, and the contents were in the politest terms, as follows :—31. "We are, in fact, aged. This is the last ceremony we can undertake (in our life). Come with all your retinue. We shall be eagerly watching for you." 32. A hired servant was engaged as a carrier, and the letters were sent by him. (In the mean time) the pious people of Pratishṭhāna were wrestling hard over the preparations for the wedding. 33. The Universe is kind to him, to whom Śrī Hari is associated as a close friend. Prosperity comes to serve him at his home, and there is no lack in worldly things. 34. The letters of invitation were sent to the distant and near relatives in the province of Vijāpur.

As soon as the letters were read to them they felt very pleased. 35. Uddhava, the wise, the perfect Vaishṇava, carried with him all his wedding preparations, and with his wife arrived at Pratishṭhāna. 36. He met the aged couple with the greatest joy. Uddhava fell at Eknāth's feet, and embraced him lifting up his hands. 37. And as they thus lovingly embraced, their minds experienced a sense of supreme rest. Their eyes filled with tears, as they realized the unusual circumstance of their meeting. 38. As to the father of the bride, who lived at a distance from Pratishṭhāna, he made preparations for food on a large scale. The packs were placed on bullocks and were sent ahead. 39. He provided garments, and ornaments for both parties. Taking the marriage party with him, he arrived at Pratishṭhāna. 40. He found a spacious *wādā* and he and his wife lodged there. Invitations were sent to people in the city, announcing that the marriage would take place on the morrow.

THE WEDDING CEREMONIES.

41. The preliminary ceremonies began, the honouring of God, feasting the Brāhmaṇs, gifts of clothing were given by Brāhmaṇs and others, playing of wedding music, the turmeric ceremony on bride and bridegroom. 42. Divinely dainty food of many varieties was cooked in the *mandaps* of each party. The feasting of the Brāhmaṇs was worthy of the occasion, as also the dining of others. 43. On the part of the father of the bridegroom, Uddhava was chief director. All the preparations he took upon himself, and he did it with the greatest joy. 44. The pious people of the sacred

city paid respect to his suggestions. Whatever plan Uddhava proposed, they acted accordingly. 45. Accompanied by the relatives, by the citizens, by the Brāhmaṇs, to the loud sound of the wedding music, they moved in procession to pay honor to the bridegroom. 46. With baskets full of the wedding meats, the bride's party of women joined the procession, and having given garments and ornaments to the bridegroom, they brought him to their wedding *mandap* in gay procession. 47. The bridegroom was duly honoured on arrival, the Brāhmaṇs held the marriage curtain between bride and bridegroom. The solemn words were intoned, "*Sāvadhānam, Sāvadhānam,* Think of Śrī Krishṇa." 48. Repeating the *Ashtakas,* the Brāhmaṇs completed the marriage ceremony, and the ultimate aim was accomplished. The wedding music sounded loud and continuous. 49. As this union of *Prakṛti* and *Purusha* took place all rejoiced. The offering of parched rice was then made, and gifts were distributed to all present. 50. The ceremonies of Sunmukh and Telvaṇ, the worshipping of the baskets, the *Dhenḍā* dance, the entry of the bride into the bridegroom's house, the worship of Lakshmi, all these were duly performed. 51. For five days the wedding festivities were continued with the proper ceremonies. Gifts of garments were distributed to all. There was no lack of anything. 52. After the bride's father had thus given away his daughter in marriage, he returned to his home. The grandparents seeing with their own eyes their grand-daughter-in-law, were comforted. 53. The friends who had come in marriage procession from the Province of Vijāpura, they also, supremely delighted at the events, returend to their homes. 54. Uddhava alone remained behind, filled with the desire to serve Eknāth, and in body, speech and mind he was ever present, ready to render service. 55. And knowing Eknāth's thoughts, Uddhava, without being told, knew what to do and what not to do. Eknāth thus had no worries of any kind, and his heart was filled with love.

EKNĀTH AND HIS WIFE GIRJĀBAI.

56. His wife, Girjābāi by name, supremely noble in character, was always at hand ready to serve Śrī Eknāth. 57. She was young in years, a mere child, but she knew well all customary household duties, and paid respect to the wishes of the grandparents, obeying whatever was told her. 58. Thus, as these aged grandparents saw the noble character of their grand-daughter-in-law, they were comforted, and said, "By the favor of Janārdan the longing of our eyes has been fulfilled." 59. The new couple adopted the method of life of living on whatever was given to them, yet clothing and food came to them in abundance. So that Brāhmaṇs received offerings and the hungry were fed. 60. In giving out food, no question of caste was raised. To Eknāth Janārdan filled the universe, and so he was all kindness to every creature. 61. Formerly Bhānudās had installed an idol of Pāṇḍuraṅg in a shrine. Eknath worshipped this idol with loving devotion. 62. Immediately after the second *prahar* of each day Eknāth gave offerings to the Brāhmaṇs, at the third *prahar* he gave a reading of the *Purāṇas,* at night there was always a *kirtan.* 63. Men and women, dwellers in that sacred city, came with love and reverence to listen, and day by day Eknāth's fame greatly increased.

THE DEATH OF THE GRANDPARENTS.

64. The grandparents saw before their very eyes, for many days, this mode of life. Then their bodily life came to an end, and they went to the Vaikuṇṭha world. 65. Śrī Eknāth, with his own hands, performed the funeral rites, and helped them on to their good ending. Although himself not under the law of *karma* or *akarma*, yet for the instruction of the crowd he performed the customary funeral rites. 66. Śrī Viṭṭhal, in the guise of a Brāhmaṇ, continued to sing in his *kīrtans*. He whom even Brāhma and the other Gods cannot apprehend, even He remained there as leader in the chorus. 67. Yogis perform their eight modes in contemplation, but that does not give them the sight of the *saguṇ* God. But because of Eknāth's *bhakti*, he was there playing on the cymbal and singing with him.

THE DEATH OF JANĀRDAN AND CELEBRATION OF THE SIXTH.

68. Suddenly some one came from Devagiri bringing the news that Janārdan Swāmi had left his body behind, and gone to the Vaikuṇṭha world. 69. Eknāth heard the news of his *Sadguru's* departure, and yet felt no sorrow whatever, for Janārdan, the Indestructible-one, the Unmanifested, the All-perfect was pervading all beings. 70. Yet taking Uddhava aside he instructed him to celebrate the Sixth of the month, and lovingly make preparations. 71. Uddhava touched his forehead to Eknāth's feet, and said, "Tell me what is the reason for celebrating the Sixth of the month." 72. Observing his purpose, Eknāth

told the whole reason. " The Sixth of the month, Uddhava, is the birthday of Janārdan. 73. On the sixth of Phālgun, during the dark half of the moon, Janārdan had the vision of Dattātreya given him, and on the same date Dattātreya gave me his full blessing. 74. On this same date also Janārdan left his body behind, and became *nirguṇ*. These, then, are the four events that have occurred, and what is to take place in the future you will soon see. 75. So make great preparations for offerings to the Brāhmaṇs." Uddhava replied, "I will do so," and made a *namaskār*. 76. In the preparations some things were received unasked. Others were bought on credit. Seven hundred rupees in coin were borrowed from *Vaṇis* and a note was given for them. 77. Uddhava wrote the promissory note in Eknāth's name, having agreed on the time for repayment, and explaining the purpose of the loan. 78. Having thus made full preparations they began with love this festival of the Sixth. The whole sacred city was invited, and food was cooked sufficient for all. 79. Pious and loving persons laboured hard with their own hands. No one felt it a burden. All worked with loving hearts. 80. Accompanied by the players on the *diṇḍi* they went first in procession down to the banks of the Gaṅgā, and here with the sweet sound of cymbals, the *vīṇā,* and the drum a *Kīrtan* was performed with great eclat. 81. Eagle banners were flying, the kettledrum sounding, musical instruments were playing festal music. The Vaishṇavas were shouting " victory, victory," and the din of the sound filled to overflowing all etherial space. 82. At noon, led in the procession by the players on the *diṇḍi* they returned to Eknāth's abode. The Brāhmaṇs then bathed, were then seated crowded in lines. 83. Śrī Eknāth, with his own hands washed the feet of the Brāhmaṇs, and as he drank the water with which their feet were washed he felt great joy. 84. He was a *bhakta* of Brāhmaṇs, wholly devoted to them. He touched his own eyes with his thumb. His strong conviction was that there is no deity superior to the Brāhmaṇ. 85. With his own hands he rubbed sandal wood paste and *buka* on their bodies. He gave them the *tulsi* leaf, and flowers. And having thus worshipped the Brāhmaṇs he served them dainty food. 86. Having prepared the melted butter, and other sauces, they were served with the cooked food on the leaf-plates. In his love he repeated the *mantra* that the enjoyer of this food was Janārdan himself, who pervades every creature. 87. The Brāhmaṇs then sipped water from the palms of their hands, and sat down to eat, all shouting together the name of Viṭṭhal. 88. Whatever pleased the taste of any one, that was brought in dishes and served to him, Śrī Eknāth, the while, requesting them to eat very leisurely. 89. After all were fully satisfied, they got up to wash their hands with expressions of love. He gave to all of them the *vidā,* and gifts of money. They then went to their homes. 90. Viṭṭhal, Uddhava and Eknāth, and the citizens who had assisted so joyfully then sat down to their meal in the very last line of diners. 91. As night came on Eknāth performed a *kīrtan.* Many people came to listen to it. His words of inspiration being marked with love, what lack could there then be of delight. 92. Thus the night passed. The same kind of festivities were held on the Seventh of the month, and on the Eighth the Gopālkālā was celebrated. 93. Led by the *dinḍi* players, the procession arrived at the bank of the Gaṅgā. Here a great crowd of pilgrims had assembled who were shouting the names of God and "Victory, Victory." 94. When the ceremony of the Gopāḷkāla was completed *prasād* was distributed to all. As night came on dramatic representations took place, and all were deeply impressed thereby. 95. After these dramatic representations were completed the Husband-of-Rukmiṇi was put to rest. And as dawn came on they honoured *sādhus* and saints. 96. In this way the festival of the Sixth was celebrated. All felt happy and exclaimed, "To save the world this noble Eknāth has come down to earth, an *avatāra*. 97. Pratishṭhāna is a sacred city full of Brāhmaṇs. All the Brāhmaṇs are scrupulously orthodox. To show them the perfect way of *Bhakti*, he has become an *avatāra* in human form (*saguṇ*.)"

THE MERCHANT WANTS BACK THE BORROWED MONEY.

98. Now the merchant, from whom things had been bought on credit, and for which Uddhava had written a promissory note, the note now being due, began to ask for his money. 99. Uddhava replied to him, "As soon as a note is received, we shall bring the amount to your house. Feel confident of this." 100. Although thus assured, the scoundrel would not listen. "You are continually receiving unasked for money," he declared, "and you spend it in feeding Brāhmaṇs. 101. Eknāth has cast aside the ordinary human life, and dances wildly in his *kīrtans*. He has made every one crazy. I will not permit this!" 102. Not content with saying things to Uddhava, this evil minded man came to Eknāth's

house. Eknāth was at his bath and prayers. Yet he uttered a curse on him. 103. "If you eat any food before you have paid me my money, then I swear by Pāṇḍuraṅg," uttering this curse he went away. 104. Eknāth, however, gave offerings to the gods and to the fire, and feasted the Brāhmaṇs as usual, but he himself would not eat, because of the oath sworn by the *Vāṇi*. 105. Neither would Uddhava or the good Girjābāi eat. The sun had set, and as yet no money had been received. 106. Uddhava laboured hard, but could not secure money anywhere. One *prahar* of the night passed and still they fasted. 107. Seeing their troubled condition Paṇḍharināth was distressed. The Husband-of-Rukmiṇi could not endure that his *abheda Bhakta* should remain fasting. 108. So Śrī Hari took the form of Uddhava and went to the house of the vāṇi, and called him to the door. "Come quickly outside," he said. 109. The merchant opened the door, and called out to him saying, "Why have you come here at this late hour of the night." 110. Uddhava replied, "Bring me the promissory note at once, and here count out all this money, which includes the interest due." 111. The merchant answered, "How can I make out the account at night? My account book and the promissory note are at my store. 112. Come early in the morning, and take away the note." Listen now, ye, his devoted Bhaktas, to what the Lord Vaikuṇṭha replied. 113. "If you are so patient, then why did you put Eknāth under that oath. I am deeply distressed by his having to fast. I am in a fainting condition." 114. When the Vāṇi heard this charge he became repentant at heart, and went to his store and there examined the account. 115. And as he counted out the money, which was the exact amount due him, he was astonished to see that every coin had on it the same superscription. 116. The Vāṇi returned the note, which Hari tore up with his hands, but brought the pieces back with him to his house, and placed them in his account book. 117. The Vāṇi now became greatly distressed in mind. Sleep would not come to him. "I laid Eknāth under an oath not to eat," he said to himself, "and I myself came home and ate. 118. Seized by the desire for the perishable, I have persecuted a saint." While thus greatly disturbed in mind the sun arose. 119. He hastily washed his face, and went to Eknāth's *wāḍā*. He made him a *sāshtāūg namaskār,* and cried out, "I have truly, wronged you." 120. Śrī Nāth replied, "It is a rule of business ethics that until one has paid one's dues, one should not eat." 121. When the Vāṇi heard this remark,he was overcome with astonishment, and turning to Uddhava said, "You paid me the money, and took away the promissory note. 122. You should have told your *Svāmi* of this. Why have you still kept him fasting." Uddhava answered, "One must never tell an untruth." 123. The vāṇi then immediately swore that what he said was true. And Uddhava (after making search) came and told Eknāth, "The cancelled note is indeed in our account book, and I now understand what has occured." 124. Uddhava turning to the Vāṇi said, "Blessed is your loving *bhakti*. Through having business relations with Eknāth you have met the Husband-of-Rukmiṇi. 125. Do not, however, speak of this mysterious event to any one soever." The merchant prostrated himself before Uddhava and hastened back to his home. 126. Śrī Nāth then made offerings to God, ate in line with the Brāhmaṇs. Girjābāi and Uddhava did also the same, ending their fasting that day. 127.

Pāṇḍuraṅg, in the guise of a Brāhmaṇ, continued to be the leader of the chorus. The *kīrtans* continued to be full of delight. All were deeply impressed, as they listened to them. 128. It pleased Purushottama thus to increase the glory of Eknāth. In the guise of a Brāhmaṇ, the Soul-of-the-World used the *kīrtans* to inspire love. 129. Twelve years passed in this way, making an epoch in his life. Let the saints now listen to what took place later on.

THE IDENTITY OF VITHOBĀ IS DISCOVERED.

130. A Vaishṇava *bhakta,* living in the sacred city of Pāṇḍhari used to sit in contemplation. He desired a visible manifestation of Pāṇḍuraṅg. Many days passed in this way. 131. His lips repeated aloud the names of God. His heart had no other desire. Suddenly one night the Husband-of-Rukmiṇi appeared to him in a dream, saying, 132. "You wish for a visible manifestation of myself, but I am under an engagement at Pratishṭhāna, where Eknāth, the *abheda bhakta* is wholly absorbed in *kīrtans* in my praise. 133. I, Pāṇḍuraṅg, have taken the guise of a Brāhmaṇ there, and lead the chorus. The world calls me Viṭhobā by name. Go quickly to the place. 134. Go to the home of Eknāth in Pratishṭhāna, and there you will see me." As he saw this vision of the night he was overcome with astonishment. 135. He started at once for Pratishṭhāna, and arrived at Eknāth's house. He enquired for the Brāhmaṇ Viṭhobā, and rushed forward to embrace him. 136. And as he made a *sāshṭāṅga namaskār,* suddenly the Husband-of-Rukmiṇi changed his form. He

took the *saguṇ* form of the four-armed, with sparkling jewels in his crown. 137. His face was glorious, his form lovely. Divine earrings flashed in his ears. On his neck was the *vaijayanti* necklace and the *kaustubha* jewel. His yellow garment was dazzlingly bright. 138. The shape of his body was beautiful and graceful. His two hands looked charming, placed on his sides. This lovely form, with his two feet placed together, was beautiful. All this the Brāhmaṇ actually saw. 139. With him some Vaishṇava *bhaktas* had also come. They also saw this visible manifestation at that time. 140. After giving them this visible manifestation, God became invisible, and all who had come from Paṇḍhari glorified Eknāth, 141. saying, "Blessed art thou, *Vaishṇava bhakta*, visible *avatāra* of Vishṇu. Pāṇḍuraṅg, in the guise of a Brāhmaṇ, himself led your chorus." 142. When the Brāhmaṇ Viṭhobā became invisible, Eknāth's mind became overcome with astonishment. He said to himself, "The Life-of-the-world has wearied himself for my sake. He has let nothing lower his reputation of greatness. 143. It is his nature to care tenderly for his slaves. He, whose limits even the Vedas do not know, even He has become the helper of his *bhaktas*." 144. That Pāṇḍuraṅg had in this way paid his debt of gratitude to Eknāth, people now heard. The deed became noised abroad, that for twelve years he had been the leader of the chorus. 145. As the honey in the flower-buds sends out its fragrance when the breeze is in motion so does the fame of the deeds of the saints, as they relate them to one another. 146. The qualities of humility and sincerity are their imperishable garments. By these their good fame is manifested to the world, and great poets sing their praise.

147. Amongst all great books the supremely great are those containing the Acts of the Saints. Only to those who are fortunate, is this a pleasing thought. 148. Continual doubters and haters, are ever enveloped in the darkness of Ignorance. They have never any leisure. All their time is spent in the occupations of their worldly life. 149. But you good people are not such. As I read, explain, and comment you listen to my crude words, and make them sweet to you. 150. By your support my soul is filled with love, otherwise I am but Mahipati, the dull minded, the sinner, and truly not a poet or author. 151. Svasti. This is the Śrī Bhaktalīlāmṛita. By merely listening to it one's desires are fulfilled. Listen then to it, ye loving, pious, *bhaktas*. This is the sixteenth delightful chapter.

CHAPTER 17.

Śrī Bhaktalīlāmṛita.

MAHIPATI'S PREFACE TO CHAPTER 17.

Obeisance to Śrī Pāṇḍuraṅg.

1. If there are interested listeners present, a speaker has a feeling of great joy. When opposition and doubts are far absent, the words of a story flow easily. 2. Just as the lotus in the lake opens its petals to the rising of the sun, so when one is before interested listeners, love wells up in the heart. 3. Or as the peacock dances in various steps, when it hears the thunder in the clouds. Or as the infant frolics, when its mother is before it. 4. Or as when Gaṇpati goes through dancing motions, when in the presence of Mriḍanipati. Or as when Sarasvati broke out

into song when she, with love in her heart, saw before her, her father Brahmadeva. 5. Just so, before you, saints, I utter in a familiar way my crude sentences. The Husband-of-Rukmiṇi knows whatever is lacking and whatever is complete in them.

EKNATH GIVES READINGS FROM THE BHĀGAVATA.

6. At the close of the last chapter there was the story of how Pāṇḍharināth, in the guise of a Brāhman, lovingly led the chorus in the *kīrtans* performed by Eknāth. 7. And how twelve years thus passing, suddenly a Brāhmaṇ arrived from Paṇḍhari, who recognized the Husband-of-Rukmiṇi, and had a visual manifestation of him. 8. And how Purushottama, the Giver-of-the-bliss-of-Absorption became immediately invisible, lest being recognized by people generally it would lead to trouble in Pratishṭhāna.

9. One day Uddhava, the *sadguru bhakta* made this request of Śrī Nāth, "A desire has arisen in my heart to listen to the reading of the Śrī Bhāgavata Purāṇa from your lips." 10. Responding to this lovingly expressed desire Eknāth began reading aloud the Great Purāṇa, and pious hearers, having performed their worldy engagements, came to listen. 11. Simple minded people, women, *śūdras,* merchants, and great and distinguished citizens as well, came there with reverence to listen. 12. According to custom the loving *bhaktas* sat close to him, and listened to his reading of the Purāṇa, Eknāth translated the text, explained its meaning in full, and thereby the snares of doubt were broken.

GOD APPEARS IN THE GUISE OF A BRĀHMAṆ, KEŚAVA.

13. Suddenly one day Paṇḍharināth, in the guise of a Brāhmaṇ, appeared, and Eknāth, seeing him, made him a reverent *namaskār*. 14. "Whence have you come, sir, he asked, "What is your name?" The Life-of-the World listened to Eknāth's questioning, and replied, 15. "Keśava is my name. Know me as one indifferent to worldly things, and I am alone. I have come here that I may listen to the reading of the Bhāgavata from your lips. 16. If your lips will give me assurance I shall always remain here with you. I have heard great praise of you, and I have therefore come here." 17. Eknāth listened and answered, "My own desire is also the same, that I may always have your company. So fulfil the desire of my heart. 18. It occurs to me that the Lord-of-Vaikuṇṭha has many forms. He takes many guises, but he, Śripati, does not make these miraculous deeds openly evident. 19. He lately took the guise of a Brāhmaṇ, and for twelve years led my chorus. He it is, who now in the form of Keśava has come to my home, but no one is able to recognize him." 20. The Husband-of-Rukmiṇi now spent many years in the company of his *abheda bhakta*. With longing desire to hear the Bhāgavata read he would sit close in front of Eknāth, listening to him. 21. If Eknāth failed to bring out all the meaning of the words or sentences he would express a doubt and raise a question, and Eknāth would clear away the doubts. The occasions were of unusual interest. 22. Uddhava also, his close friend, and full of reverence, sat close in front of Eknāth listening to him.

These two were the chief listeners. The others sat all around them. 23. The inhabitants of that sacred city, who came to listen, all became *bhaktas* of Vishṇu, and forgiveness, mercy, peace, and detachment from the world, dwelt in them. 24. Through Eknāth's preaching they put away all dishonest business. Zeal for religion filled their minds, and great enthusiasm for repeating the names and attributes of God. 25. The sandalwood trees of Mount Mailā have close to them the common *babul* and *khaira* trees. The fragrance of the former pervades the wood of the latter, and no difference then exists between them. 26. Just as by virtue of association with the good, one's pitiful state of ignorance is changed and immediately one gains the experimental knowledge of demonstrated truth; 27. Just as in the *Dvāpāra yuga* to Śrī Krishṇa, in his historic form, Uddhava was very dear; so in the present instance the same bond of love existed. 28. To love, ever new, ever developing and growing, is to be given the name *Bhakti*. By means of it the hearts of the listeners were deeply impressed, and the illusions of this world disappeared. 29. As a rule every day at the third *prahara,* the reverent people came to listen. The *Vaḍi* would become crowded, and the extatic love shown was extraordinary.

THE BRAHMAṆS ARE ENVIOUS OF EKNĀTH.

30. As the loving hearers saw Eknāth's emotion, they were pleased, but the Vedic Brāhmaṇ paṇdits were moved to hatred. 31. Many of them indeed sitting idly on the little hillside, reviled Eknāth, saying " He has set up

his shop in this sacred city, and is seducing all the pious people. 32. As to oratory he does not excel, but in his *kīrtans* he seems to cast a spell over the minds of men. Explaining word by word, one after the other, and gives them a *prākrit* [Marathi] version of the Sanskrit text. 33. He leaves aside the many other *Purāṇas,* and has chosen the Bhāgavat. He explains its meaning in full, and by it the hearts of all are deeply impressed. 34. By listening to the religious teachings of the Bhāgavata, all have become desireless of worldly things. No one now carries on business simply to fulfil worldly desires. All are absorbed in gaining philosophic knowledge. 35. Our patrons used to carry on worldly business, and projects for livelihood, but now all of them have been seduced by Eknāth, through his reading to them Prākrit books. 36. He casts aside the commentary of Śridhar (on the Bhāgavata) and constantly reads the Dnyāneśvari, explaining in melodious language the excellence of *Bhakti.* 37. By listening to Eknāth's preaching the whole universe will be absorbed into its own self, then what will the creator do? This is what troubles us greatly. 38. We, Vedic Brāhmaṇ paṇdits, learned in the Four Vedas, have none to pay attention to us, Eknāth having so deeply impressed the people. 39. As to his knowledge, it is merely that of the *Prākrit,* and yet abundance of money and grain flow to his house. He feeds hundreds and hundreds of Brāhmaṇs, and lacks nothing at all. 40. We are all learned Shāstris, but Truth does not work, if one sits still. We have always to act so as to please our patrons. 41. It is true that people say that Eknāth is an *avatār* of Vishṇu, but we think he has a grudge against us. He has ruined all business that has

Desire as its end. 42. Our patrons used to carry on many worldly businesses, but now they also are associating with Eknāth, and listening to his reading of *Prākrit* books." 43. In these words the Vedic paṇdits, who dwelt in the sacred city, reviled Eknāth, adding also, "He has put a stop to the Way of *karma,* and propounds the way of *Bhakti* as the only way. 44. Let alone the state of others, the wives of us Brāhmaṇs of the mendicant order, learning that the worldly life is false, is indeed *Māyā,* spend their time at Eknāth's feet. 45. Just as in the *Dvāpāra Yuga* the wives of us, Brāhmaṇs of the mendicant order, learning so these, our wives, stealthily steal away to listen to Eknāth's *kīrtans.* 46. Eknāth preaches the religious teachings of the Bhāgavata to our patrons, and thereby they have become desireless of worldly things. No one now performs those rites that look for the fulfilment of worldly desires, and so our profits are gone." 47. With such words the Brāhmaṇs, dwellers in the sacred city, all flung their insults, but they did not think of Govind in their hearts and experience loving delight. 48. Eknāth was a respecter of Brāhmaṇs, and so with reverence for them he continued to serve them with feelings of love. 49. Whether any one reviled him or praised him, he looked upon every one as Janārdan in visible form. So while some honored him, and others dishonored him, he paid no attention to the joy of the one or the pain of the other. 50. "Janārdan fills mankind," he said. "It is He who causes both the insults and the praise." Enlightened by this conception all his feelings disappeared. 51. All the Brāhmaṇs, dwellers in the secred city, began now to persecute him in many ways. If they saw anything of his that they wanted, they asked him for it, and Eknāth never refused them. 52. If the Brāhmaṇs saw any specially fine garment or vessel, and asked for it, he at once gave it to them. If unexpected guests appeared in town, they were told, "There is one Eknāth here, a generous giver. 53. Though thousands of guests come, he gives them food to their full satisfaction. The *Siddhis* are favorable to him. So hasten there." 54. At their own homes there was an abundance of wealth, but these Brāhmaṇs never gave food to others. With a hateful mind they would point out to the hungry the house of Eknāth.

HOSPITALITY OF EKNĀTH AND GIRJĀBĀI TO FOUR BRĀHMAṆS.

55. Now it happened one day that rain began falling in torrents. For seven days, day and night, it rained slabs of stone. 56. Houses became soaked, and leaked everywhere. No dry spot could be seen on the face of the earth. No one could collect kindling wood, and so no cooking could take place. 57. Although there might be plenty of money and grain in their houses, still no kindling wood could be collected. Suddenly, as the night passed into the second *prahar*, four Brāhmaṇs appeared in town. 58. They wished for a full meal, and to obtain it they were wandering from house to house. The Brāhmaṇs of the town informed them, saying, "There is a man here of courageous integrity. 59. His name is Eknāth," and from a distance pointed out to them his house. The travellers went there, and said to Eknāth, 60. "We four are in the pangs of hunger. We have come to

you, because we have heard of your fame. So cook us a meal in your house, and appease our hunger." 61. Hearing what they had to say, Eknāth pitied them from his heart, and ordered Girjābāi to cook a meal for them. 62. She replied, "There is no fuel whatever." Eknāth answered, "This house has wooden sides." He then called to Uddhava, 63. "Rip up a section of the house, and give her plenty of these lathes." Uddhava replied, "It will take too long a time to do so." 64. Nāth then himself ripped off the tape from his bed, and broke up immediately the frame work of the straw rick. In this way he supplied the needed fuel and the cooking was done. 65. He heated water, and gave it to the Brāhmaṇs hot for their bath. And because of the cold he kindled for them the hand-warmer. 66. Girjābāi, with her own hands, served the food on their plates. When their hunger was satisfied, they uttered words of thanks. 67. By the favor of Pāṇḍuraṅg may your heart keep its beautiful character." Eknāth then gave them *pān supāri* for the cleansing of their mouths, and said, "Now go and rest."

EKNĀTH'S HOSPITALITY TO THREE MAHOMEDANS.

68. After some days had passed, the day for the worship of his Ancestors arrived. Brāhmaṇs had been invited to the feast, and the viands were being prepared at the house. 69. The day dawned. It was now a *prahar* and a half. The Brāhmaṇs had been invited to go and take their baths. The cooked viands were ready, but the Brāhmaṇs were late in returning. 70. Eknāth finished

his own religious observances, and then fixed his gaze on the path by which the Brāhmaṇs were to return. Just then the three Gods felt a desire to test his goodness of heart. 71. So Brahmadeva, Vishṇu and Maheśvara appeared in the form of Mahomedan *fakirs,* with heavy beards, bloodshot eyes, and anklets with bells and crystals. 72. They had rosaries in their hands. Their bodies were enveloped in skins. They had long matted hair on their heads. Appearing in this disguise 73. they said to Eknāth, "We three are hungry. We want food to fill our stomachs" This is all they said. 74. Śrī Nāth listened to their request and at once replied, "Surely," and brought in a dish of food that had already been prepared in the house, and served it to them. 75. He sat down close to these Mahomedans, and filled their plates. And when they had washed their hands after the meal, he passed the *pān supāri* to them. 76. In this way they definitely tested Eknāth's conviction of God being in every creature, and his love for them. The three Gods then took their visible divine form, and gave Eknāth a visual manifestation of themselves. 77. And as Eknāth saw their *saguṇ* form he exclaimed, "You have made me *sanāth,* one protected." The Gods then retook their Mahomedan guise of *fakirs,* and started to leave. 78. Just then the Earth-gods (Brāhmaṇs,) having finished their ablutions returned to Eknāth's *vādi.* The fakirs, seeing them, let them hear the belchings of their loaded stomachs. 79. And in their Mahomedan language they bestowed their blessing on Eknāth, saying, "You have satisfied our hunger. May God bless you." 80. With these words the Mahomedan *fakirs* passed outside.

THE BRĀHMAṆS PERSECUTE EKNĀTH

The Brāhmaṇs began now murmuring among themselves. "This mingling of different castes has grown to an extreme." 81. And so they said to Eknāth, "This is the anniversary day in honour of your ancestors, and you have feasted those Mahomedans with the oblation food before you have feasted us." 82. One of the Brāhmaṇs added ironically, "The good deeds of his ancestors must have been many, and hence these hungry fakirs have come here for their midday meal. 83. The anniversary ceremonials having now been fully completed there is no longer need of us here." With these words they all turned to go away. 84. Eknāth came forward before them, and made them a *namaskār* explaining, "The fakirs were famished with hunger. I therefore fed them. 85. But we have brought fresh unpolluted water and a second cooking has been prepared in the kitchen. So forgive my fault I beseech you svamis, and perform the ancestral worship ceremonies." 86. Eknāth pled hard with them, and besought them again and again, but those Brāhmaṇs would not listen. They exclaimed, "You are a violator of the prescribed rituals." 87. The Brāhmaṇs then went to their religious head who lived in the sacred city, and acquainted him with the affair, telling him how Eknāth had fested the Mohamedans before first performing the ancestral anniversary ceremonials. 88. The Religious Head together with the leading Brāhmaṇs arrived at Eknāth's house in haste. The family priest (seeing them coming) said to Eknāth, "They are coming to excommunicate you." 89. The Brāhmaṇs gibed Eknāth, "To day is your ancestor's worship anniversary day. Were they Mahomedans by caste, that you should have feasted these Mahomedans?" 90. Thus with many insults the Brāhmaṇs mocked him. But Śrī Nāth was a great ocean of calmness. He did not feel the least bit of anger. 91. The surging billows of man's insults came rolling over him, but to this ocean-of-calmness these billows were no more than a mouthful of water. He had destroyed the very path of Desire and Passion, an act extraordinary and unequalled. 92. But Eknāth regarded these Brāhmaṇs as forms of Janārdan, so he made them a *sāshṭāṅg namaskār,* and exclaimed, "Be gracious to me, O Svami and perform the ancestral worship ceremony." 93. The Religious Head replied, "Your good deeds seem so many, your fathers in heaven will surely come down and themselves partake of the feast. 94. Śrī Nāth answered in a very novel way. "A Brāhmaṇ's word is a marvel. Your word cannot fall to the ground. Eeven seemingly impossible things can take place. It is not so very difficult. 95. In the Great Sacrifice, God, together with Indra, has his hunger satisfied when the *Svāmi* utters the ejaculation, *Svāhā, Svadhā.* 96. A Brāhmaṇ's word is a marvel indeed. By a word of his, God becomes manifest in a stone idol. Mādhava clasped Śrī vatsa to his heart. What might not happen to a mere human wretch like myself." 97. To this the Brāhmaṇs replied, "No more of your long-winded oratory. If your heavenly fathers do not descend to the feast, we shall excommunicate you." 98. So saying they placed three seats on the floor. Then, as Eknāth uttered the word, "Come," suddenly the heavenly fathers descended. 99. They appeared to the Brāhmaṇs in a form supremely glorious and radiant. The Brahminical thread shone upon their necks. They wore golden rings on their hands

All this the Brāhmaṇs saw. 100. The heavenly fathers took their seats, and began loudly to repeat from the Vedas. The Brāhmaṇs marvelled as they saw this sight. 101. They realized that this extraordinary event was due to Eknāth, and filled with shame, they hung their heads and sat down with their faces between their knees. 102. Then together with the Religious Head, these Brāhmaṇs arose, and in silence departed. Those Brāhmaṇs, however, who had been invited to the feast, and who had purified themselves, they remained. 103. The ceremony of the ancestral worship having been duly performed, they all dined with the heavenly fathers, who after receiving the *vida* and gifts, departed on their way back to heaven. 104. The Brāhmaṇs, seeing this miracle, were supremely astonished, and going to the Religious Head, related what had happened. 105. How that the heavenly fathers had eaten in their presence and then departed upwards to Heaven. The Religious Head became much ashamed, and exclaimed, " We have made ourselves of no account. 106. We have persecuted Eknāth in many ways, but God has been his helper. We have suffered defeat. What plan shall we now adopt? 107. When Durvāsa was attacking Ambarish, he was himself pursued by the *chakra*. So today history has repeated itself, and we feel much ashamed." 108. While on the one side the Brāhmaṇs were talking thus among themselves, on the other nothing could awaken either joy or pain in Eknāth. 109. He did not feel troubled in mind that the Brāhmaṇs thus persecuted him, nor did he even keep in his memory the miracle of his heavenly fathers having come down to dine. 110. The conviction that God filled mankind, so impressed his mind that when he heard himself insulted or praised, to both he was indifferent. 111. At the third watch of the day, the listening to the reading of the Purāṇs was continued. At night Hari kīrtans took place, and the hearts of the pious men of Paiṭhaṇ were deeply impressed.

BRĀHMAṆ ENVY STILL CONTINUES.

112. By day and by night crowds constantly gathered at Eknāth's house, but the Brāhmaṇs seeing his glorification, burned with envy. 113. Saying among themselves, "The people of Paiṭhaṇ, listening to Eknāth's *kirtans* have become deeply impressed. All are worshipping Śrī Rām. All have become Vaishṇavas. 114. No one now spends money on religious rites for the attaining of their desires. So our means of livelihood are cut off. The people are living according to the teachings of the Bhāgavata." Such was their complaint to one another. 115. Just as when a thief becomes enraged when he sees the moon shining bright, so the spread of Eknāth's glory fanned the fire of the Brāhmaṇs' wrath.

BRĀHMANS TEMPT EKNATH UNSUCCESSFULLY.

116. As day and night they watched for some weakness in him, they soon saw an opportunity to tempt him to a fault. There lived there a Brāhmaṇ named Krishṇadās. He was a special worshipper of Bhavāni. 117. The goddess seeing his painful austerities, visibly revealed herself to him. He asked of her the boon of poetic power, and began his great work. 118. He wrote a Prākrit

version of the Yuddha kāṇḍ of the Rāmāyaṇa, delightful in its similes. The Brāhmaṇs were delighted. 119. They remarked, "Eknāth produces a great deal of poetry, but his style is crude. It passes, however, with women, *Śudras* and other simple folk." 120. They even came and sat down by Eknāth and talked in his presence in the same way. Listen now to how they praised Krishṇadas Loḷyā. 121. "Eknāth, listen," they would say, "Many people write poetry, but Krishṇadās has composed the Rāmāyaṇa, and its style appears most delightful. 122. The Goddess has favored him. No single verse is written without careful thought. Neither the past nor the future has such a poet. 123. Hearing this praise of Krishṇadās, Eknāth felt greatly pleased and exclaimed, "Oh the infiniteness of God's glory! Truly one cannot know its limits!" 124. The Brāhmaṇs thus attempted to arouse in him a feeling of hatred, but such a feeling could not enter his heart. Astonished at this those earth-gods returned to their homes.

KRISHṆADĀS WARNED THAT HE MUST DIE.

125. Now I ask your attention to another event. As Krishṇadās was composing his version of the Rāmāyaṇa, and had not quite completed the Yuddha Kāṇḍ, suddenly the Goddess appeared to him. 126. Bhavāni said, "At exactly the third watch to-morrow you will surely die. Let your mind therefore be on its guard." 127. As he came back to consciousness he felt exceedingly sad, saying, "The book is not yet finished. What shall I do?" 128. Taking with him as much of the book as was written, he went to Eknāth's house. As soon as Śrī Eknāth saw him,

he arose and went forward to greet him. 129. Krishṇadās, in great humility touched his forehead to Eknāth's lotus feet. Eknāth, seating him, said, "It is very gracious of you to visit me this day." 130. Krishṇadās, with expressions of affection, related his story from beginning to end, adding, "Tomorrow death will come to my body. From this there is no escape. 131. I am preparing a *Prākrit* version of the Yuddha Kāṇḍ of the Rāmāyaṇa. Some of it remains to be done. I ask you to complete it" 132. Thus affectionately pleading, he placed the book before Eknāth. Loving thoughts filled Eknāth's mind, and he began to consider what to reply. 133. He read a chapter of the book, and was greatly pleased with it. "It is beyond my power," he said, "to complete these verses. 134. You have begun the book well. Finish it yourself." Krishṇadās replied. "But I have before me fear of tomorrow." 135. Śrī Eknāth then asked him how many days it would require to complete the book, and added, "Until then Death will not so much as touch you, Saint." 136. As Krishṇadās heard this assurance of Eknāth's, he felt a sense of trust, and exclaimed, "Right here will I sit day and night. The book will then be completed." 137. Eknāth answered, "Go rather to your own home. If there should be the slightest sign of Death's approach, I will hasten to visit you." 138. Krishṇadās listened to this reply, and his heart was filled with joy. He made a reverent *namaskār* and returned to his home. 139. There he related to his people the assurance given him by Eknāth. The night passed, and the sun began to rise. 140. Krishṇadās duly performed his bath, and his customary devotions. As the appointed hour for his death approached, he became deeply depressed. 141. Just at that moment

Eknāth appeared, and reassured him. He passed his hand over him, and then gave a command to Death, 142. "For eleven days from to-day do not touch his body." All wondered as they heard this command. 143. And Death, respecting Eknāth's command hastily turned away. Krishṇadās came to himself and began composing the Rāmāyaṇa. 144. The people were all astonished at this miracle. The report of it reached the ears of the chief Brāhmaṇs of Pratishṭhāna. 145. And they discussing the matter among themselves said, "If Krishṇadās dies on the eleventh day, then only shall we regard the miracle as true, otherwise as false."

KRISHṆADĀS COMPLETES HIS BOOK AND THEN DIES.

146. Thus, these evil minded ones, were watching for some defect. In the meantime, on the tenth day the book was completed. 147. And the moment this Yuddha Kāṇḍ was completed,* Krishṇadās gave gifts to Brāhmaṇs, worshipped Sarasvati, and exalted the greatness of Eknāth. 148. On the eleventh day Krishṇadās performed his bath, and observed all his customary devotions. And Eknāth, realizing that the time for Krishṇadās' departure had arrived, went to visit him. 149. With fragrant powders, flowers, and garlands Krishṇadās worshipped Eknāth, and

---

* *Note.*—There seems to be some doubt at present as to whether this Yuddhakāṇḍa by Krishṇadās Loḷyā is extant. (See Mr. Bhave's notes in Mahārāshṭra Sārasvat, pages 136, 137, first Edition and 274 in second Edition.) A Yuddhakāṇḍa by Krishṇadās Mudgal is known, but his identification with Krishṇadās Loḷyā is not yet proved.

made him a *namaskār*. Then without the least distress of mind, he arrived at the life-Beyond. 150. The Brāhmaṇs now said among themselves, "After all our extolling of Krishṇadās Loḷyā, in the end it is we who have truly suffered defeat. What plan shall we now adopt? 151. The more we devise evil against him, the more his fame spreads among the people. Eknāth's deeds are miraculous. Our hatred only adds to them." 152. Others said, "In his former birth he was great. Hence, God being his helper, he has now increased greatly his fame. 153. Superstitious believers fall at his feet, but we do not like his deeds." Thus the Māyā of Vaishṇava yoga prevented their understanding Eknāth.

A RICH MERCHANT HAS AN IDOL OF PAṆḌURAṄG MADE.

154. It now happened that in the Province of Karnāṭak, there was a rich merchant. He was constant in his worship of Śrī Paṇḍuraṅg. He was pious, generous, and of good report. 155. A desire having come to him to make a metal image of Viṭṭhal, he did so, and its pose, and smiling countenance, created a sense of peace in those who looked upon it. 156. Now let us take note of what he did, with his smiling face, the Giver-of-boons-to Puṇḍalik, the Husband-of-Rukmiṇi, with his feet placed together, and his hands on his hips. 157. The merchant had made all preparations, and was waiting for a good and auspicious day for the ceremony of bringing life into the image, and for feasting the Brāhmaṇs. 158. When fast asleep at night, the life-of-the-World appeared to him in a dream, and said, "On

the bank of the Gaṅgā, in the sacred city of Pratishṭhāna, there lives one, called Ekā Janārdan. 159. *Bhakti,* knowledge, and absence of worldly desires are characteristics that are deeply impressed upon him and adorn his personality. Take this image of God in *saguṇ* form, which you have made, and give it to Eknāth there. 160. If you do not obey my command, and if you should perform the dedicatory rite here, you will suffer many evils. You will not escape thereby the ills of this life, difficult to overcome." 161. This vision, in the dream of the night, caused him deep distress. He could no longer sleep. And now the sun arose. 162. He immediately told of the vision to Paṇḍits, Brāhmaṇs, *Sādhus* and *Sants,* and as these omniscient ones deliberated on the meaning of the vision, they also were in doubt. 163. The *Purāṇiks* and priests finally gave their opinion, that he should have patience for a few days. If the vision was repeated, then the image should be at once taken to Pratishṭhāna. 164. The merchant acquiesced to the suggestion of these omniscient ones. For three nights in succession he had the very same dream. 165. Accordingly the Brāhmaṇ came to Pratishṭhāna, bringing with him the image of Pāṇḍuraṅg. He rested awhile on the bank of the Gaṅgā, to bathe. 166. He had come richly clothed and adorned. He had with him a large retinue of men and horses. The chief Brāhmaṇs of the sacred city were highly pleased when they saw him. 167. "He must undoubtedly patronize us," they said, as they came bringing the record books. "Who is your priest?" they enquired. The merchant replied, 168. "There is one Ekā Janārdan here in this city, who is a Vaishṇava *bhakta.* God revealed this to me in a dream, and I have therefore come to see him." 169. On hearing this there arose in their minds deep disquietude, and murmuring they said, " Eknāth has bewitched the whole universe." 170. Deeply irritated, they exclaimed, " Eknāth has bewitched the people of this town, and to those elsewhere he gives dreams." They changed their speech in order to secure gifts of money. 171. They therefore said to the merchant, "If you have this earnest desire to meet Eknāth, then you surely are our patron". And with this hope in mind, they began to repeat the word of the bath ritual. 172. The rich merchant, finding them crowding around him in their officious intermeddling, gave them some money gifts, and then entered into the town. 173. He enquired of the people where Eknāth lived, and soon arrived at his house. Here he saw Śrī Eknāth seated on his mat and Uddhava before him. 174. With reverence, love and respect the merchant made him a *sāshtāng namaskār*. Eknāth at once arose and greeted him. 175. "From whence have you come?" he asked. "Kindly tell me the reason. Inform me what country and city you are from." 176. The merchant replied to the *Svāmi*, "I have made an image of Śrī Viṭṭhal. I was about to have performed the ceremony for bringing the divine life into it, when I had a dream by night. 177. The vision said to me, "There lives in Pratishṭhāna one Ekā Janārdan. Go and give this image to him." I had this same dream for three nights. 178. Therefore, with this purpose in mind, I have come to see you, *Svāmi*. I must have laid up in a former birth many good deeds, which now at last are bearing fruit." 179. So saying, the merchant produced the image of Pāṇḍurang with its smiling, gentle face, to look on which created in him a sense of peace. 180. Eknāth took up

7

the image, and pressed it to his heart, exclaiming, "Controller-of-the-Universe, Giver-of-absorption-into-Brahma, this is Thy miraculous doing." 181. As Uddhava, also saw the lovely face of the image, he too felt a sense of peace. Eknāth then requested him to begin at once the preparations for the rite. 182. The astrologers were called immediately, and an auspicious day for the ceremony for bringing the divine life into the image was named. Uddhava undertook all the preparations, and caused the ceremony to become known in the city. 183. The inhabitants of the city exclaimed, "Seeing the devotion of Śrī Eknāth the image of Viṭṭhal has indeed come here from the country of Karnāṭak." 184. Eknāth continued the reading of the Purāṇ during the third *prahar* of each day, and the *kīrtans* in the evenings. The merchant listened and felt a sense of peace. 185. Remarking to himself, "All minds are deeply stirred by Eknāth's eloquence. He is surely Pāṇḍuraṅg himself, descended to save the world." 186. The preparations for the ceremony were completed. On the morrow was the auspicious day. So during the last *prahar* of the night the cooking for the expected multitude was begun. 187. Skilled women cooks, whose husbands were living, cooked the feast with their own hands. Food, in abundance, and of great variety, was prepared. 188. As soon as the morning dawned, the worship of the image was begun. The Vedic priests came and duly performed the rites and ceremonies. 189. The image was bathed with the five nectarous substances, and the *mantras* were repeated for bringing the divine life into the image. It was then duly anointed, and clothed in golden brocade. 190. It was adorned with pearls, diamonds and rubies, and then with garlands of flowers and the tulsi leaves, this Ruler-of-the-World was worshipped. 191. Incense, lamps and the five lamp tray were waved over it; festal music was played at the door of the shrine. The Vaishṇavas loudly uttered God's names and attributes, and sang verses of praise. 192. Food cooked in ghee and dainty food were lovingly presented as offerings to it. Vedic mantras were recited, and handfuls of flowers were offered. 193. Eknāth then took a lump of butter on the palm of his hand, and placed it to the mouth of the idol, saying, "O Viṭṭhal, eat this now. 194. As Krishṇa *avatār* you stole butter, and ate it greedily. Our eyes are ravenously hungry to see you do so again. 195. If you will show so wonderful a miracle, your glory will greatly increase in this place." Hearing these words of Eknāth the image smiled. 196. And putting out its tongue licked up the butter in Eknāth's hand. The Vaishṇava *bhaktas*, seeing this miracle, gave shouts of "Victory Victory." 197. They then walked around the image, and lovingly made before it *sāshtāng namaskārs.* The sun had now reached the noon hour, and the Brāhmaṇs sat down in lines to eat. 198. Śrī Eknāth respectfully worshipped them. With his own hands he washed their feet. He anointed them with sandal-wood oil and other fragrant perfumes, and waved the incense and lamps before them. 199. He served many dainty dishes, impartially, on their leaf plates, at the same time uttering the mantra that the real enjoyer of the feast was Janārdan in each of them. 200. Thus the Brāhmaṇs of the city were all well feasted, and receiving the *pān supāri* and gifts, were highly pleased. 201. The merchant seeing the success of the festal occasion was much gratified, and said to himself, "I must plan some way of getting Śrī Eknāth to come to my home."

THE MARRIAGE CEREMONY OF PAṆḌURAṄG AND RUKMIṆI IS PERFORMED.

202. So making his obeisance to Eknāth he said, "After I now return to my country, I am going to make a beautiful image of Rukmiṇi. 203. Bring all your retinue with you. I invite you to perform the marriage ceremony of Śrī Pāṇḍuraṅg with Rukmiṇi." Eknāth was greatly pleased at this invitation. 204. And after conferring with Uddhava accepted the invitation. The merchant, after presenting rich gifts, took leave and departed. 205. On returning to his home he had an image of Rukmiṇi made, and completing preparations for the wedding, appointed the marriage day. 206. Then writing a letter of invitation, embellished with saffron, he sent it to Eknāth at Paiṭhaṇ, in which he said, "I ask you to come soon, bringing the bridegroom and the bridegroom's mother in marriage procession." 207. Eknāth had already received a hint of this invitation, and had made his preparations for going. He invited the blind, the lame, and the poor to go with him to the marriage. 208. He furnished them with new wedding garments, and, urging them to accompany him, the bridegroom marriage procession started on its way, led by the din of festal music. 209. The Bridegroom, namely the idol of Viṭṭhal, was carried in a palanquin. Girjābāi (as mother of the bridegroom) rode in a carriage. The others rode on horses, all acclaiming the praise of Eknāth. 210. The men and women of

the towns they passed through exclaimed, "God had become the son of his *bhakta,* and as bridegroom, He is going to a far distant place for His marriage." 211. Thus pleasantly Eknāth journeyed along, and the people along the way seeing the marvellous splendour of the procession, flocked to see him. 212. When the marriage procession arrived at the outskirts of the merchant's town, they encamped. And as soon as he received word of their arrival, he hastened to welcome them. 213. All the inhabitants of the town also hurried out to join in the welcome, and reverently and affectionately touched their foreheads to Eknāth's feet. 214. Uddhava, and all the other guests were also greeted, and clothing and adorning the idol bridegroom, all rejoiced. 215. They gave gifts of raiment to the priest, and then worshipped Śrī Pāṇḍuraṅg. From there with great eclat the procession wended its way to the lodgings prepared for the guests. 216. After the ceremony of installing the household gods and the feasting of the Brāhmaṇs, the marriage of Viṭṭhal and Rukmiṇi took place. The Brāhmaṇs held the marriage curtain between the two, and intoned the words "*Sāvadhānam, sāvadhānam*" (Attention, Attention.) 217. As they ended the marriage formula with "Om Puṇyāha" (May it be a day of Happiness) the din of musical instruments began. The *bhakta*s shouted, "Victory, Victory," and the day was made a great festal occasion. 218. Then they sought to honor the mother of the bridegroom, all of which was received by Girjābāi. The merchant touched his forehead to Eknāth's feet, and then said. 219. "May we now hear, to our heart's content a *kīrtan* from your lips." Śrī Eknāth accepted the invitation, he having brought with him all that was needed.

220. The sound of cymbal, lute, and drum was swelled with the acclamations of the audience. The *kīrtan* aroused the passion of love. The hearts of the hearers were deeply moved. 221. He lovingly sang of the deeds of God in his visible form (*saguṇ*) and related the *Paurāṇik* stories, every now and then causing them to repeat aloud with heartfelt love the names and attributes of God. 222. Eknāth remained there a month, and turned every one to the worship of Vishṇu. Finally he began taking leave of the merchant that he might hasten back to his own country. 223. The merchant, highly gratified by the visit, gave many marriage gifts to the bridegroom. He spent a large amount of money in gifts of garments to the wedding guests. 224. Eknāth, having thus accomplished the purpose of his visit, returned to Pratishṭhāna. When the inhabitants of the sacred city saw him, they flocked to his feet. 225. And when night came they carried the Husband-of-Rukmiṇi in festal procession. And here, I, Mahipati, a servant of servants, sing the praises of His goodness. 226. Svasti. This book is the Śrī Bhaktalilāmṛita. By merely listening to it one's desires are fulfilled. Listen then to it ye loving pious *bhaktas*. This is the seventeenth delightful chapter.

CHAPTER 18.
MAHIPATI'S INVOCATION.

Obeisance to Śrī Gaṇeśa. Obeisance to Śrī Rāma Krishṇa.

1. This is the Supreme Brahma, standing on the brick at whose sight bodily consciousness disappears, and to obtain whom the Husband-of-Mṛidāni sits in the cemetery.

2. Blessed are those citizens who out of the love of their hearts live in the sacred city of Paṇḍhari. They, in their love, see there the Supreme Brahma actually manifested in visible form. 3. Those who look upon the river Chandrabhāgā, acquire, in so doing, all that other sacred waters can bestow. The greatest of sins even are washed away. Such is its glory, the Purāṇs declare. 4. Those who, with supreme affection in their hearts, feel drawn to visit Paṇḍhari, return not hither (after death) through birth, but there comes to them Deliverance through absorption (into Brahma.) 5. Blessed indeed are those Vaishṇavas who go on pilgrimages to Paṇḍhari, for at the temple door of Puṇḍalik they arrive at the pleasures of Heaven. 6. As is the glory of Paṇḍhari, so is the glory of the sacred city of Pratishṭhāna. Here, because of the perfect bhakti of Śrī Eknāth, the Husband-of-Rukmiṇi came.

EKNĀTH PLANS A PILGRIMAGE TO PAṆḌHARPUR.

7. In the last chapter there was related the interesting stories of how the Brāhmaṇs persecuted Eknāth, and also how his heavenly fathers in visible forms came down from heaven. 8. Further on, how the image of Pāṇḍuraṅg came from the Karnāṭak, and how, later, after celebrating his marriage returned to his own town. 9. How, with exceeding joy and pomp, the Lord-of-Paṇḍhari was carried in procession. That indeed was a most auspicious day when the Soul-of-the-World was placed on His throne. 10.

And Eknāth, having invited all the Brāhmaṇs of the sacred city, feasted them with many kinds of savoury food. 11. After the above events Śrī Eknāth told Uddhava in private, of a secret wish. He said, "Although we have rendered Him no service, yet Pāṇḍuraṅg in his idol form has come to our house. 12. In all my life, I have never visited Pāṇḍhari, and yet even without my rendering him any form of service, this Recliner-on-the Serpent (Vishṇu) has come to our house. 13. Just as the clouds in the sky thunder, even though the *chāṭaka* has not opened its mouth (to the rain). Just as the moon rises, even though the *chakor* may be yet wholly unawake. 14. Just as the sun reveals himself in the sky, even though the lotus may not be thinking of him. Just as a mother cares for her child while it is playing in the yard (unconscious of her.) 15. So although I have not been to Paṇḍhari (to render service), the Husband-of-Rukmiṇi has felt kindly towards me, and suddenly came here to my home from the Karnāṭak country. 16. So now this thought has come to me, that I must see Paṇḍhari with my own eyes, that Vaikuṇṭha upon earth, that home of the saints." 17. As Śrī Eknāth thus spoke, Uddhava bowed low. And as this was to be Eknāth's first pilgrimage (to that place) a good auspicious day was chosen for starting. 18. With *dinḍi* and flags woven with gold and silver thread, with the sweet sounding cymbal, lute and drum, Śrī Eknāth, and other pilgrims prepared to start on their journey. 19. Because of the effect of association with his goodness, inhabitants of the sacred city prepared to accompany him, with supreme joy in their hearts, enthusiastically shouting the names and attributes of God.

EKNĀTH STARTS ON HIS PILGRIMAGE TO PAṆḌHARPUR.

20. This assemblage of Vaishṇavas, singing and dancing, started on their pilgrimage, clapping their hands to their shouts of, "Victory, Victory," and the sounds they made filled the very heavens. 21. Singing God's praise Śrī Eknāth journeyed on foot. A great crowd of people from the city accompanied them a part of way. 22. Eknāth instructed Uddhava how to care for affairs at home. And Uddhava, solemnly promising to do so, prostrated himself at Eknāth's feet. 23. After Eknāth was out of sight Uddhava returned home. The other citizens also returned to the city. 24. Uddhava carried on all the affairs at Eknāth's home just as he had established the custom. In the afternoons at the third *prahar* there was the reading aloud of the *Purāṇs.* At night *kīrtans* were performed. 25. The worship of Vishṇu, and the feeding of the poor that Eknāth was accustomed to perform, Uddhava followed. "Blessed, Blessed," cried the dwellers of the sacred city. "Nothing whatever is lacking (from the customary usage.)"

THE JOURNEY TO PAṆḌHARPUR.

26. But now as to the pilgrimage. Eknāth, and the many who were accompanying him, were on their way to Paṇḍhari. They journeyed along the path joyously. At every stage in the journey *kīrtans* were held. 27. On account of being in the company of Śrī Eknāth no one felt weary or exhausted. In the excess of joy they repeated the names of Hari. 28. The weak and the

needy, both in the front and the rear (of the procession,) were assisted. Every now and then there were bursts of song with feelings of love in praise of the Husband-of-Rukmiṇi. 29. Śrī Eknāth himself was an *avatār* of Pāṇḍuraṅg, come to save the world, yet for the sake of mankind, he at no point overstepped human limitations. 30. For whatever example saints set, that the pious follow. In this way the latter become free from faults, and no longer are in bondage to this world. 31. Whenever Eknāth met distinguished Vaishṇavas he made them a *namaskār*. He was a man of great humility. He had not the least pride. 32. He was like the sun that rises in the sky, and pours his brightness over the earth, yet feels no pride of his own glory. 33. With feelings of deep love, these simple minded Vaishṇavas, journeyed along the path, praising God in song. 34. As they approached the city of Paṇḍhari, and saw the pinnacle of the temple their hearts rejoiced, and they lost all bodily consciousness. 35. That very night Paṇḍharināth appeared to the officiating priests (of the temple) in a dream and said, "Tomorrow there is coming here on a pilgrimage Ekā Janārdan, the *abheda bhakta*. 36. Therefore, taking along with you diṇḍis and banners go out to meet him, and on the fourteenth day of the moon let Eknāth perform a *kīrtan* at the chief door of the temple." 37. It soon became known in the sacred city that such a vision had been seen, and all the people hurried to the Chandrabhāgā (river) for an ovation (of welcome.) 38. Saints, *mahants,* and distinguished Vaishṇavas, sang praise to God with rejoicing, so that the whole etherial space was filled with the shoutings of God's names, and cries of Victory! Victory!

EKNĀTH ARRIVES AT PAṆḌHARPUR

39. When Śrī Nāth saw before him the city of Paṇḍhari, he fell prostrate on the ground. Tears of joy flowed from his eyes. All embraced one another, 40 Saying, " Blessed is this cream of all days, in which we have seen Paṇḍharpur, truly very Vaikuṇtha on earth, the mother-home of the saints. 41. Thus extolling the glory of the city, they waved incense to (God) the Being-of-Supreme-Goodness, Being-of-Infinite-attributes, Selfjoyous, to whom no limits can be ascribed. 42. The whole crowd of pilgrims now crossed the Bhimarathi (river). And no sooner had they crossed, than the saints and *mahants* approaching, welcomed them. With affection they embraced one another. 43. " Blessed is this day," they cried, " in which we have met Eknāth." After bathing in the Chandrabhāgā, Eknāth went through all his usual devotions. 44. Śrī Eknāth then went to view the tomb of the Muni Puṇḍalik, that chief of all *bhaktas,* and lovingly worshipped him. 45. The temple priests then suggested that he should next go to the chief entrance of the temple, there first to meet the Husband-of-Rukmiṇi, and then be free to go to his lodgings. 46. Eknāth had absolute confidence that the voice of the Brāhmaṇ was the voice of God, so with their *dinḍis* and banners they marched along (to the temple.) 47. At the Eagle-platform they prostrated themselves to the ground with love. And while the saints and *mahants* were singing the praises of God, they bowed at their feet also. 48. Paṇḍhari is the city of Śrī Vishṇu. It is Vaikuṇṭha itself on earth. It is where men and women live, who are four-armed and who have no differences or distinctions between themselves. 49.

There are truly very many sacred watering places on this earth, but those who visit them become filled only with greater pride. 50. Not so with Mother Paṇḍhari. At the mere sight of her one's evil nature and pride pass away. Bringing repentance to the heart of the wicked, she starts him on the way to the chief end of man. 51. He who can destroy the evil pride of the heart, which is the real root of birth and death, he is to be recognized as the Supreme. Yogi. 52. Yogis direct their sight to the tip of their noses. And such is the appearance of (this image of) the Supreme-Being. He stands on the bank of the Bhimā (river), with both hands on his hips. 53. The Yogis conquer their egotism and obtain the highest place. So is not the Husband-of-Rukmiṇi. He delivers all ignorant beings. 54. This God-of-Gods, this Giver-of-Absorption-into-Brahma, Eknāth saw with his own eyes. With a heart full of joy, he embraced him with love. 55. Graceful in his posture, lovely in his appearance, his beautiful hands on his hips, his face fascinating, alligator-shaped earrings in his ears. 56. A divine yellow silk garment fastened at his waist, his neck with a garland of *tulsi* and *manjari*, His feet together on a brick. Merely to look at him is to have all consciousness of body dissolve away. 57. Eknāth gazed at him with feelings of love, and touched his forehead to his feet. Then with his lips he sang hymns of praise, and worshipped this Lord-of-Heaven. 58. And this *saguṇ* form, which he saw with his eyes, he treasured in his memory. He then went to worship Satyabhāmā, Rāhi and Rukmiṇi. 59. After making a pradakshiṇā of the sacred city, the while singing songs of praise to Pāṇḍuraṅg, he made his way to his lodging.

EKNĀTH MEETS WITH THE BHAKTAS AT PAṆḌHARPUR.

60. Let us now turn to what was in the heart of the *bhakta.* All the Brāhmaṇs of the scared city were given an invitation (to a feast). Savoury dishes were prepared, and the next day they sat down to a breakfast. 61. Then on the fourteenth day of the moon the Husband-of-Rukmiṇi (in a vision) made known his wish to all the saints, saying, " I am very fond of Eknāth's *kīrtans.*" 62. As soon as this wish was revealed in the vision to the priests, they said very respectfully to Eknāth, " We request you, Great Svami, to perform a *kīrtan* at the Eagle-platform. 63. It is Śrī Paṇḍuraṅg's wish. You have been honored for this purpose. " When Eknāth heard of this gracious honor, he made great preparations for the occasion. 64. Flags and streamers, and the seven colored banners, the cymbal, *viṇà,* and drum, all were ready. 65. Saints, *mahants, sādhus, ṛishis,* Vedic paṇdits, and the people of the sacred city sat down with reverence to listen. Their hearts were filled with delight. 66. They had already heard of Eknāth's wide-spread fame, and all were anxious to listen to his eloquence. 67. Among them there was also a great number of pilgrims, those brave, loving, heroic Vaishṇavas, and other men and women pilgrims, making a dense crowd. 68. Eknāth now stood up, and began with a hymn of invocation (to God,) and declaring that both listeners and speaker were Janārdan, bowed in worship. 69. As he thus spoke, there was clapping of hands to the name of Viṭṭhal, and with the tumultuous noise of these shouts of praise the etherial space was filled to overflowing. 70.. " Krishṇa, Vishṇu, Hari, Govinda,

Achyuta, Infinite-one, Source-of-Happiness, Supreme-Being Sachchidānanda, Śrī Mukunda, Guru-of-the-World, 71. Keśava, Nārāyaṇa, Mādhava, Lover-of-Bhaktas, Ocean-of-Mercy, Lord-of-the-Cowherdesses, God of Gods Thou dost quench the entire fire of this life's delusion. 72. For the sake of the dull, the stupid, the ignorant, Thou standest here on the bank of the Bhimā. Here thou dost welcome sincere *bhaktas,* and dost protect them with thy pitying glance." 73. Thus they sang the names (and attributes of God) with hearts full of love, and dancing to his praise the whole audience lost all consciousness of body. Ecstasy arose to its highest pitch.

EKNĀTH RELATES A STORY OF HIS GREAT GRANDFATHER, BHĀNUDĀS.

74. At this moment some one made Eknāth a request. "The life of your great-grand-father, Bhānudās, is exceedingly interesting. Let us hear it told in song." 75. Śrī Eknāth was greatly pleased on hearing this suggestion, and said, "I had that very thing in mind, when you, Svāmi, gave the command," (and he sang the story of Bhānudās, as follows.)

76. King Rāma, with his followers, was ruling in Vidyānagara. Travelling in state, he came one day to this sacred city of Paṇḍhari. 77. While looking at the beautiful image of Pāṇḍuraṅg, a strong desire filled his heart. Said he to himself, "I want to take the Husband-of-Rukmiṇi to my city of Vidyānagara." 78. With this thought in mind he fasted for seven days. Krishṇa then appeared to him in a dream, and bid him as follows; 79.

"Because I saw the extraordinary devotion of Pundalik (to his parents) I took up my abode here at Paṇḍhari, and according to the promise I made him, I here meet men of piety. 80. I enjoy this place. There is no place of rest like this. My abode in the Ocean-of-Milk and Heaven itself seem inferior places to this. 81. Here pious and loving *bhaktas* are constantly coming on pilgrimage. Here, free from all worry, I, Krishṇa, live in their company. 82. This being so, King Rāma, you make your persistent request in vain. Still I will tell you, how I may be carried to Vidyānagara, and what you must do. 83. I will only go there on condition that Brāhmaṇs, making themselves ceremonially pure, carry me along in their hands, and nowhere on the journey place me on the ground." 84. Seeing this vision of the night, the king was overjoyed in his heart. He called his ministers together and conferred with them in private. "Advise me," he said, "what plan I can adopt?" 85. The ministers replied, "Give the Brāhmanṇs of our country large gifts, and station them along the route. 86. Then passing the image from hand to hand we can quickly bring it to our city." The king listened to this proposal, and it pleased him greatly. 87. He wrote humbly-worded letters to the Twice-born of the various villages, and soon collected a multitude of Brāhmaṇs along the route. 88. At certain regular distances he made arrangements for water and food, and the Brāhmaṇs seeing in all this a service rendered to God, were glad. 89. The king then made his *namaskār* to the God, and thus besought Him, "Do me now this favor, O Pāṇḍuraṅg, and come with me immediately."

90. Thus besought by the king, the image was lifted to be passed from hand to hand. Against this act the

special servants and priests of the idol protested violently, but the king would not listen to them. 91. The monarch had authority and no one had the strength to prevail against him. Men and women (of the city) watched what was going on, and tears filled their eyes. 92. The king had no sooner taken the image away, than Paṇḍharpur seemed like a deserted city. It looked like a body without life.

93. We turn now to King Rāma. Causing the image to be passed from hand to hand, he arrived at his city. 94. He collected all the distinguished Vaishṇavas together, and had a *kīrtan* performed. There were *dinḍis* and banners in profusion, and beautiful garlands of flowers. 95. With affection they worshipped and anointed the image of Pāṇḍuraṅg, and placed it on a throne. The king proclaimed a great festival. He could not contain himself for joy. 96. The king honored the distinguished Vaishṇavas with rich gifts of garments and ornaments, and distributing money lavishly he made the Brāhmaṇs happy. 97. Adorning the Husband-of-Rukmiṇi with ornaments set with jewels, costly raiment and strings of pearls, he worshipped Him, and the etherial space overflowed with joy. 98. Now while the king was asleep in his palace the image of Pāṇḍuraṅg appeared to him in a dream, and said, "You have brought me to this place. I will tell you the conditions on which I shall stay here. Listen. 99. In accordance with the laws of justice and equity you must carry on a kingdom of righteousness. If the least injustice takes place, I shall remain here no longer. 100. I delight in loving *bhaktas*, and if you should persecute any of them, when innocent, I shall return to Paṇḍharpur, my former

abode." 101. The king having received this vision by night from Paṇḍharināth, he was greatly alarmed, and was continually on the watch.

102. The priests came in the early mornings and affectionately worshipped the idol. The king first performed his bath, and then came to watch the worship of the idol and listen to the songs of praise. 103. Because the idol was adorned with priceless ornaments, there was great fear of thieves. Locks, therefore, were placed on the doors of the temple, during all the eight watches of the day, even from morning to night. 104. Until the king came to the temple no one in the city could obtain a sight of the idol, so carefully was it guarded. 105. The king regularly worshipped it, using the sixteen rites. Thrice a day savoury food, with a dressing of melted butter was offered to it. 106. Around it burned constantly rows of camphor lights. Flowers, musk, and many other fragrant materials were placed upon it. 107. But separation from Paṇḍhari pierced the heart of the God like an arrow, and he was ill at ease. "I am imprisoned here," he said to himself. "When shall I be delivered from here?"

108. Now let us turn to Paṇḍhari, where in the month of Ashāḍh a crowd of pilgrims had gathered. The saints, *mahants,* siddhas and *ṛishis* were in great distress. 109. Only the most courageous Vaishṇavas had gathered here. The others, worldly minded, said to themselves, (Why go there?) Paṇḍharināth has gone away. 110. And thus minded they all remained at home. The saints, *mahants,* however, made Paṇḍhari beautiful by their

presence. 111. Just as when it rains heavily on the earth, one mistakes side gullies for rivers. But when the hot season comes, there is not a drop of water left in them. 112. That crystal which alone endures the blow of the hammer, is considered a priceless diamond. Experts know that other crystals would be smashed to powder. 113. When tested by intense heat, that which appears brilliant, is recognized as gold. Brass appears dull. Such is the method of testing them. 114. If the gem [taken from a cobra's head,] is wound around by a cotton thread and then thrown into the fire, and the thread does not burn, then the gem is a sure antidote to snake poison. 115. So in times of adversity, amid the many whirlpools of fiery trials, he whose determination in no wise fails, he alone deserves the name of saint. 116. He whose love does not weaken in times of distress, but who with tenacity of purpose performs accustomed duties, such a *bhakta* is dear to the Good-Being, as one loves one's own soul.

117. Well, enough of these long drawn out remarks, but the composing of similes is a poet's business. No sooner had King Rāma taken Paṇḍharināth away, than there arrived pilgrim saints. 118. Not seeing the Husband-of-Rukmiṇi on his throne, Paṇḍharpur seemed to them like a deserted city, like the ceasing of the functions of the senses, when the body is without life. 119. Like an army without a king, like the night without the moon, like the poetic inspiration without the grace of God. 120. Or, again, like a house without the master of the house, so Paṇḍharpur appeared. All were troubled, but no one was able to suggest any remedy at all.

121. Just then * Nivṛitti, Dnyānadeva, Sopāna, Nāmā, Sānvatā, all Vaishṇavas, Muktābāi storehouse of goodness, arrived on their pilgrimage. 122. Also Kabir, Rohidāsa, Gorā the potter, Goṇābāi, Jani, the servant of Nāmā, and Rājāi, all noble *bhaktas.* 123. This company of pilgrims was seated by the Eagle-platform, and Nāmadeva was performing a *kīrtan,* when Bhānudāsa suddenly approached. 124. On his shoulder he carried the Brahma lute, and he came along playing the lute, singing, dwelling on the Husband-of-Rukmiṇi in his heart, and repeating his names (and attributes). 125. In this manner Bhānudās arrived at the Eagle-platform. He at once saluted the saints and *mahants* and reverently made them a *namaskār.* 126. He found all these distinguished Vaishṇavas greatly troubled in their hearts, thinking over how the Husband-of-Rukmiṇi had been taken away to Vidyānagara. 127. Some argued that the God-ofGods, seeing the devotion of King Rāma, had gone from Paṇḍhari. One said, "Then why should not we, who are many Vaishṇava *bhaktas,* go and bring Keśava back." 128. To this proposal of Dnyānarāj, no one responded. Some said,

---

* *Note.*—Neither Viṭṭhal Kavi, nor Mahipati in his Bhaktavijaya 43, 136-147 name the *bhaktas* present at Paṇḍharpur. Keśavasvāmi, in his *Eknāth charitra* 14, 75-78, and followed by Mahipati here, makes Bhānudās a contemporary of Dhyāneśvara and the group of saints that tradition usually associates with him. This anachronism may perhaps be best explained by the probable fact, that neither Keśavasvāmi, nor the author from whom Keśavasvāmi obtained his information, knew the dates of Bhānudās or Dnyāneśvara, and therefore had no difficulty in making them contemporaries to him, all belonging to the distant past.

"There is no way of going against the will of God." 129. Another spoke from the non-dualistic point of view. "God is within us. God fills all animate and inanimate things. There is no place empty of Him." 130. Another said, "If we go there, the king will be angry with us, and put us, in prison. Then what would we do?" 131. The cowardly minded remarked, "That is none of our business." Just then Bhānudās bowed prostrate before those saints. 132. "If you will command me," he said, "I will speedily bring Paṇḍharināth back. You may put away all anxiety. I bid you to remain here.

133. With these words to them, Bhānudās departed. And just as Māruti rejoiced in going to search for Sitā, so Bhānudās rejoiced. 134. In his heart he dwelt on the image of Paṇḍuraṅg. With his lips he sang the fame of His name. Day and night he repeated his name (and attributes) with peace of heart accompanied with love. 135. Under the influence of the wonderful thought of bringing God back, his heart was joyous. He lost the consciousness of body. He forgot thirst and hunger. 136. He asked for no food, but if anyone happened to give it to him, he ate it with contentment and continued his journey. 137. Travelling in this way along the route, Bhānudās finally approached Vidyānagara, and enquired of the people, whether it was here that Pāṇḍuraṅg had been brought. 138. For fear of the king, he found, no one would reply to him. But finally he met a good man, a Brāhman, who told him every thing. 139. "King Rāma," he said, "brought the image of Pāṇḍuraṅg here, and has installed it in the temple, but no one is allowed to see it. It is constantly kept under lock and key." 140. Bhānudās thought

to himself, "Then I must see the God privately. I will go there after the hymns of praise are sung, that put him to rest for the night." 141. That evening the king came to the temple as usual, hurried through the evening hymns of praise, and returned to his palace.

142. Bhānudās, the distinguished Vaishṇava, now came to the door of the temple. He found the priests outside, overcome with sleep. 143. To the rooms within rooms there were four doors. Each door was fastened with heavy locks. But the Husband-of-Rukmiṇi performed a miracle, and caused the locks to fall. 144. Seeing all the doors unlocked, Bhānudās was happy indeed, "My desire is fulfilled," he thought to himself, and at once entered. 145. There stood the Lord-of-the-World, His feet close together on the brick, both hands on his hips, his eyes fastened on the tip of his nose. 146. Bhānudās saw its beautiful face, and was filled with rapture. But pretending outwardly that he was angry, he began to scold the God.

147. "Husband-of-Rukmiṇi, Lord-of-Paṇḍhari, what is the meaning of these badges fastened to your feet? Your deeds do not correspond with your promises. I realize this now from experience. 148. You gave Puṇḍalik a promise that you would for ever remain at Paṇḍharpur, to save the dull minded and the ignorant. Apparently you have not the slightest recollection of that promise. 149. You have chosen for yourself a very fine private place in the king's palace, and adorned yourself with fine raiment, and many ornaments. You are receiving offerings of savoury food. 150. It is for this that you are staying here in enjoyment. You have forgotten us in

your heart." Bhānudās then immediately composed an *abhang* to which I ask this wise audience to listen.

The Abhang of Bhānudās.

1. On the bank of the Bhimā river, standing on the brick, Vithobā was ruling in Paṇḍhari.

2. Ṛiddhi and Siddhi wait upon Him with their retinue. Thou art not obtainable even to Brahmadeva and other Gods.

3. Yet leaving all that you have come here. Who has beguiled you, Kānadiyā?

4. The conchshell, the kettle drum, the hand drum, and the horn sound, and keep you, O God, awake.

5. You are sprinkled with *champaka* oil, smeared with fragrant oils, rivulets of Bhivarā sandal wood oil are flowing on you.

6. Rambhā, Tilottamā, Urvaśi, and Menikā, and many other heavenly damsels have come with you.

7. On golden *paryeli* jewelled lamps are waved over your beautiful and glorious face.

8. But Mother Rakhumāi has naturally become depressed and how silent has Puṇḍalik become.

9. *Bhaktas* and Bhāgavatas are displeased, and without you, have become speechless.

10. Blessed is Pandharpur, the mother-home of the Universe. Blessed is the sand-bed on the bank of the Bhimā.

11. Come along with me, says Bhānudās. Let the God remember the debt he owes through the promise He made. 151. With this pleading request, Bhānudās fell at the God's feet. "Tell me now," he cried, "Who has beguiled you, O king God?" 152. As Chakrapāṇi listened to this pleading, He was deeply moved. He embraced Bhānudās, and drew him close to his heart. 153. "I am confined in a prison here," Pāṇḍharināth exclaimed, "and you also have hardened your heart, and have not taken me back to my home. 154. O loving *Bhakta,* do not desert me here, and go away. I truly cannot endure a single moment without you." 155. Thus speaking, this Being of Mercy, gave Bhānudās a love-token. He put around Bhānudās' neck his own garland of *tulsi* leaves and flowers. 156. "Tomorrow," He said, "come and take me along with you." At this request of the Husband-of-Rukmiṇi, Bhānudās was overjoyed. 157. Along with the garland of flowers, however, there came the string of nine jewels. But Bhānudās was not aware of this, as he quickly passed out. 158. The moment Bhānudās left, the Life-of-the-World miraculously relocked the doors. Now as soon as it was dawn the king hastened to the temple.

159. As he was waving the lights before the God, he failed to see the string of nine jewels on His neck. "A thief must have been here," he thought, and he poured out his rage on the priests. 160. Detectives rushed in every direction to discover the thief. Suddenly they saw Bhānudās, the distinguished Vaishṇava. 161. He had bathed in the Gaṅgā, and was sitting repeating the names and attributes of Viṭṭhal. On his neck the servants of the king noticed the radiant string of divine jewels. 162.

They seized this distinguished Vaishṇava, and brought him quickly before the king. Showing him the string of jewels, they said, " We have caught the thief and have brought him here." 163. The king became furious with rage, and angrily addressed him. Then to his officers he said, "You have caught the thief, and have brought him here. Now impale him." 164. Without proper consideration, and without justice, he gave this order to his officers. He was not aware of what was to take place. His mind was enveloped by the illusions of Māyā. 165. So they gave Bhānudās, the distinguished Vaishṇava, a severe beating; placed the stake on his shoulder, and śendur on his forehead. 166. But Bhānudās, with love in his heart, held in his mind the image of Pāṇḍuraṅg, exclaiming, " God-of-Gods, Husband-of-Rukmiṇi, how nobly you are treating me. 167. Because I have come to carry you back, you put this necklace around my neck, and now you are giving me up to be impaled. You have not the slightest love. 168. Well, since it thus lies in your mind, death will come to my body, but never, never will I forget Thee." And with this he broke out into the following *abhang*.

1. Though the heavens should roar with thunder; though the sphere of the universe should crash into pieces; though fire devour the three worlds, yet will I wait on Thee, O Vithobā.

2. Though the seven oceans should flow into one; though the five elements be dissolved, yet, Thou wilt be with me, O Vithobā.

3. Though any disaster whatever, may fall heavily upon me, yet may my repeating of Thy name never cease,

just as a devoted wife does to the Lord of her life. Says Bhānudās, Hear me, O Vithobā.

169. Thus expressing his purpose, he became choked with emotion. When suddenly Paṇḍharīnāth manifested his presence. Listen how he did it, ye pious *bhaktas* of His.

170. The sharp stake that had been fastened upright in the ground, suddenly burst into branches and leaves, beautiful flowers and fruit, to the astonishment of all. 171. The king was informed by his servants that the impaling stake had become a living tree. The king heard the report and was startled. 172. Repentant, the king hastened to see the sight. And there he saw Bhānudās with his eyes closed, repeating the names and attributes of the King-of-Paṇḍhari. 173. Seeing him in this attitude, the king, prostrated himself on the ground before him, exclaiming, "You fearless Vaishṇava, I sinful and dull of understanding, did not recognize you." 174. Bhānudās now opened his eyes and looked about, and beheld the stake had become a great tree. "The Husband-of-Rukmiṇi has manifested His presence for me," he exclaimed. "A miracle has taken place." 175. The king now took Bhānudās by the hand, and led him to the temple. And there they saw the image of Pāṇḍuraṅg with dejected countenance, and tears streaming from his eyes. 176. Seeing him so, the king made a *sāshtāng namaskār,* and then with palm to palm before the God, he pled with him in tender words. 177. "I have done wrong in many ways," he exclaimed. "I have persecuted your *bhakta.*" Hearing King Rāma's plea for mercy, the Lord-of-Paṇḍhari replied. 178. "Remain here in peace, but ever bringing my form to your remembrance. I am going back with Bhānudās to behold

Paṇḍhari. 179. If you use any pressure to prevent this, great calamity will befall you here." Accepting this reply of Śāraṅgadhara, the king, ceased to speak further.

180. Bhānudās now said, "Husband-of-Rukmiṇi, what means shall I employ (in carrying you back?). Mine is not a kingly power, that I can collect a multitude of people to carry you." 181. The Husband-of-Rukmiṇi listened to his question, and then a miracle followed. Suddenly the image became small in size, to the amazment of the king. 182. Bhānudās was delighted, and placed the King-of-Paṇḍhari in a little bamboo basket. Then exclaiming, "Victory to Śrī Viṭṭhal!" he carried along the Husband-of-Rukmiṇi. 183. Enclosed within the basket, the Supreme Being, told Bhānudās his deep inner thoughts. "The universe is filled with joy to-day, for I shall see the saints." 184. Thus, journeying along the route, Bhānudās, arrived near the city of Pāṇdhari, and this Vaishṇava *bhakta* descended into the Padmatirtha to bathe. 185. He washed his *dhotar,* and spread it out to dry on the stone wall of the tank. Suddenly the God assumed again his large form. 186. The cover of the basket above his head, and the side at his feet were broken to bits. Bhānudās was amazed. The Husband-of-Rukmiṇi then said. 187. "The saints and *mahants* have been waiting for me unceasingly at the Eagle platform. Go quickly, and tell them (I am here). They will come immediately to welcome me." 188. At this request of the Lord-of-the-World, Bhānudās, glad of heart, hastened to the Eagle-platform, and with smiling countenance made the announcement. 189. "I have bought back truly the image of Viṭṭhal as far as the Padmatirtha." As they heard this announcement, all rejoiced at heart.

190. And all went out to welcome him, carrying with them a palanquin. They had with them *dinḍis* and banners in profusion, and the festal musical instruments were played. 191. The Vaishṇavas sang the praise of Hari, singing and dancing in their love. All the inhabitants of the sacred city, great and small, followed in the procession, 192. Exclaiming as they went along, "How can we ever repay our obligation to Bhānudās. Blessed is this fearless Vaishṇava hero. He has brought back our Śāraṅgadhar." 193. The whole crowd now approached the Padmatirtha. As soon as they saw the image of Pāṇḍuraṅg, they prostrated themselves to the ground. 194. Bhānudās gave a helping hand, and Paṇḍarināth was placed in a palanquin. The *bhaktas* shouted, "Victory, Victory," and scattered fragrant powders in the air. 195. Thus in pomp the Husband-of-Rukmiṇi was brought to the Chandrabhāgā river. Here they bathed him, and then brought him to the temple. 196. On a happy auspicious day, the image was replaced on its throne. Immediately the God, Giver-of-bliss-of-Absorption, spoke to Bhānudās a word of promise. 197. "I cannot repay your kindness. You have again brought Paṇḍharpur to my sight. I shall assuredly become an *avatār* in your family line." 198. At this promise of the Saviour-of-the-World, the *bhaktas* shouted "Victory, Victory," and to all the inhabitants of the sacred city there came great joy. 199. As rain from a cloud in the time of a drought, as life returning to a body at the point of death, so feeling this to be a joyous time, gifts were given to the people. 200. Men and women of their own accord distributed sweets from house to house. The Vaishṇavas at the Eagle-platform nodded their heads in unison to the loud music of praise.

201. Thus Ekā Janārdan sang the story of Bhānudās, and the saints and *mahants* listened to the *kīrtan* with rapt attention. 202. He thus sang the interesting story of his ancestor, Bhānudās. The sound of Brahma was incarnate there. Loud were the strains in which the *kīrtan* was sung. 203. Finally the last hymns of praise were sung and lights waved before the Husband-of-Rukmini. I, Mahipati, the servant of servants, now distribute the sweetmeats. 204. Svasti. This book is the Śrī Bhaktalilāmrit. By merely listening to it, one's desires are fulfilled. Listen then to it, ye loving, pious *bhaktas*. This is the eighteenth delightful chapter.

CHAPTER 19.

BHAKTALĪLĀMṚITA.

Mahipati's Invocation.

1. Obeisance to Śrī Gaṇeśa. Victory, Victory to the Merciful, to the Everlasting-Sleeper-(on-the-Serpent,) Bumble-bee-in-the lotus-heart-of-his-*Bhaktas,* Pervader-of-the-Universe, Ocean-of-Goodness, Supreme-over-All. Saviour-of-the World. 2. Thou thyself, O Thou-with-the-eyes-of-a-lotus, hast caused the beautiful life of Thy slave to be related. I am not an independent relater. I am dependent on Thee, subject to Thee. 3. Just as the wind sways the hay scare-crow, so the inspiration to my mind comes from Thy power, O Pāṇḍuraṅg. 4. The pipe plays many tunes, so the ignorant say. With undiscriminating mind, they fail to recognize the player. 5. The earth supports the tree. According to the soil there springs up the tender shoots. So, whether my narration lacks, or is perfect, the

cause is to be found entirely in Thee. 6. The soil that produces a tree does not always produce a cypress tree. So at the beginning or at the end, whatever it be, Thou Śāraṅgapāṇi, art He upon whom we rest. 7. Thou art both speaker and hearer, both in one. There is nothing else but Thee. So, now, looking upon us with eyes of favor, may God cause us to cross safely the ocean of life.

EKNĀTH RETURNS TO PAIṬHAṆ.

8. In the last chapter there was related the remarkable story of how Eknāth went to Paṇḍhari, and in a *kīrtan* lovingly sang the wonderful life history of Bhānudās. 9. The saints, *Mahants,* and other pious folk had listened with great joy of heart, and exclaimed, "Blessed is the sacred city of Pratishṭhāna, for it enjoys the sight of Śrī Nāth. 10. Eknāth is not a human avatār. He is, in very fact, Pāṇḍuraṅg himself, descended as *avatār.*" No sooner did Eknāth's ear catch this praise of himself, than he arose and went out. 11. He proceeded to the temple, and lovingly met there Pāṇḍuraṅg. Here he made gift offerings to the Brāhmaṇs, and taking God's leave departed. 12. Night and day Eknāth thought upon the extraordinary greatness of Paṇḍhari, and proclaimed to the people the noble fame of the city. He then started to return to Pratishṭhāna.

13. As he was approaching the city, Uddhava heard the news of his coming, and all the inhabitants of that sacred city hastened out to welcome Him. 14. Regarding Eknāth as the image of Pāṇḍuraṅg, they reverently made him *namaskār.* They embraced him with loving emotions,

and could not contain themselves for joy. 15. All lifted aloft emblems and banners, and marched along, while Eknāth sang the praises of God. On the route booths joined booths. An extraordinary crowd had gathered. 16. Thus accompanied with shouts of joy, Eknāth entered his home. Here also singing sweet songs of praise, he waved lights before the Husband-of-Rukmiṇi. 17. Thus successfully ended the pilgrimage to Paṇḍhari. With Uddhava, the loving disciple, always sitting beside him, 18. The customary worship of Vishṇu, the listening to the reading of the *Purāṇs,* the feeding of the poor, the song service in praise of Hari, all this went on as before. There was no failure in anything.

THE GREAT SANYĀSI, ŚRIPĀD.

19. Now there was in the sacred city of Pratishṭhāna a great *sannyāsi,* named Śripād. He had conquered the six enemies of the soul, and had become a Paramahansa. 20. He recognized God in every creature. He recognized no distinctions of less and more. To him beggar and king were alike. 21. A mosquito and an elephant, a four-legged or a two legged animal were all alike to him. Whatever creature he happened to see, he prostrated himself before it. 22. The Brāhmaṇs of the city said among themselves, "Although Śripād is a great man, he has not the least pride. He makes *namaskār* to everyone. 23. An outcaste or a Brāhmaṇ, a cow, a cat, a dog, a pig, or a bird, if he sees any of these he reverently bows to them. 24. Whether one is of low caste or high, does not at all come into his thoughts. Truly he is out of his head, through the influence of some *mantra.* He is certainly possessed."

25. Some said, " Each one knows himself only. He is no concern of ours. A Paramhansa does not have to consider in the least the differences of caste." 26. Thus of the inhabitants of the sacred city, some reviled him, some praised him, but from this he experienced in his heart, neither pleasure nor pain. His state was that of one unconscious of a body (conscious only of soul.) 27. He had adopted a regular habit of visiting Eknāth, and with fixed attention, lovingly listening to his *kīrtans*. 28. Thus bowing prostrate before every creature, and constantly visiting Śri Nāth, his heart was ever at peace, and filled with joy.

ŚRIPĀD WORSHIPS A DEAD DONKEY.

29. Many days thus passed, when a most extraordinary event occurred. The prostrating *Svāmi,* making his obeisances (*namaskār*) as he went along, arrived at the banks of the Gaṅgā (the Godāvari) for his bath. 30. A donkey had drowned in the river. The dead animal had floated down, and when the freshet had spent its force, the bloated carcass lay on the sand. 31. The prostrating *Svāmi* arriving at the spot made his *namaskār* to the carcass of the donkey. The Brāhmaṇs all laughed to see this prostration, for it was to a lifeless thing. 32. " O Svāmi," they exclaimed, "All-knowing-one. Who is it, to whom you have made this obeisance?" Hearing this question of the Brāhmaṇs, he looked to see what it really was. 33. It was indeed the carcass of an animal greatly bloated. The Brāhmaṇs added, " If you will bring this carcas to life, then indeed your feelings of reverence are justified. 34. Regarding this world, as if

it were but soul (ātmā), you make obeisance to every creat-ture. If you raise this donkey to life, then we are ready to acknowledge that your belief is proved true." 35. The Paramhansa listened to the proposition of the Brāhmaṇs, and replied, " The soul (ātmā) pervades all animate beings." Then to the Ātmā he prayed. 36. " God-of-Gods, King of Paṇḍhari. You have disappeared out of this thing. And so long as the body of this donkey appears in the form of a carcass, so long prostration before it seems in vain."

THE DONKEY IS BROUGHT TO LIFE.

37. He had no sooner thus spoken, when an extra-ordinary miracle took place. The carcass of the donkey, lying there, suddenly came to life. 38. Shaking itself, it snorted, flapped its ears, and in a moment was on its feet. The sight amazed the Brāhmaṇs, and they exclaimed, " This is an extraordinary miracle." 39. Putting aside their pride, the Brāmaṇs, made him a *namaskār*. Great crowds of people gathered to see what had happened, filling with their numbers the whole sand-bed of the river. 40. Men and women were astonished at the great acquired power of the prostrating Svāmi, and exlaimed, " So great a saint is not to be seen elsewhere on the earth." 41. The Brāhmaṇs said to one another, " This is indeed so. This Eknāth of our town is ever performing *kīrtans* in the *prākrit,* and beguiling all the people. 42. But he has no power to raise a carcass to life. It is only empty know-ledge which he is constantly preaching with his lips to the pious people." 43. While the Brāhmaṇs were thus reviling him, Śrī Nāth happened to approach. He just

happened to be coming to the bed of the river for the purpose of reciting the Vedas (Brahmayadnya.) 44. When the Brāhmaṇs saw him they let loose hateful words at him, and praising the prostrating Svāmi, said "Blessed, Blessed is he. 45. It is foolish to call anyone a saint who cannot perform a miracle, and indeed it does not seem commendable to endure such a so-called saint among men." 46. With these remarks all the Brāhmaṇs returned to their homes. Suddenly the prostrating Svāmi approached Śrī Nāth, and prostrated himself before him.

EKNĀTH REBUKES ŚRIPĀD FOR HIS MIRACLE.

47. Eknāth looked at this superior ascetic, and made him a *namaskār*. Then he thus addressed him. "You have created to-day a serious predicament. 48. To begin with this is the evil *Kaliyuga*. Mankind is filled with suspicions and hate. In addition to this the king is a Mahomedan. One sees therefore difficulties in the way of practising Yoga. 49. If the king hears of your powers, he will confine you in prison, so that if any of his household should die, he might cause them through you to come to life. 50. And every where there are men with selfish desires. They will be asking you continually of the past and the future. Through this you will be interrupted in your manner of life. What is the remedy for this?"

ŚRIPĀD IS BURIED ALIVE BY EKNĀTH.

51. The Prostrating *svāmi* accepted Eknāth's nectar-words, humbly besought him that he would give him a burial alive. 52. Śrī Nāth replied, "That you should

receive a burial-alive seems the best suggestion." Some Kāmatis, therefore, were quickly called, and a hole was dug by them. 53. In this hole the bodily-unconscious ascetic sat. There was a moment of worship, and then the sand was filled in over him. Śrī Eknāth then bathed and returned to his home. 54. The affair soon became known in the sacred city, that the Prostrating *Svāmi* had received a burial alive. On this the Brāhmaṇs all assembled and took counsel together. 55. The Paṇḍits, and the Vedic religious heads summoned Eknāth to Pimpaleś-vara, saying, "You have performed this most unusual deed without informing us. 56. You had a hole dug in the Gaṅgā river, and you buried the distinguished Yogi alive. Who repeated the *mantras* there? You performed the deed without the prescribed rites. 57. Using pressure, you told him to take this burial alive. This Paramhansa is now buried, and the charge of murder most certainly hangs over your head. Therefore you must be encommunicated. 58. In what *Śāstra* is it written that one should force a sannyāsi to be buried alive. If there is such a *Śāstra*, show it to us." All the Brāhmaṇs then exclaimed.

BRĀHMAṆS ACCUSE EKNĀTH OF AN UNLAWFUL ACT.

59. "The *sannyāsi* easily raised the dead donkey to life. You could not endure the sight of such miraculous power in him. Therefore you killed the sannyāsi. We know your secret inner motive." 60. One added, "A brave man indeed! A very great expert indeed, in the Bhāgavata religion! Turning aside from the path of right-eousness, he has set up a market for selling his doctrines."

61. Another said, " By some hocus pocus he knows some bewitching *mantras.* He, only in mere form, sings the names of God, while really seducing the pious and robbing them." 62. One very impudent man openly declared, " This fellow is assuredly a violator of our religious laws. He violates the path laid down in the Vedic commands, and commits unlawful and eccentric deeds. 63. In killing this *sannyāsi* he has committed murder, yet his mind is not disquieted thereby. He still carries on his worship with a joyous heart. His heart is as hard as a stone. 64. Without possessing it himself he preaches knowledge to others. There was no pity aroused in his heart when he murdered the *sannyāsi.*"

THE BRĀHMAṆS DEMAND A MIRACLE OF EKNĀTH.

65. The Brāhmaṇs then said to Eknāth, " The charge of murder falls on your head. Perform now a miracle, and thus save yourself from excommunication. 66. If this stone bull here before our eyes shall eat *kadabā* stalks from your hands, then you are without the least blame, and we will withdraw our purpose of excommunicating you." 67. Eknāth listened to the words of these chief Brāhmaṇs, and placed his forehead at their feet, saying, " That which passes your lips, Svāmis, can never prove unture. 68. Formerly by the pitying glance of Vasiṣṭha's eye his cane became heated to brilliancy equal to that of the sun. The Supreme being never lets a Brāhmaṇs' word come false." 69. The

Brāhmaṇs exclaimed in reply, "You are talking a lot of longwinded stuff. If you show us a miracle, then only we shall regard your statements as true." 70. At this they ran, and brought some sheaves of *kadabā* stalks, and placed them before Eknāth. Eknāth, seeing their persistence, said to the stone bull, 71. "To-day, of my own accord I seated the *sannyāsi* in his grave. If there is no fault whatever in this act of mine, then eat these *kadabā* stalks." 72. As these words escaped Eknāth's lips, a most strange thing happened. The stone bull ran out its tongue, 73. And drawing a sheaf of *kadabā* stalks into its mouth rapidly devoured it. All the Brāhmaṇs saw this sight, and were filled with amazement. 74. And said, "Eknāth, Sir, you have performed a miracle. Therefore, you are free from the penalty of excommunication which we had intended to inflict upon you." 75. Eknāth listened to these words of the chief Brāhmaṇs, and made them a *namaskār,* saying, " I am indeed dull of understanding. I am not acquainted with the Vedic Śāstras. 76. By drinking the water with which your feet are washed I am purified. And in your feet are all the *tirthas,* vratas and *siddhis.*" 77. The Brāhmaṇs, however, remarked among themselves, "This miraculous deed performed by Eknāth is an act that cannot be acquired through the practice of Yoga. This astonishing deed comes from *Bhakti.* 78. Because of his former devotion to his Guru, his service to saints, and his loving worship of Śrī Hari, Pāṇḍuraṅg has become pleased with him, and protects him moment by moment." 79. Thus conversing among themselves, all the chief Brāhmaṇs returned to their homes. As the affair became known in the sacred city, the people marvelled. 80. The loving pious ones sang Eknāth's praises. "The Lord-of-Heaven has descended to save the universe," they said.

SOME BRĀHMAṆS DISBELIEVE THE MIRACLE.

81. But some of the suspicious and spiteful people of the town declared the affair false. Among them the chief Brāhmaṇs who had remained behind in the sacred city; they now hurried to Pimpaleśvara. 82. They examined carefully the stone bull, but it was a stone just as before. "How could he have eaten the *Kadabā* stalk?" they exclaimed. "The story does not impress us." 83. Then calling Eknāth, they said, "Unless you show us the same miracle you performed yesterday, you are excommunicated. Not all of us saw the miracle. 84. You were here yesterday certainly but we were not, and we are unwilling to listen to the story. They then put some sheaves before Eknāth saying, "Feed this to the Stone bull (*Nandi.*) 85. If you do not show us this miracle, then the authority of the *Śastras* will be employed in this contention, and the curse will surely be visited upon you for having buried the *Sannyās*i alive." 86. As Eknāth listened to this demand of the Brāhmaṇs, his thoughts became troubled, and turning to the Nandi (stone bull) he prayed. Listen, O hearers, to his prayer. 87. "How long wilt Thou be willing to be constantly eating *Kadabā*? There are a great many more Brāhmaṇs remained in the city. 88. Tomorrow they will come and demand the same thing of me, so I must quickly devise some way by which the doubts of all may be removed."

THE STONE BULL LEAPS INTO THE RIVER.

89. Eknāth had no more than uttered this prayer, when a remarkable event took place before the sight of those Brāhmaṇs, and other men and women. 90. The stone bull rose up, and running jumped into a deep hole in the Gaṅgā river. It is there to this day. 91. As the Brāhmaṇs saw this great wonder they marvelled and said, " Eknāth's greatness is beyond our comprehension. It is a deed that does not belong to man. 92. Formerly in this town of our ancestors Dnyāneśvara made a buffalo repeat the whole of the Vedas. 93. And when Chāṅgadeva, the Siddha, came to visit him, he made the lifeless wall move forward. In like manner Eknāth has performed now an extraordinary deed." 94. Thus conversing among themselves, they then said to Eknāth, " There is now no excommunication for you. You may return to your home. 95. Blessed is your loving devotion. You have brought life to a stone Nandi (stone bull). The God-of-Gods is pleased with you. We now recognize the real meaning of what has happened." 96. Śrī Eknāth heard this praise, and reverently bowed at their feet, saying, "This that has happened is through the power of your favor. As the humblest of all I come to your protection." 97. With these words of Janārdan's Eknāth, the Brāhmaṇs were gratified, and the people of Paiṭhaṇ, great and small, came to see the *Nandi*. 98. At that spot the *Nandi* is still there, and when the sand gets removed the *Nandi* is plainly visible to the sight. Let no one doubt this in his heart. 99. Śrī Nāth returned to his home. The pious folk were filled with joy, and day by day Eknāth's good fame became known further far and wide.

EKNĀTH GOES TO ALANDI.

100. It now happened at a certain time that Śrī Nāth was about to go to Alankāpuri. He left his faithful disciple, Uddhava, at home, and started with his retinue of followers. 101. Influenced by the thought of such good company, a great crowd started with him on this pilgrimage. They journeyed along the road listening the while lovingly to loud songs of praise. 102. Arriving at Alankāpuri, they rested on the bank of the Indrāyaṇi. Here Dnyānadeva, appearing to him in a dream by night, said to him, 103. "The roots of the Ajāna tree have reached my neck. Dig into my tomb and push the root aside." 104. Śrī Nāth did so, and there beheld Dnyānadeva. He made a prostrate *namaskār* before him, and pushed aside the root. 105. He then closed up the tomb again, and performed a *kirtan.* Also on the eleventh of the moon there was an all night praise service, participated in by all the pilgrims.

GOD MIRACULOUSLY PROVIDES FOOD FOR THE PILGRIMS.

106. At that time Alankāpuri was a depopulated town. There was no rice and other food materials to be obtained there. God Paṇḍarināth performed a miraculous thing. Listen, O, ye pious *bhaktas,* to what he did. 107. The Husband-of-Rukmiṇi, compassionate to the needy, became a Kānadā Lingāyat. He erected a booth, and sat there with all the needed articles of food. 108. He would say to the pilgrims, "Take away with you all the articles you need. I do not ask for any money now. I am well acquainted with Eknāth." 109 Thus remarking, the

Husband-of-Rukmiṇi would measure out all the needed articles of food, wheat, flour, dāl, rice, ghi, vegetables and salt. 110. After four days had passed, he, suddenly, there and then, became invisible. This Merciful-One would not let his servant lack in the very least thing. 111. The pilgrims came immediately to Eknāth, and told him that they had bought their food materials on credit, but that the merchant was now nowhere to be seen. 112. As they thus naively related this story, Eknāth understood its secret, inner meaning, and exclaimed, "What has God of the Eagle-banner wrought, He who protects his *bhaktas* from mortification!" 113. Thus completing their pilgrimage they started to return home. As they came back near to the sacred city of Pratishṭhāna, Uddhava came forward to welcome them. 114. Also a great crowd of pious inhabitants of the sacred city, both men and women, came to welcome them, and filled with love, made their *namaskār* to Śrī Nāth. 115. All carried aloft eagle banners, emblems, and flags, and sang aloud songs of praise, relating the story of Dnyāneśvara. 116. The clang of the cymbal, the *viṇā,* and drum swelled in harmony with the acclamations of the crowd. The sound of Brahma was incarnate there. The servants of Hari danced as they went along. That day was a blessed, happy day. 117. Thus singing, they returned home. Then they sang *ārati,* and reverently waved lights before Śrī Hari. 118. On the next day there was the giving of gifts to Brāhmaṇs, and a feast of many kinds of dainties was provided for them. 119. With the *viḍā* and the generous gifts all were satisfied. Then Eknāth, with his own lips, described the greatness of Alankāpuri.

*EKNĀTH CORRECTS THE TEXT OF THE DNYĀNEŚVARI.

120. It happened one day that Śrī Nāth, with affection and joy for his task, sat down to correct the text of the book, Dnyāneśvari. 121. Although existing copies had been made with loving care, still mistakes had been made by copyists, until finally the meaning and grammatical relations becoming unintelligible, the book had ceased to be commonly known. 122. It was for this reason that Śrī Dnyāneśvara became an *avatār* in the form of Eknāth at Pratishṭhāna, and corrected the text of the whole book, 123. Then looking with loving eye upon Uddhava, Śrī Nāth told him the unfamiliar fact that Dnyāneśvara, with deep insight, had made a Marāṭhi translation of the Gītā. 124. And that, "Through the mercy of Janārdan I have corected the text of the book. The pious minded people should, therefore, assemble together, and hear the book

---

* *Note.*—There is very strong documentary evidence that the statement here made, that Eknāth corrected the text of the Dnyāneśvari, is a historic fact. Nearly all *Mss* of the Dnyāneśvari contain a colophon, stating that Eknāth made the corrections in Śaka 1506 (A.D. 1584.) A very old manuscript of the Dnyāneśvari in the Tanjor Library was written in Śaka 1515 (A.D. 1593), and contains the colophon regarding Eknāth. As this copy was actually made during the life time of Eknāth, and cnly nine years after the date assigned for the correction, the evidence it affords is exceedingly strong. The copy was made by one Paraśarāmātmaja at Ahmednagar. The exemplar from which he made his copy was of course older, and therefore it is possible that that colophon was written by Eknāth himself.

read." 125. Hearing these words from Eknāth's lips, Uddhava was greatly delighted, and the Husband-of-Rukmiṇi, in the form of Keśava, was one of the attentive listeners. 126. Before these two, Śrī Nāth constantly read the Dnyāneśvari. But in addition to these there were also present pious men and women who came to listen. 127. Śrī Nāth would clearly explain the deep meaning of the Dnyāneśvari, so that no question remaining unanswered, the whole became intelligible to all, from child to adult. 128. Every day at the third watch he began to read aloud this work of Dnyāneśvara. Keśava and Uddhava were the two principal listeners, and there was great enthusiasm. 129. When the reading of the book was finished they worshipped Sarasvati, waved auspicious lamps, and distributed sweets.

GOD IN THE FORM OF KEŚAVA ASKS PERMISSION TO DEPART.

130. And with this ending of the reading of the Dnyāneśvari, the Lord-of-Paṇḍhari, who had been there in the form of Keśava, asked Eknāth's permission to depart. 131. "I have spent twelve years happily with you here," he said, "but I am now homesick, and I ask you to give me permission to go away." 132. To this request of the Life-of-the-World, Eknāth assented, but added, "I hope you will be pleased to let me see you again here." 133. Keśava-in-visible-form listened to this request, and then suddenly became invisible. But the Lord-of-Heaven said to himself, "I must come here again sometime." 134. The thought came into the mind of the Husband-of-Kamalā, "Eknāth has served me in many ways. I must in some

way repay his kindness." This thought pleased the God greatly. 135. Thus thinking to himself, the Lord-of-Dvārakā, immediately became invisible. The *bhakta*, Uddhava, now said to Eknāth, "I will always remain with you." 136. And so when the *kīrtans* were performed, with love and enthusiasm he would follow in the refrains, keeping time with the cymbals, and thus bringing extraordinary animation to the music. 137. And from the child to the aged, men and women were constant listeners to these lively *kīrtans*.

THE PIOUS OUTCASTE, RĀṆYĀ MAHĀR, AND HIS WIFE.

Now there was in that sacred city a very pious man, an outcaste.

138. This Yogabhrashṭa in a former birth had been a distinguished Vaishṇava. Through some fault he had been born a Mahār, an outcaste. 139. His wife was supremely virtuous. She loved the image of Śrī Krishṇa, and both, performing loving acts of worship, would repeat his names. 140. As Śrī Nāth performed his nightly *kirtans*, both of them used to come, but sat outside. They listened with fixed attention, lost to all bodily consciousness. 141. When the *kīrtans* closed, and the people had left the *wādā*, they would bow to Eknāth and then go back to their home. 142. And now as to how they used to serve Eknāth. They would always sweep the path which he used to use when going down to the bank of the Gaṅgā to bathe. 143.

And when Śrī Nāth was taking his bath they were accustomed to look towards him and make him a prostrate namaskār from afar, regarding him as Vishṇu-in-visible-form.

144. It now happened one day, a Hari day, that Eknāth, with great joy, was performing a *kirtan,* and was relating how Śrī Krishṇa showed himself to Arjun in the form of the Universe. 145. As the distinguished Vaishṇava was expressing in song that event, he repeated the beautiful verses of Dnyāneśvara, used in his commentary. 146. At that juncture Rāṇyā Mahār propounded with his own lips this question to Eknāth, "When Śrī Hari, who pervades all animate and inanimate things, assumed the form of the universe, 147. Where was I, at that time, outcaste as I am now." Śrī Nāth replied, "You were wholly attached to Krishṇa". 148. Hearing these nectar words from the lips of Eknāth, he became lost in contemplation. His ideas of difference and non-difference passed away. The conception of duality vanished. 149. Whatever animate or inanimate things he now saw, he became one with them. He now knew no longer any differences of color or caste. 150. He became convinced in his mind that Eknāth was the supreme Brahma-in-visible form. Then freeing themselves from all their domestic entanglements, both of them went and took up their abode in the *kāsanā.* 151. It was their thought that by doing so, when Śrī Nāth came there to bathe in the Lakshmi *tirtha,* the opportunity of seeing him would come to them without effort. 152. It was for this opportunity that they abandoned their own place, and now came to live near the bank of the Gaṅgā river.

RAṆYĀ MAHAR'S WIFE WISHES TO INVITE EKNĀTH TO DINE.

It happened one day that the wife of the Unmentionable said to the Lord of her life, 153. "Eknāth is in very truth Pāṇḍuraṅg, who has become *saguṇ* to save the universe, nevertheless my mind has conceived the purpose of inviting him here to eat in our home. 154. If you will go and invite the *Svāmi*, I will make the needed preparations." Rāṇyā Mahār listened and replied to his wife, "I will go." 155. Finding Eknāth alone, Rāṇyā told him the secret of his heart, "My wife has conceived the purpose," he said, "of serving you at a feast. 156. If you will give me permission, I will make the needed prepartions at my home." Recognizing his kindly feelings, Eknāth did not refuse. 157. And said, "Through the grace of Janārdan, the wish of your heart will be fulfilled." Rāṇyā listened to these assuring words, and received from them a sense of peace. 158. He informed his wife of the encouragement Śrī Nāth had given him. In worldly goods they were exceedingly poor, yet they collected together the materials necessary for a feast. 159. By the side of their door they placed the *tulsi* altar. They washed their garments, and cleaned their vessels. Both of them regularly performed their daily baths, and the names of God were ever on their lips. 160. They laid in a store of wheat, flour, dal, rice, ghi, and vegetables, and fasting on Hari days, they became regular listeners at Eknāth's *kīrtans*. 161. When there was an all night Hari praise service, they spent all that time in listening to the *kīrtan*. Only when it was dawn would they return to their home.

EKNĀTH IS INVITED BY RĀṆYĀ MAHĀR AND HIS WIFE.

162. The Unmentionable's wife was an exceedingly pious and virtuous woman. She said to the lord of her life, "Let us now invite the Svāmi to a feast." 163. I will do the cooking here at home. Hasten, and sit by the bank of the Gaṅgā, awaiting the coming of Eknāth. 164. When the Svāmi comes there for his bath, seek an opportunity when he is alone, and very humbly give him our invitation. 165. "I will do so," said Rāṇyā, and at once went and sat down on the bank of the Gaṅgā. Śrī Nāth soon arrived, and Rāṇyā reverently made him a *namaskār*. 166. Eknāth acknowledged his loving *bhakti*. After he was seated for a moment the Unmentionable affectionately addressed him. "I have a special request," he said. 167. "But I am one without caste. I have no right to invite you, and I hesitate to do so, yet will you come and take a meal at my house?" and with this he fell at Eknāth's feet. 168.To this request Śrī Nāth replied. "You are a loving Vaishṇava *bhakta*. Śrī Krishṇa has seen your sincerity and is pleased. 169. A Brāhmaṇ may be thoroughly conversant with the Vedas and Śastras, and yet be without devotion to Śri Hari. Though he may be adorned with the twelve noble qualities, yet an out-caste can be superior to him. 170. Although he is an out-caste, he may be very acceptable to God." And here Eknāth repeated a Sanskrit Śloka from the Mahābhāgavata.

Bhāgavata Purāṇa VII. 9. 10.

Translation.

A dog-eating outcaste who has made an offering to God of his mind, his words, his actions, his property and his very life, is to be considered far superior to a Brāhmaṇ, who, although gifted with the twelve charateristics of a Brāhmaṇ, has turned away from the feet of God. The former purfies his whole family, not so the latter puffed up with pride.

EKNATH RECITING A ŚLOKA TO RĀṆYĀ EXCITES THE ANGER OF THE BRĀHMAṆS.

171. Eknāth had repeated only this one *śloka* in the presence of the Unmentionable, but there were some Brāhmaṇs near by, who became greatly enraged. 172. Then all the Brāhmaṇs came about Eknāth, and loudly vociferating, closed around the loving *bhakta*. 173. The chief Brāhmaṇs said to Eknāth, "That *śloka* was not from the Bhāgavata, but from the Vedas. Why did you repeat a *śloka* from it to this unmentionable? 174. An outcaste has no right to that potent philosophic knowledge. This being so, you have done a very improper thing. 175. Your deed appears like that of serving dogs with spiced custard, like rubbing sandalwood oil on an ass, or presenting a miror to a blind man. 176. The Brāhmaṇs further said to Eknāth, "In repeating that *śloka* to this outcaste a great sin rests on your head. The performing of a penance is therefore your due." 177. Śrī Nāth listened to these words of the Brāhmaṇs, and placing palm to palm, he made a *namaskār* to them, replying in conciliatory words. 178. "Rāṇyā Mahār," he said, "is a Vaishṇava *bhakta*. He is fondly attached to the worship of Śrī Hari. He has conquered all the six enemies of the soul. One should not, therefore, call him an outcaste. 179. When

one looks at the character of this Unmentionable, not one good quality is lacking in him. One sees in him all that the Bhāgavata religion enjoins. 180. I am convinced that he has the right to the philosophic knowledge. By his reverent devotion he has made the Supreme Brahma, existing in the form of Śrī Hari, subject to him. 181. Seeing his earnest desire I repeated merely a short line. I ask your Greatnesses to forgive me my trasgression." With these words, he prostrated himself before them. 182. To this the Brāhmaṇs replied, "You are very impudent, you stiffnecked fellow. You have openly preached to one without the right to listen, thus departing from right doing. 183. If you refuse to perform a penance for removing your fault, we shall excommunicate you." So said all the chief Brāhmaṇs. 184. Śrī Nāth, the Supreme-Brahma-in-visible-form, did not in the least resist. He assented to the demand of the Brāhmaṇs, and said, "Prescribe the penance." 185. So saying, he stepped into a deep pool in the river, and remained standing. The Brāhmaṇs brought cowdung and ashes and repeated over him a *mantra*. 186. The Unmentionable saw all this, and in silence returned to his home. His wife was engaged in cooking. Quickly she enquired of him the result of his errand. 187. "Did you invite Śri Nāth?" When she said this he replied, "Ours is broken fortune. 188. Because Eknāth spoke to me, all the Brāhmaṇs are enraged. They have made him stand in a pool of the Gaṅgā, and are giving him a penance. 189. The good we have laid up in a former birth is not sufficient to bring about the service of saints." The wife sobbed with emotion saying, "We might as well give up life." 190. Thus exclaiming, she threw herself on to the ground and her tears flowed so copiously that the earth was wet with them. 191. Seeing her in this condition, her husband called her to himself by the motion of his hand, and said, " Eknāth is an ocean of mercy. He will not pay disrespect to the poor. 192. I will go to him again, and give him again our invitation. If he refuses to come, then indeed there is no use in living, and we may then give up our lives." 193. With this determination of mind, he hastened to the bank of the Gaṅgā. He made a prostrate *namaskār* before Eknāth, and said, " I ask you to come to-day and eat at my house."

EKNĀTH ACCEPTS RĀṆYĀ'S INVITATION TO DINE.

194. Seeing his earnestness, Eknāth, who had voluntarily assumed this human body, replied to him, even though there were Brāhmaṇs standing near by, " I will come." 195. "As soon as your cooking is ready, I will come, about noon time." The Unmentionable returned delighted to his home. 196. The Brāhmaṇs now murmured among themselves. " He is laying a course of defilement. Through him there will now come about the mixture of castes. 197. Because he repeated the *śloka* to the Unmentionable, we had to give him penance, and now he has accepted the invitation of the unmentionable and is going to eat at his house. What is it that we can do! " 198. The Brāhmaṇs then assembled secretly, and planned among themselves to set spies and catch him in the act (of eating at the Mahār's). 199. The whole circle of Brāhmaṇs therefore, set itself to watching here and there. They made a study of his form (so as to recognize him.) 200.

Some stood in the lanes, others sat by his door, talking to each other under some pretence or other. 201. Some sat down on the bank of the Gaṅgā river repeating *mantras*, with rosaries in their hands. Others went to the house of the Unmentionable, and concealed themselves near the door. 202. Thus putting aside their usual private business, all these Brāhmaṇs turned their attention to spying. But they failed to perceive that Eknāth was the *avatār* of Mahārāj Vishṇu. 203. The Brāhmaṇs said to one another, "Let us give no hint to Eknāth. The unmentionable will come to call him, and we can then catch him in the very act of eating at his house."

GOD IN EKNĀTH'S FORM EATS AT THE MAHĀR'S HOUSE.

204. Now as to Eknāth. After he had duly performed divine worship, he had a reading aloud of the Purāṇa at his house. The sun had now reached the zenith. 205. Uddhava, in the mean while, was rendering worshipful service to the Brāhmaṇs, and religious mendicants. Having offered holy water and fragrant unguents, he began to serve the various dishes.

206. Turning now to the house of the Unmentionable, after all the cooking had been finished, his wife requested him to hasten and bring Eknāth back with him. 207. This *yogabhrashṭa*, but a true Vaishṇava, had smeared the floor, and thoroughly cleaned the house, and with his own hands had beautifully marked the floor with designs with coloured powders. 208. He had provided fragrant unguents, rice, garlands and the materials for

worship, and was now waiting expectantly with a heart full of joy. 209. The Unmentionable came to Eknāth's door and humbly besought him, "Will the Svāmi now come with me to eat?" Eknāth replied to him. 210. "You go on, and I will follow you quickly." At this the Brāhmaṇs began to make signs to one another by the motions of the eye. 211. Now what did God Pāṇḍuraṅg do, but take the form of Eknāth, and appeared at the house of the Unmentionable, to his surprise. 212. He exclaimed to his wife, "Śrī Nāth has come to our house." She, full of pleasure, reverently made him a *namaskār*. 213. She felt like one, who about to die, drinks the nectar of immortality. She gave him the board seat to sit on, and lovingly washed his feet. 214. Then promptly with loving devotion she touched her own eyelids with her thumb, applying the sandalwood pigment, and placed a garland of *tulsi* around his neck. 215. On his forehead she drew the *tilak,* and on it rubbed the fragrant powder. All this the Brāhmaṇs, who were sitting as spies, distinctly saw. 216. Some of them remained sitting there, others ran to Eknāth's house. Those who had been in the street exclaimed, "Coming by what street did he escape our observation?" 217. One of the Brāhmaṇs replied, "He must have changed his guise and moving stealthily like a thief, escaped our observation, and knowledge." 218. Another said, "He has bewitched our eyes. From early dawn we have been sitting here, closing the street." 219. Those who had been in the Mahārwāḍā went to Eknāth's house, and lo! there was Eknāth on his board seat, with the rosary in his hands. 220. When the Brāhmaṇs saw this uncanny sight, they were overcome with astonishment, and informed those in the house of their wonderful tale. 221. "The marvels done by this defiled one," they exclaimed, "are most extraordinary. He is here and he is there; he is in both places." Then they all rushed together to the Mahārwāḍā to look. 222. And there sat Eknāth on the board seat with all the materials for worship in profusion before him. The Brāhmaṇs rushed back and forth, and lo! in both places they saw him. 223. Just as there does not appear the least difference between an object and its reflection, so was it between Pāṇḍuraṅg and Eknāth. There was no difference whatever. 224. As holy water and common water are two in name, but there is no difference as to their oneness. And who is there who can chose between the sun and its brightness? 225. As the blue of the sky and the sky itself, as the flower and the honey in it, are one, so Eknāth and Pāṇḍuraṅg in human form were seen to be of the very same shape. 226. That Eknāth had become a *saguṇ* avatār in order to save the world; this, those Brāhmaṇs, failing to recognize, were lost in perplexity. 227. This made them exclaim, "How is it that at the same time he is seen here and there in both places?" Until the third watch they vainly rushed back and forth. 228. But they could see no difference between the two, of less or more. He was seated in both places. The Unmentionable had worshipped Eknāth. and was arranging the food on the dishes before him. 229. His wife with affection served Eknāth with all kinds of savoury food, regarding God Janārdan as the partaker of the food. Eknāth then sipped water. 230. Śrī Hari, who is hungry for devotion, was fully satisfied. Whatever his taste craved, he would ask for, and received on his plate. 231. In this way the meal passed. She then with love gave him water to cleanse his hands, and making the *viḍā* with her own hands gave it to him. In doing this she experienced a sense of great satisfaction. 232. The couple then made Eknāth a *pradakshiṇā,* and a prostrate *namaskār,* exclaiming, "You have fulfilled our earnest desire. Blessed art Thou Mighty-one, Guru-of-the-World. 233. We were without devotion, without *Bhakti,* without intelligence, without caste, but you have fulfilled our earnest desire, and purified us in this present life." 234. Śrī Nāth reassured them, and then suddenly vanished from their sight. The man and woman then ate what was left on his plate as his gracious gift. 235. The Brāhmaṇs utterly astonished in their minds, went down to the brink of the Gaṅgā to bathe, and then going to Eknāth's house watched him there. 236. While these events were taking place (at the Unmentionable's house) Eknāth with Uddhava was also eating at his own house. And the Brāhmaṇs exclaimed, "We are not able to fathom this defiled man. 237. We have wearied ourselves rushing back and forth in vain. In both places he is the same." Listen now to what one, with an evil imagination, suggested. 238. "Learning magical *mantras,* he has gained the favor of the king of the demons, and putting this mighty demon forward, he has made this extraordinary miracle to appear." 239. Thus remarking the Brāhmaṇs returned to their homes.

Mahipati, the true bard of the saints, herewith proclaims, as a public crier, Eknāth's great fame. 240. Svasti. This book is the Śrī Bhaktalīlāmṛita. By merely listening to it one's desires are fulfilled. Listen then to it, ye loving, pious *bhaktas.* This is the nineteenth delightful chapter.

Chapter 19. Ovis 240. Śloka 1.

CHAPTER 20.

BHAKTALILĀMṚITA.

Mahipati's Invocation.

Obeisance to Śrī Gaṇeśa.

1. Victory to Thee, Śrī Hari; Everlasting-recliner (on the serpent.) At Thy door I come as a beggar. I have conceived a desire within me. What it is I will tell Thee. Listen O Pāṇḍuraṅg. 2. I desire O Husband-of-Rukmiṇi, constant association with Thy *Bhaktas*. This is the longing of my heart. So fulfil this desire of my heart, O glorious Lord. 3. I would be a beast in the homes of those who go on pilgrimages to Paṇḍhari, for I would then carry on my back their provisions, and they would bring me to Thy door. 4. I would be the stone pavings in the sacred city of Paṇḍhari. The feet of the saints would then touch me with their purifying touch. 5. If Thou puttest me into a human body, place me there, but make me craze for Thee, so that without hindrance I may remember for ever in my soul Thy feet. 6. I want not metalphysical knowledge, nor learnedness in the *Śāstras*, Give me not the homage of men. Give this to me, O Paṇḍharināth, that my affections may be centered in Thee. 7. I am fond of the lives of the *Bhaktas,* dear to Thee, to whom the universal soul and self are one. So, Thou Eagle-bannered—One, give to me to recollect their lives. Give me an apprehending mind.

BRĀHMAṆS ACCUSE EKNĀTH OF WORKING THROUGH DEMONS.

8. In the last chapter there was related the miraculous story of the loving feelings and piety of the Unmentionable; how God dined at his house, and how the Brāhmaṇs did not understand the Māyā aspect of it. 9. Eknāth was a deedful *avatār*. He manifested many kinds of deeds, but the Brāhmaṇs conceived in their hearts evil surmisings. "He has learned magical *mantras*," they said. 10. "By gaining the favor of the chief goblin, he has made his one form to appear as two. He has taken us by craft. We can catch him in nothing."

EKNĀTH AND TOUCHSTONE.

11. There was a Brāhmaṇ living in the city of Pratishṭhāna a very pious man. He used to perform regularly his morning and evening devotions, his purifications, and abounded in good deeds. 12. By good fortune, acquired in a former birth, he had found a touchstone (*parīsa*.) By its means he enjoyed happiness of mind, and every form of wealth. 13. No one in the world seemed as happy and as favored by every circumstance as he. As people watched him, good thoughts were aroused in them. 14. Day after day thus passed when suddenly his son and wife died. He was greatly depressed by this, and found no relief whatever. 15. Where a household lacks food, there will be found an abundant progeny. Where painful vows are made for the purpose of having a child, there a sickly infant is born. 16. One gains a beautiful wife, but the husband is very ugly. A young man may be very

noble, and yet his wife may die. 17. One possesses sons, a wife and wealth, but a horrible disease developes in his body. The generous minded possess no wealth. There are the wealthy, but they are misers. 18. If a man acquires a beautiful body, still it is short lived, a righteous king he may be, but he lives but a few days. 19. There is the desire in the mind of one to bestow gifts, but he meets no one worthy, or noble enough to receive them. Such are the strange experiences in this life. All know this from personal experience. 20. Thus it was that by fate and fortune the man had no sooner obtained his touchstone than he lost his wife and those belonging to him, and he became greatly distressed in mind. 21. Seeing how this worldly life deceives one, he became depressed in mind, and thought to himself, "I must go on a pilgrimage to a sacred watering place," and this desire seized him. 22. Then he thought to himself, "With whom shall I entrust this touchstone? I see no one who is trustworthy." He then went to Eknāth's house. 23. Finding an opportunity of being alone with him, he reverently made him a prostrate *namaskār*, and said, "I have conceived the purpose of going on the great pilgrimage. 24. I have been wondering who will care for this invaluable object which I have with me. You are a true *bhakta,* and a great ascetic. You seem to me the one only honest man." 25. When Eknāth heard this remark, he replied. "Wherever your trust is, that is the place for your object." 26. Receiving this assurance, the man placed the touchstone in Eknāth's hands. Looking at it Eknāth was surprised and said to him. 27. "This appears to be but a stone, and yet you call it a priceless object. Tell me quickly what is the good quality it possesses?" 28. The man took a bit of iron in his hands, and at once applied it to the touchstone, when suddenly it turned into gold. "This is a touchstone," he explained. 29. "After I return from the Great Pilgrimage give me this back again. The Eagle-bannered-one is favourable to you. You will have no use for this." 30. Śrī Nāth tossed it under his seat, and the man having made his namaskār, started immediately on his pilgrimage. 31. But it passed from Eknāth's recollection that he should carefully guard the priceless object. The cloud may rain upon the ocean, but the ocean pays no regard to it. 32. Or again, the sun, complete in his brightness, does not so much as cast a look at the light of a lamp. One who has obtained nectar, pays no attention to a medicinal plant. 33. And so to Eknāth, who had attained his soul consciousness, gold and cowdung were alike. He, therefore, did not remember carefully to guard the touchstone. 34. After a year had gone by the man returned from his pirgrimage. The first thing he did was to make obeisance to Śrī Nāth, and lovingly embrace him. 35. Eknāth asked him all the particulars of his successful pilgrimage. The man thought to himself, "He will give me back the touchstone without my asking for it." 36. With this idea the distinguished Brāhmaṇ sat quietly for an hour or two, but Śrī Nāth had not the slightest recollection about the touchstone. 37. The man then said to himself, "To-day is our first meeting together. For that reason doubtless he passes the subject by. I will come to-morrow and see to it." 38. Thus thinking to himself, the Brāhmaṇ went back to his home. But his mind was not at ease. "I see no good outcome to this," he said. 39. "I gave the object to him, because he seemed one without worldly desires and affections. Why is it that he hesitates to give me back my own." 40. Bringing such thoughts into his mind he was troubled the whole of the night. As the sun was rising he finished his early morning bathing. 41. While Śrī Nāth was performing his worsihp of God, the man came and bowed to him, and in answer to his questioning about the journey related it from its beginning to its end. 42. But Eknāth still made no reference whatever to the return of his touchstone. Finally the man becoming bold, recalled the matter to Eknāth's mind. 43. Then Śrī Nāth remembered it, and asked where he had placed it. The man replied, "You tossed it under your seat," and pointed there with his hand. 44. Both of them hunted diligently, but the touchstone pebble was not there. It was customary for the offerings of flowers to collect for a fortnight, and then on Hari day to be thrown away. 45. Eknāth said to the Brāhmaṇ, "The touchstone must have gone with the stale flowers." At this suggestion of Eknāth's the man's heart beat violently. 46. "I have only returned home, because of the desire to have the touchstone back again," he said. "I had no tie of wife or son, and my mind is now greatly distressed." 47. Śrī Nāth started with him for the Gaṅgā river, saying, "Let us go quickly, and see whether it may not have been thrown in there." 48. Śrī Nāth comforted him as they went along saying, "The withered flowers were thrown into the Gaṅgā." Eknāth stepped into the water, and took up five or seven pebbles. 49. He then said to the man, "Choose from these your touchstone." The man took a piece of iron from his pocket and applied it to the pebbles to see what would happen. 50. And Lo, every one of the pebbles had become a touchstone, to his great astonishment. And the greedy desire arose in his heart to possess them all. 51. But Śrī Nāth said to him, "Recognize one of these as yours and take it. The remaining I will offer to the Gaṅgā. They will be well cared for there." 52. The man selected one from them. The rest Eknāth tossed back into the Gaṅgā. Eknāth then bathed and returned to his home. 53. The poet's mind is unequal to the task of extolling the glory of Śrī Nāth. Where the Veda itself says, "Not that, Not that," what is the mosquito Mahipati there! 54. Śrī Vishṇu became an *avatār* to save the universe, and as Eknāth he lived a life of good deeds in truth, with devotion for the sake of mankind.

EKNĀTH'S DAILY LIFE.

55. Eknāth was accustomed to rise at a very early hour at dawn, to perform his toilet, to wash his face and teeth, and then to go down to the Gaṅgā to bathe and offer oblation to he sun. 56. After performing these regular duties he used to include the worship of the image of Pāṇḍuraṅg, before whom he waved the platter with incense and lights with sweet songs of praise. 57. After this there was the listening to the reading of the Purāṇa, explanation of its meaning, and grammatical constructions. Then came again a visit to the Gaṅgā, to make loving offerings to ancestors. 58. At the house there was the practice of good deeds. There was infinite love in his worship of the Brāhmaṇs. He drank with pleasure the water touched by their feet. And in all this he experienced great satisfaction. 59. After the Brāhmaṇs had been feasted he would himself partake of a scanty meal. At

the fourth watch of the day he would himself read aloud Śridhar's commentary on the Bhāgavata. 60. As the sun was setting he would go to the Gaṅgā for his evening devotions. On returning to his home he would perform the waving of incense. 61. At night there would be the spirited services of song. A crowd of pious people would be present to sit and listen with reverence. 62. Eknāth's lips would describe the many acts of Rām and Krishṇa in the joy of love. And the pious folk, from the child to the aged would wag their heads in approval with joy.

GOD COMES TO SERVE ŚRI EKNĀTH AS ŚRI KHAṆḌYĀ

63. Thus with due rites Hari *kirtans* took place at night, and at all times there was the repeating of God's names. Because of all this the Life-of-the-World was deeply pleased. 64. And as He saw this service of Eknāth's he felt the immense weight of a debt, and said to Himself, "I can never repay Eknāth's kindness." Keśava loved Eknāth greatly. 65. So Krishṇa, taking the form of a Brāhmaṇ, immediately started from Dvārakā, and arriving at Pratishṭhāna bathed in the river bed of the Gaṅgā. 66. Hari then went and stood before the door of Ekā Janārdana. There he reverently made his *namaskāra,* and said, "I have come with the fixed purpose of serving you. 67. Because of your worship of Vishṇu, your service to Brāhmaṇs, and your devotion to Vaishṇavas I have a longing desire to have constant association with you. 68. My life long I have given loving service to the saints. I ask no wages from you. All I care for is enough to eat. 69. I have

no further wants than a blanket, a garment, and maintenance sufficient for my stomach, and your constant good company." Thus the glorious-Lord spoke. 70. But because of a divine Māyā outside of Eknāth's control, he did not recognize the Husband-of-Indirā, and so asked him "What is your city? Have you wife and dependants?" 71. What is your family line? What is the name of this body of yours? Hearing these questions of Eknāth the Life-of-the-World replied. 72. "I am absolutely alone. I have no snare of wife or son. This body of mine has the name of Krishṇa Śrī Khaṇḍyā. I wander everywhere over the country. 73. I am a Rigvedi Brāhmaṇ. My home is wherever my mind is pleased. I have conceived the desire of serving you." Thus spoke the Husband-of-Rukmiṇi. 74. And Eknāth replied, "I have no desire to ask that you serve me. Accept food and raiment here, and in peace seek the supreme attainment." 75. Hearing Eknāth's nectar words, the Giver-of-supreme-Bliss responded," I will accept food earned by toil, and remain in your home. 76. By your grace I have abundant strength in my body, and I have this purpose in mind to serve saints. 77. I might sit and eat, but that would be only for this perishable body. I want to do kindness to others, for thereby it would be put to the highest purpose." 78. Thus saying the Soul-of-the-world briskly took up the *kāvadi* on his shoulder, and filling its vessels with the water of the Gaṅgā, poured it into the great earthen jar. 79. He, whom Brahmādeva and the other Gods regard as worthy of worship. He, whose feet are praised by Śiva and the other Gods, even He, the Life-of-the-World, a deedful actor in this drama, became a Brāhmaṇ. 80. In attempting to extol whose fame the Vedas and Purāṇs are frantic, even He collected what remained on the plates of the Brāhmaṇs for he had a marvellous liking for service. 81. In the Ocean of milk there lies the Island of the Sun. Here the Recliner-on-the-Serpent has his heavenly abode. Yet He it was who used to arise as soon as it was early dawn, and who thought lightly of his hard physical toil. 82. He, for whom, in acquiring the eight branches of the Yoga, the yogi wears himself out, even He used to rise early and brightly polish the vessels used in the worship of God. 83. The Dark-complexioned, fine-featured Husband-of-Rukmiṇi, Giver-of-union-with-Brahma, and World-renowned, even He with his own hands joyously performed every needed work. 84. He, from whose feet the river Bhāgirathi flows, even He, the glorious Lord, would lovingly fill the jars with the clear water of the first dip, for the worship of God. 85. He, whom the eighty-eight thousand Rishis worship, even He would reduce to paste the sandal-wood on the stone slab, and fill the ointment box. 86. He, whose night-and-day slaves are the eight Powers, along with Lakshmi, even He, Hrishikeshi, would weave garlands of flowers, and place them ready for the worship of God. 87. He, through whom the moon and the king of the constellations, the sun, become a mass of brilliancy, even He, Adhokshaja, would bring forward the lamps, and feel no shame in his heart for doing so. 88. If Eknāth ever called out to him, "Krishṇa", he immediately appeared before him. He failed in nothing whatever, and was always on the alert. 89. Because he made the sandal-wood paste the Brāhmaṇs called him Śrī Khaṇḍyā. All the inhabitants of the town marvelled at him. 90. Saying, "There is a Brāhmaṇ serving at Eknāth's house. He takes no wages, and yet does every thing with zeal." 91. Unknown to Eknāth the Lord-of-Dvārkā was accustomed to enter the kitchen and lovingly and joyfully render domestic service to his wife. 92. The Dark-complexioned One was infatuated by Eknāth's spirit of *bhakti*. Forgetful of all his divine glory, the Tender-hearted-one, stood before Eknāth, ever ready to serve. 93. In this way the Lord-of-the-World spent twelve years there, when suddenly a wonderful thing happened. Listen to it, ye pious devotees of his.

THE DIVINE IDENTITY OF ŚRI KHAṆḌYĀ REVEALED.

94. There was a Brāhmaṇ in Dvārkā, who lovingly practised his religious ceremonies. That he might have a direct revelation of God he was always repeating His names. 95. Twelve years thus rolled along, but he had no direct revelation of Him. Finally one day, he, after fasting, to an extreme limit 96. Mother Rukmiṇi informed him in a dream, "You are fasting to the extreme limit, but Krishṇa is not here. 97. In the city of Pratishthāna there is an *abheda bhakta.* The Lord-of-Vaikuṇṭha has gone there and is serving him. 98. Chakrapāṇi Krishṇā, as Śrī Khaṇḍyā brings water for him in a kāvadi; makes, and gives him, the fragrant pigments, and is ever ready to render service to Brāhmaṇs. 99. Therefore, you should go at once to Pratishṭhāna. There you will find Śrī Lord Krishṇa." Having seen this vision, the Brāhmaṇa awoke. 100. And as he thought over the matter in his mind, he said, "Rukmiṇi has given me the sign by which I may recognize him." So he hastened to

Pratishṭhāna, and bathed in the Gaṅgā. 101. Just then Śrī Khaṇḍyā came down to the bank of the Godā (Godāvari), bearing the kāvadi on his shoulders. He at once recognized the Brāhmaṇ, and said to himself, "Why has this creditor of mine come here! 102. I had chosen a worthy place here, and have been spending my time happily. It is Rukmiṇi who has made this public, and sent him here." 103. Thus thinking to himself the Lord-of-Dvārkā felt extreme chagrin. He filled his jars, however, with water, and went home. 104. He entered the god-room and sat making the fragrant pigment, when suddenly the Brāhmaṇ, enquiring his way along, entered Eknāth's *wāḍā.* 105. Śrī Nāth saw the Brāhmaṇ and reverently made him a *namaskār.* They at once embraced one another. 106. Eknāth gave him a seat, and thus questioned him. "Tell me, where have you come from? What is your occupation?" 107. The Brāhmaṇ made an affectionate *namaskār,* and told him his story. He said, "I went to Dvārakā, and there worshipped before the image of Śrī Krishṇa. 108. I performed there the rites whereby I might have a direct revelation of Him in bodily form. Suddenly Rukmiṇi appeared to me in a dream, saying, 'Śrī Krishṇa has gone to Paiṭṭhaṇ. 109. There, at the house of the loving *bhakta* Eknāth, he is acting as a servant.' On seeing this vision I have hastened here. 110. Now let me see him at once." And with this he fell at Eknāth's feet. Śrī Nāth was amazed, and replied. 111. "Down to the smallest atom Śrī Krishṇa ever pervades every thing. Answer me, what space is empty of Him?" 112. The Brāhmaṇ replied, "Eknāth, I have no liking whatever for this philosophy about Brahma. Let me now see Krishṇa, Śrī Khaṇḍyā, the Brāhmaṇ. 113.

Recognizing your affection, O Vaishṇava *bhakta*, God felt Himself under a very heavy burden of debt, and for twelve years has been serving you here. There is no limit to the Divine." 114. Hearing the Brāhmaṇ's remark, Eknāth was amazed, and lovingly said to Uddhava, "Summon Krishṇa, the Brāhmaṇ." 115. When Uddhava called out, Śrī Hari was in the god-room. At once he assumed his four-armed form, equipped with the shell and disk. 116. He had on him his resplendent crown before whose brilliancy the sun seemed pale. Dark—complexioned, beautiful, King-of-Heaven, whom but to look upon is rest for the weary soul. 117. His brilliant earrings flashed. Around his neck was the jewel-necklace with the Kaustubha stone. One's eyelids closed at the dazzling light of his yellow raiment. 118. On his feet were ornaments, the *nepur*, the *vanki* and *todar*. Both hands were anointed with fragrant oil. As the Brāhmaṇ saw the Lord-of-the-World standing at the door of the god-room he sprang towards Him. 119. He lovingly greeted Him, embracing His feet. As to Eknāth, he was filled with remorse, saying, "I have been the cause of weariness to the Recliner-on-the-Serpent." 120. Embracing God, he said, "Śrī Hari, was this a right thing for you to do? You, yourself, became a Brāhmaṇ and unstintingly wearied yourself for me. 121. In describing Thy glory, O Lord, the four Vedas themselves became weary in the attempt. Brahmadeva became amazed. What greatness have I? 122. Thou, Purifyer of the Sinful, hast fastened the *todar* to thy feet. May this not prove false to the end of Time! This comes as an experience to my soul." 123. As Eknāth thus praised Him, and again and again made Him a *namaskār,* the Husband-of-Rukmiṇi exclaimed to him, " Blessed is your pure *bhakti."* 124. Once before this I took the form of Viṭṭhal and for twelve years led your choruses. Then in the form of Keśava, I listened to the whole of the Bhāgavata Purāṇ from your lips. 125. Thus I have already spent twenty-four years laboring here for you, but you did not know it." Thus spoke the Soul-of-the-World. 126. Eknāth replied, "O Life-of-the-World, O Pervader-of-the-Universe, O thou Ornament-of-the-*bhaktas,* O, Bewitcher--of-the-mind, through Thy deeds, Thou whose nature even Virinchi does not know." 127. The conversation having proceeded thus far, Śrī Hari suddenly vanished from sight. The Brāhmaṇa embraced Eknāth's feet and exclaimed, "You are the only blessed one, in the world." 128. Eknāth replied to the Brāhman, " Although Krishṇa was actually near me, I did not recognize him. It was you who to-day have caused me to see Him." 129. The ascetic, with his soul full of joy, dined with Eknāth, and remained there with him a number of days, listening to the Hari *Kīrtans.* 130. The worship of Vishṇu, listening to the Purāṇa, and bathing in the Gaṅgā, were his regular habits, and with deep reverence he became convinced that Śrī Eknāth was in reality Krishṇa Himself.

EKNĀTH AND THE FOUR THIEVES.

131. And now pious folk, listen with respect to another delightful story. As Śrī Eknāth was once performing a *kīrtan,* an audience of good people had assembled. 132. There were many men and women who had come together,

so that the *wādi* became densely crowded. The names of God were loudly sung, so that the very air became dense with sound. 133. With shouts of, "Victory, Victory," they clapped their hands. The assembly of worshipers manifested their joy, and unseen by men many of the gods were present. 134. They shouted aloud God's names, "Krishṇa, Vishṇu, Dark-complexioned-One, Achyuta, Ananta, Purushottama, Bali-Bandhana, Trivikrama, Victorious-Rāma, Raghupati." 135. These names, Eknāth, full of love, repeated aloud in his *kīrtan* and his soul so united itself to the Names, that he no longer had the least bodily consciousness. 136. While this kīrtan was going on, four thieves entered and sat down saying to themselves, "After the people have gone away, we shall carry on our operations." 137. No one had the least idea of their hypocritical designs. Near the close of the *kīrtan* the thieves concealed themselves. 138. The lights of the wave offering were lighted and waved before the glorious Husband-of-Rukmiṇi. Sweetmeats were distributed among the audience, and all left for their homes. 139. The thieves had hidden themselves behind a wall, and they sat quietly for four hours or so. Uddhava locked the large outer door, and immediately after retired to sleep. 140. Śrī Eknāth continued sitting on his seat with his rosary in his hand. Neither sleep nor drowsiness came to him, as he sat filled with happiness. 141. Uddhava and Girjābāi had fallen asleep. The thieves now entered the inner apartment and began examining the various things. 142. Paṇḍharināth now performed a wonderful miracle. Hear the story, ye fortunate listeners. All the thieves became blind, totally blind. 143. The lights were burning in the house, but they could see nothing whatever.

They now began to whisper to one another, "What shall we now do?" 144. They could not make out where the doors were, the lintels or the steps. They bumped their heads against the posts. "This is all unpropitious. We see in this the wrath of God," they exclaimed. 145. Repentant in heart, they said to one another, "Eknāth is a Vishnu *bhakta.* This misfortune has come upon us, because we have come here to steal. 146. Life is useless without eyes. We had better give up life at once. In doing harm to this servant of Vishṇu, we have angered the Husband-of-Rukmiṇi." 147. Thus conversing together the thieves wandered about the *wādi,* when suddenly they found themselves in the god-room, and standing before Eknāth. 148. Then again another miracle took place. The sight of the thieves was restored. And now deeply repentant, they bowed in reverence before Eknāth. 149. Because of Eknāth's goodness their evil hearts left them, and joining palm to palm, the four thieves stood lovingly before him, praising him. 150. "We, evil minded ones, not knowing you to be the image of Śrī Pāṇḍuraṅg, came here to injure you. Because you are a saint, forgive us this wrong." 151. Eknāth replied to them, "Who are you? Why are you praising me? Tell me what are the desires of your hearts?" 152. They answered, "We are thieves. We came here to steal. As we were looking for booty, we suddenly lost our sight. 153. All of us, crazed by this loss, have been wandering about the *wādi,* and now we have been brought to this conviction that we have committed a great sin." 154. As the thieves thus spoke, the heart of Eknāth, that Ocean of peace, and mercy, melted within him, and he exclaimed, "You have suffered much. 155. You came into my house with high hopes. Do not go away now with averted faces." Thus pleading with them. 156. He took them into his treasure room and showed them everything; remarking, "Take away with you whatever may please you." 157. Give to your life peace and forgiveness. It is in living a life of good deeds, that you will be without blame. This is my injuction." 158. As the thieves saw Eknāth's calmness, his word of instruction sank deep into their hearts. They coveted his property no longer. They expressed a desire only for a blessing of food to satisfy their hunger. 159. Eknāth immediately awoke Uddhava and Girjābāi, and said, "Prepare a meal quickly." 160. Thus requested by Eknāth, they very quickly cooked a meal. He served the thieves with his own hands, affectionately and kindly helping them to eat. 161. Just as people of the world honor their sons-in-law, and the parents of their sons-in-law with respect, so he treated these thieves, pressing them to eat. 162. Eknāth prepared the *vidā* with his own hands, and passed it to them, He then saw them on their way, making them gestures of respect. 163. From that day the thieves gave up all their habits of stealing, and with supreme reverence gave themselves to the worship of Hari. 164. This shows Eknāth's state of mind. He thought of the universe as himself. His feelings towards enemy and friend were alike. His actions, therefore, were out of the ordinary, and not to be compared with those of others. 165. The man who acts as he, talks as he, is, indeed, an *avatār* of God. By the very sight of him souls are saved. 166. In even listening to his praise the greatest of sins are destroyed, and one gains the Ultimate Release, and no longer has rebirths. 167. Blessed is the scared city of Pratishṭhana, where Eknāth came down as an *avatār*. Blessed are its people for they saw his deeds with their own eyes.

EKNĀTH'S MERCY TO AN OUTCASTE THIEF.

168. There was a certain outcaste who stole for a living. After many days, he was, on a certain occasion, caught in the act of thieving. 169. The owner of the house at once seized him, and took him before a court of justice. He was roughly beaten and his feet were placed in stocks. 170. He paid out money until stripped of all he had, but found no one who would release him. Many days thus passed, and finally he was unable to obtain food. 171. His body consequently became emaciated. He appeared to people like a bundle of sticks. Finally thinking that he would die in a few days, the prisoner was released. 172. By the hand of a carpenter the nails of the stocks were extracted and the outcaste was set free. As he had no strength to run away no guard was placed over him. 173. As night came on, the unmentionable thought to himself, "While the stocks are in this broken condition, I had better quietly steal away. 174. And yet I have no strength. How can I run away." Then he remembered God, and cried, "O Merciful One, save me from this place. 175. I am helpless. I am altogether a sinner. I have lain here many days in imprisonment. O Dark-complexioned One, in Thy mercy take me at once from here." 176. As he was thus thinking to himself, he suddenly heard the distant sound of a *kirtan*. He immediately began to crawl away, yet fearful of his life. 177. He went along staggering in the direction of the

Hari kirtan. As he heard it he suddenly saw the open door of Eknāth's *wāḍi.* 178. He entered the *wāḍi* and sat quietly in a corner. And as he attentively listened to the music of the kīrtan, his soul felt peace. 179. Both body and soul of the audience were pierced to the quick as they listened to the words of Eknāth. "Blessed, Blessed," all exclaimed. "This is, indeed, the place of rest for the weary." 180. Two watches of the night thus passed, and now the lamps for the wave offering were lighted. "Victory, Victory," shouted the *bhaktas,* and then made their final *namaskār* to Eknāth. 181. He distributed sweetmeats and all the people returned to their homes. Uddhava locked the outer door, not seeing the Unmentionable. 182. The helpful, true disciple Girjābāi now retired to sleep. Eknāth, however, continued sitting on his seat, and happened to cast his glance towards where the outcaste was sitting. 183. When he came near to look, he beheld a person like a corpse, but still alive. There was no strength left in his body. Such was the sight that met his eye in the *wāḍi.* 184. The compassionate Eknāth felt his heart melt with pity. He sought to question him, but the man made no reply other than that of a sign, by putting his hand to his mouth. 185. Śrī Nāth understood its meaning. "This fellow is suffering from hunger," he said, and at once going into the house, awoke his wife. 186. Girjābāi reverently touched her forehead to his feet, exclaiming "Tell me your wish." The *videhi* replied. 187. "A sick and starving man is sitting out in the yard, so whatever you can prepare in a moment's time, and suitable for him, get it ready at once." 188. No sooner was the command given, than she quickly lighted the fire in the *chul.* She had some wheat flour at hand and this she cooked. 189. She added sugar and milk to it, and came out with it into the yard. Śrī Nāth then with his own hands served it to the man from his dish. 190. And lest the man, having been starving for so many days, should die from eating too freely he lovingly fed him small quantity at a time. 191. He gave him water in an earthen dish, causing him to drink every now and then. Finally the man's life, that has its origin in food, came back to him, and what were the prisoner's first words? 192. "O merciful one to the poor, O friend of the helpless. Blessed, Blessed one. I have experienced your kindness. You have taken me, a helpless one, to yourself, and have quickly relieved me of my distress. 193. I am an outcaste, a Mahār. I became a thief for my stomach's sake. When my deed became known in the court of justice I was severely beaten. 194. My body became emaciated. They then released me from the stocks. Hearing the sound of your *kirtan,* I ran away here." 195. Eknāth listened to the Unmentionable's reply and quickly assured him that he might remain there until his strength returned. 196. He then gave him clothes, and a place to sleep in the manger. Eknāth then reentered the house and sat repeating the names of God. 197. For a very short time he paid his respects to Sleep, and awoke very early in the morning. He returned from his bath in the Gaṅgā, and performed all his customary rites. 198. He then at once sent information to the mayor of the town, saying, "Your prisoner came to my house last night." 199. The mayor replied, "Your Greatness, you have accepted him. It is not now for us to punish him." Such was his only reply. 200. After the Brāhmaṇs had dined Śrī Nāth served the prisoner with food. At night the prisoner lovingly listened to the *kirtan*. Finally full strength came back to his body. 201: He ate the food of Eknāth. His evil mind left his body. He began to worship Śri Hari with affection.

202. The narrator of the beautiful story in the next chapter is the glorious Husband-of-Rukmiṇi. Mahipati has recorded in this book his words of comforting assurance and grace. 203. This book is the Śrī Bhaktalilamrita. By merely listening to it one's desires are fulfilled. Listen then to it, ye loving pious *bhaktas*. This is the twentieth delightful chapter. Chapter 20, verses 203.

CHAPTER 21.

BHAKTALILĀMṚITA.

Mahipati's Invocation.

Obeisance to Gaṇeśa.

1. As the giver is the support of the asker, or as the seer is the refuge of the blind, so Pāṇḍuraṅg is the light of the Mind. I have no other refuge but Him. 2. He is fond of the stories of *bhaktas*. He has, therefore, adopted a subterfuge. He fondly occupies my heart, and permits no difficulties to my mind. 3. If it is sleeping, He awakens it. He gives me memory in my dreams. Śrī Hari is fond of the stories of the saints. Without question He has entered into the depths of my heart. 4. In order, assuredly to save the world, Paṇḍharināth Himself became a *bhakta* of God, doing those things that make

the good manifest among men. 5. "The Life-of-the-World, skilled in the use of Māyā, is both the author and the destroyer of fear," So says Dvaipāyana in the Vishṇusahasranāma.

BRĀHMAṆS FIND FAULT WITH EKNĀTH'S KINDNESS.

6. In the last chapter there was narrated the delightful story of how Eknāth tenderly cared for the Unmentionable. His kindness was praised by those free from worldly desires, pious and loving. 7. But the greatest of the Brāhmaṇ paṇdits, religious rulers, and learned *śastris,* talked disparagingly. "Eknāth has done what is improper," they said. 8. He has kept the Unmentionable thief in his *wādi* for many days. By such action caste pollution takes place. He has added defilement to his other faults. 9. If there is need for benevolent acts, are there not other castes? What is the value of nourishing a thief. One only increases evil thereby. 10. You may caress a scorpion, but that will not change its habit. You may feed a serpent with milk, still it will not cease to bite. 11. So if one nourishes a thief in one's own house, he will later steal all the more." Such were the disparaging remarks used by the religious rulers.

EKNĀTH AND THE BRĀHMAṆ GHOST.

12. Bearing the above event in mind, some one approached Eknāth and spoke to him. When suddenly an extraordinary event took place. Let good people listen

to the story. 13. Along the path that Śrī Nath was accustomed to take when going to his bath there was a banyan tree. Out of this tree a ghost of a Brāhmaṇ suddenly appeared. 14. And as Śrī Nāth was going down to his bath the ghost stood before him joining palm to palm, and said, " By the sight of you, I, a sinful being, have been saved. 15. Through hating a Brahman I came to this birth. I have no further desire but to make one request of you. 16. For a long time you have been feeding Brāhmaṇs. And the othtr night you fed the Unmentionable prisoner. Both of these good deeds are in your possession. 17. If you will place in my hand one of the two, symbolized in the form of water, I shall at once be saved. 18. You have indeed become an *avatār* in order to save the world." When Eknāth heard this humble supplication he replied. 19. " I see no such thing as sin or righteousness. Whatever you wish for ask from me." The Brāhmaṇ ghost comprehended his meaning, and lovingly asked. 20. " You protected that prisoner. Bestow on me that deed of benevolence." Śrī Nāth took water in his hand and presented it to him. 21. The moment the water touched the palm of his hand the malevolent creature attained deliverance. The Brāhmaṇs of tht sacred city witnessed the scene and were amazed. 22. Receiving a celestial body, the malevolent creature went up the path to heaven. All the people shouted aloud the names of Hari, and praised the greatness of Eknāth. 23. Those who had been speaking disparagingly of him had their mouths stopped. " Victory, Victory," cried the people as they saw this extraordinary event. 24. All experienced the very great goodness of benevolence. The Unmentionable, whom he had cared for, was now a loving worshipper of God. 25. After strength had come back to his body he returned to his home. Such was Eknāth, the benevolent, the saviour of the world, who had become an *avatār*.

EKNĀTH'S PILGRIMAGES TO PAṆḌHARPUR.

26. In the month of Āshāḍha, Eknāth was accustomed to go on a pilgrimage to Paṇḍhari, and after bathing in the Chandrabhāgā, to go to meet Śrī Pāṇḍuraṅg. 27. Along with Śrī Nāth a great crowd of pilgrims would make their way listening as they went, with affection and love to Eknāth's Hari *kirtans*. 28. It was Bhānudās, who had established this custom of annual pilgrimages to Paṇḍhari, and Eknāth continued that practice without any failure. 29. The inhabitants of the sacred city of Pratishṭhāna listened constantly to his Hari *kirtans,* to his gracious words, and his remarkable parables.

EKNĀTH'S LITERARY WORKS.

30. Śrī Nāth wrote commentaries on Sanskrit works. Listen lovingly to their names, you fortunate people. 31. By the command of the *sadguru,* Eknāth was the first to make the Chatuśloki Bhāgavata to be easily understood, the meaning of which is exceedingly difficult. 32. Besides this, he wrote many verses as *padas,* and in other meters. In his *abhaṅgs* are amusing compositions. Furthermore, he wrote the most excelltnt Prākrit commentary on the Hastāmalaka. 33. Then there is the Śukāshṭaka, and after that the Svātmasukha, with its wonderful

expression of his personal experiences, which the pious listeners thoroughly enjoy. 34. Furthermore, the saints, the good and pious people, reverently and earnestly besought Eknāth to write a commentary on the Bhāgavata, because of its dealing so largely with the mysteries of *bhakti*. 35. They said, " the Bhāgavata is the greatest of the Purāṇas. If from your lips we can have the Uddhavagita in Prākrit, it will be of great use to many." 36. Eknāth listened to this request, and was truly glad, and began his Prākrit commentary on the eleventh chapter of the Bhāgavata Purāṇa.

A BRĀHMAṆ TAKES A COPY TO BENARES.

37. In a few days he had finished two chapters. There was in that city a man, a noble twice-born, who, when he saw it, was highly pleased. 38. He made a copy of it, and began to read it regularly. After a while he conceived the idea of going on the Great Pilgrimage, to Benares. 39. He chose an auspicious occasion, and taking leave of Śrī Nāth, he, with his family, started on their way. 40. They journeyed along the road with other pilgrims, and finally reached the great sacred city of Benares. They bathed in the Bhāgirathi and worshipped the Lord-of-the-Universe. (Viśveśvara.) 41. He performed fully all the prescribed rites of the holy place, and remained there four months, during which he was accustomed to read aloud from the two chapters of the Bhāgavata, composed by Eknāth. 42. He bathed in the Maṇikarṇikā, and placed his seat on its bank, himself adorned with the twelve adornments, of *gopichandan tulsi,* etcetera. 43. He had with him the two

chapters of the Bhāgavata, and these he there lovingly read aloud. When suddenly there arrived on the scene the cause of trouble.

THE BRĀHMAṆ IS ATTACKED FOR READING PRĀKRIT TRANSLATION.

44. On the same bank there resided a great *sannyāsi*, engaged in the study of the *Śastras*. Two of his disciples came down to the water to bathe. 45. To their surprise they saw there this man from Pratishṭhāna, who had placed his seat there. Seeing his noble appearance, they said to one another, " He must be a Brāhmaṇ paṇdit. 46. Let us find out at once what *śāstra*, what book, he is reading." Thus saying, they came near the man and sat down beside him. 47. They used the Sanskrit language in conversing with him. " Tell us," they said, " what *Sāstra* are you reading aloud? " 48. The man replied to them, " It is a prākrit commentary on the eleventh chapter of the Bhāgavata, that I am reading." 49. The paṇdits replied, " Read it aloud to us." The man was pleased to receive this request, and began to read it with delight. 50. To begin with, Eknāth's style was pleasing, and the man's voice was most excellent. There were no faults in the translation, nor in the exposition of its meaning. 51. The paṇdits therefore, exclaimed, "Blessed is the power of utterancy of that good man, but if this book becomes widely known, no one will care to read the Bhāgavata in its original Sanskrit." 52. The two disciples then said to one another in Sanskrit, " We had better report the matter to the *Svāmi*, and have this

thing forbidden." 53. They made signs to one another, and one remained on guard, while the other hastened to the monastery and related the news to the *Svāmi.* 54. "On the *ghāt* of the Maṇikarṇika," he said "a Brāhmaṇ is sitting reading lovingly a Prakrit version of the Bhāgavata. 55. You, *Svāmi,* are the chief authority among the inhabitants of this sacred city. Therefore, it is for you to punish him. If his *Prākrit* version is acceptable to all, who will respect us *Purāṇiks.* 56. As he listened to the words of his disciple, the sannyāsi became enraged, and said, "Bring him here, and whatever punishment should be given him, I will give it." 57. This command was no sooner given, than five or seven disciples started on a run and angrily spoke to the man, who was sitting reading the book. 58. "Come, bring your book along with you," they cried, "and come along quickly to the monastary of the *Svāmi.*" The man was greatly frightened, but bethought himself of Eknāth's feet. 59. He enfolded the book in its cloth, and hastened along. He entered the monastary of the *Svāmi,* bowed to him, and stood before him.

THE BRĀHMAṆ APPEARS BEFORE THE SANNYĀSI.

60. With a motion of his eye the *sannyāsi* invited him to be seated. The Paṇdit spoke to him in the Sanskrit, but he was unable to understand him. 61. Regarding him, therefore, as a fool, he addressed him in the *Prākrit,* "Where lives the great poet, the author of this commentary? 62. Or perchance it is your own intellect

that has produced this *Prākrit version.* Tell the whole truth without holding anything back." 63. The man replied in turn. " On the bank of the Gaṅga, in the sacred city of Pratishṭhāna there lives a great and good man by name of Nāth. 64. He is constant in the worship of Vishṇu, in his Hari *kīrtans,* and offerings. He lovingly worships Brāhmaṇs and drinks the holy water of their feet. 65. By the means of the gift of his Guru's blessing he has received the poetic inspiration and he has lovingly begun a commentary on the eleventh chapter of the Bhāgavata. 66. Two chapters were finished. These, I, an ignorant man, hastened to copy, because of my reverence for it, and I am reading it, comparing it with the Sanskrit text. 67. The *sannyāsi* then declared, " This man is altogether blameless. We must call Eknāth here and punish him.

EKNĀTH IS SUMMONED TO BENARES BY THE CHIEF SANNYĀSI.

68. In the sacred city of Pratishṭhāna, on the bank of the Godā, there must be pandits and religious rulers. How is it that they have permitted a Prakrit commentary on the Bhāgavata." 69. With this declaration the *Sannyāsi* commanded his disciples to write a letter to the Brāhmaṇs at Pratishṭhāna. 70. As follows. " Vyāsa, out of the churning of the Vedas, extracted the Śrī Bhāgavata. And this Uddhvagīta consists of the very essence of the Upnishads. 71. One, Eknāth by name, a great poet, an inhabitant of your town, has written a *Prākrit* commentary upon it. This seems to us exceedingly

improper. 72. You, the all-knowing, and chief Brāhmaṇs, should all become of one mind, and after punishing him, send him immediately here. 73. I have sent herewith two of my disciples. Give them your support. They are to vanquish him in discussion." 74. Such were the contents of the letter written to the religious rulers, requesting them to send their town's Commentator to him at Benares. 75. He also sent a letter to Eknāth saying, "Come here immediately, and bring with you your Prākrit manuscript of the Bhāgavata." 76. Such were the contents of the two letters he wrote. He then commanded two of his disciples to go to the Deccan, and bring Eknāth, 77. Further more he snatched from the hands of the man the two chapters. The two disciples journeyed along merrily and arrived at Paiṭhaṇ.

THE TWO DISCIPLES ARRIVE AT PRATISHṬHĀNA WITH SUMMONS.

78. They duly performed their morning devotions, and then met the religious rulers. The Brāhmaṇs were hastily assembled and duly informed of the events. 79. The disciples presented the letter and as it was read aloud, all the Brāhmaṇs listened. They then discussed the matter among themselves. 80. "This defiled man lives in our city," they said, "and performs eccentric deeds. But the chief religious ruler here openly praises him. 81. Eknāth has thrown a spell over the influential and moneyed men of the city, and over other piously inclined castes. He has made them subservient to him. 82. For this reason we have no influence whatever. Therefore

12

vanquish him in discussion. All of us, dwellers in this city, will render you assistance on that occasion." 83. One proposed that Eknāth should be called immediately and vanquished in discussion. Another remarked, "He must go to the sacred watering place and suffer punishment. 84. He has undertaken the composition of this Prakrit version of the Bhāgavata for his own glory. At the great sacred city (Benares) he will certainly be ignominiously disgraced." 85. The disciples from Benares showed their pride in many ways. They said, "We can vanquish him. What an evil minded man he is." 86. And so, accompanied by the Brāhmaṇs of the town, they came to Eknāth's *wāḍi*. As Eknāth saw them coming, he arose to receive them, and made them a *namaskār*. 87. They embraced one another, and in a gracious manner he caused them to be seated. "Tell me, you image of mercy," he said, "In what city do you live." 88. The disciples in reply, delivered into Eknāth's hands the letter of the *sannyāsi*. Eknāth affectionately bowed his head, and read the letter aloud. 89. Eknāth then became filled with joy, and looking towards the Brāhmaṇs said, "The Lord-of-the-universe has remembered me, and therefore, he has summoned me." 90. Eknāth determined at once to hasten to Benares, and calling Uddhav, requested him to manage all his affairs in his absence. 91. To carry on the worship of Vishṇu, the reading of the Purāṇas, hospitality to guests, worship of Brāhmaṇs, and the nightly Hari *kirtans*. "All these things I leave in your keeping," he said. 92. Uddhava assenting, made a reverential obeisance. Eknāth was filled with joy at the thought of going on the Great Pilgrimage. 93. Eknāth urged upon the disciples of the *sannyāsi* that they sit down at once to eat. "You are wearied by your many days of travel," he said. 94. "It is because of me that you have had this wearisome journey here and now back." The two Brahmaṇ disciples listened and replied. 95. "We have just dined at the house of the religious ruler, but we have our full satisfaction in seeing you." Thus thy replied. 96. And the purpose they had conceived in their minds of addressing him impudently, that evil purpose passed away the moment they looked upon Eknāth. 97. "Blessed, blessed in his *bhakti*. Blessed, blessed is his character," so whispered these disciples to one another. 98. There were present there some secret spies of the religious rulers and they hastened away to report all the happenings. 99. "At the very sight of Eknāth" they reported, "the Brāhmaṇs from Beneras became humble. While we were looking on, they became meek. He has thrown a spell upon them." 100. When the religious rulers heard them they were amazed, and said, "Eknāth has evidently discovered the method of killing an enemy by means of courtesy. 101. The God Vishṇu received all the glory by patiently enduring the mighty kick of Bhṛigu. So Eknāth has discovered the art. He ever possesses the spirit of gentleness. 102. Whoever comes to persecute him ends by falling at his feet. Thus wrath departs, through his acts of kindness, 103. If some mischief is devised against him, it turns out to his advantage. If dishonour is planned, it turns out to his praise. God is his helper." 104. Thus the Brāhmaṇ inhabitants of the city murmured in their hearts. Let the good people now listen to the events that later took place.

EKNĀTH GOES TO BENARES.

105. Eknāth started on his journey along with the Brāhmaṇ disciples, who had been sent to bring him. He took with him the manuscript of five chapters of the Bhāgavata. 106. He had, neither horse nor baggages with him, because he had started immediately on his journey. But Uddhava sent after him two Brāhmaṇs to serve him. 107. By his own choice he journeyed along the way with the men from Benares. Finally, one day, they arrived at Anandavana. 108. After bathing in the Bhāgirthi Śrī Nāth naturally sat down, and the two disciples went to the *Sannyāsi* and made him a *namaskār*. 109. And said, "Through your might indeed, we have been to Pratishṭhāna and have brought back with us the Commentator. What is your further wish?" 110. The *Svāmi* replied to this question, "I am just starting out to beg. Seat him within the monastary (until my return)." Such was his command. 111. Having thus instructed them, he started out to beg. Accompanied by his three hundred disciples, he took his departure. 112. The two disciples went to the bank of the Gaṅgā and brought Eknāth back with them. "Be seated in the monastary until the *svāmi* returns," they said. 113. "Assuredly," was Śrī Nāth's reply, and so saying, quietly sat down, even he in whom there was absolutely and eternally neither exaltation nor inquietude.

EKNĀTH BEFORE THE SANNYĀSI.

114. Now let us turn to what happened after the begging was over. The Mahant gave instructions to his three hundred disciples to go within the monastery, and

"Listen to my strict command," he said. 115. "The great poet of Paiṭhaṇ, author of the Prākrit Bhāgavata, has been brought here by my two disciples. I wish you to chastize him. 116. You are three hundred disciples. Each of you is to give him five blows. If he survives this, I will further consider what to do." 117. Bowing their heads to their *sadguru's* command, the disciples hastened away, but as they went along the way, they bethought themselves thus. 118. "The *Svāmi* is powerful and worthy of respect and has commanded us. But if in beating the Brāhmaṇ he should die, our penance will be most severe. 119. We had better take into consideration what Eknāth's methods are, what his standing is, what his worship is, and how he has acquired his knowledge." 120. Thus discussing, they stood near the door of the monastery. Finally they said, "Let us, one by one, go to the door, and look at him." 121. That being determined, one by one the *sannyāsis* entered the monastery. There they saw Eknāth sitting quietly, and appearing to them in the form of Krishṇa. 122. Reverently they bowed to him, and stood with their hands palm to palm, exclaiming, "He is the *saguṇ avatār* of the totality of Satchidānanda." 123. To all the three hundred *sannyāsis* he thus manifested himself in the monastery. They further exclaimed, "This is truly the image of Nārāyaṇa, manifested to save the world. 124. Janārdan has taken possession of man. For our sakes He has taken His abode in the human heart. If we had listened to the command of our Svāmi, an awful calamity would have taken place." 125. With these exclamations all the *sannyāsis* bowed low to Eknāth, and standing before him with hands palm to palm, said, "Truly he is the Lord-of-Heaven. 126. Then one of the disciples went and said to the *Svāmi*, "You have sent the *sannyāsis* to beat Eknāth with clubs. 127. But they have broken your command. They are all bowing to him, and standing before him with hands palm to palm. This seems to us very extraordinary." 128. When the Mahant heard the news, he became hot with rage, just as Hiranyakaśipu became furious in heart when Pralhād came as a suppliant to Śrī Hari. 129. Or as Rāvaṇ trembled with rage and violently crunched his teeth, when Bibhīshaṇa, seeing the might of Rāma, came as a suppliant to him. 130. Just such was the *Svāmi's* state of mind, and he exclaimed, "These *sannyāsis* are of my own sect, and yet have broken my command and have gone as suppliants to him. 131. What science of magic has Eknāth so fully learned that the moment he is seen he casts a spell." He then gave a command to his disciple. The substance of it I will tell you, Listen. 132. "Where my usual seat is hang there a curtain. I do not wish the sight of one who composes a *Prākrit* book." 133. With this command of the *Svāmi*, the disciple hastened ahead and hung a curtain opposite the *Svāmi's* seat. The *Svāmi* entered by another door. 134. He spread his skin mat and seated himself. The three hundred disciples were still standing by the door with eyes fastened on Eknāth's form. 135. And as they viewed his four armed form their consciousness of body vanished. They no longer thought of I and Thou. All were gazing intently at Eknāth. 136. And in love were crying out, "Eknāth, Eknāth." All were praising him with their lips, he was that Lord-of-Heaven for whom a great penance is required. 137. They had received the kind favor of their *Svāmi*, hence they could see this *saguṇ* appearance. Just as Śiśupāla and Vakradanta were saved by their very hate. 138. As the *Svāmi* listened to the exclamations of his disciples he was astonished. "He has cast a spell upon all, but how I cannot understand," He said. 139. The *Svāmi* then moved his seat close to Eknāth, with only the curtain between them. The chief *Mahant* of the *sannyāsis* then addressed Eknāth. 140. "Among all the great debaters among the *Sannyāsis* I am the most distinguished. I will crush your deceit and have you at once publicly punished." 141. Sri Eknāth, ocean of tranquility and kindness, listened to these conceited words, but was not in the least troubled thereby, and returned a soft answer. 142. "O *Svāmi*, great and powerful, I reverently place my head at your feet. Do me, a helpless one, the kindness of permitting me to see you. 143. You have conceived the desire to see me, a mere child, and have summoned me here to see you. I have come here by a long journey. Why have you drawn this curtain? 144. If I have committed any wrong, forgive me now. If you will examine my intelligence, you will find that it does not comprehend the Sānskrit. 145. I am without devotion, without *bhakti*, without knowledge, without indifference to this worldly life. I have not read the *Śāstras*. I have not studied the *Vedas*. 146. It is through serving you that I have received even this slight poetic inspiration, through which I have composed verses as best I could, beginning with the Bhāgavata. 147. I have prepared only five chapters of the Eleventh Chapter of the Bhāgavata. Will the *Svāmi* kindly look it over carefully and take into consideration its meaning? 148. If you find in the manuscript, as far as I have gone, any fault in its interpretation of the Bhāgavata, then sink it in the Maṇikarṇikā, for then there would be no reason for its existence. 149. You are Nārāyaṇa in visible form in this great sacred city, and rich in knowledge. If you do not approve of this idea, how will others approve? 150. So now show me kindness and put your anger far away. Save me a helpless one, by the sight of you." 151. These nectar words of Eknāth were no sooner heard by the *Sannyāsi* than his anger left him, and the quality of goodness manifested itself in his soul. 152. The darkness of the night of Ignorance had densely filled his soul. But when the sun appeared, giving him knowledge, the darkness faded away. 153. The light penetrated his soul. The *sannyāsi* said to himself "Śrī Nāth is not man, but the Supreme Brahma in visible form. 154. That which is the complete content of the Vedānta, the totality of Satchidānanda, the qualityless and changeless. He appears evident to the senses as Nārāyaṇa. 155. And for the salvation of the world, this Dweller-in-heaven has descended as an *avatār,* and coming to this monastery in visible form, unsought by us, has given us a sight of himself. 156. He is truly not man but a deedful *avatār.* Remove now at once the curtain and let me see this divine being." 157. Thus the *Svāmi* listened to the word of his good disciples, and his heart melted within him. He had the curtain at once removed, and Lo, to his eyes Krishṇa appeared.

THE SANNYĀSI IS CONVERTED.

158. And as he saw the *saguṇ* form before him, the same as the form for contemplation, which the great poet,

of loving *bhakti* had described in the Bhāgavata, he became repentant in heart. 159. "Save, me," he now cried, and overflowed with the eight emotions, he lost all consciousness of body, and made Eknāth a *sāshtāṅga namaskār*. 160. Śrī Nāth now reassumed human form, and lifted the *sannyāsi* up while he was shouting aloud, "Victory, Victory, I am saved to-day." 161. But Eknāth on the other hand exclaiming, "Obeisance to Narāyaṇa" made a *namaskār* to the *Sannyāsi*, saying "*Svāmi*, this seems wrong. You are the superior in this monastery." 162. The *sannyāsi* listened to Eknāth's words and was overcome with amazement, exclaiming, "He has shown marvellous deeds before our eyes. He shows reverence in the interpretation of scripture." 163. Thus enjoying ecstacy of soul the *Svāmi* took his accustomed seat and seating Eknāth close to him had him unfold the cloth containing the book. 164. The meaning of one *śloka* he read in the five chapters, and exclaimed, "What irresistable knowledge!" And as he listened he felt a sense of peace. 165. Then all, in conjunction with the *sadguru* consulted together, and standing before Eknāth with hands palm to palm, made him this request. 166. "You have already composed five chapters of the Bhāgavata. We ask you to complete the Eleventh *skandha* here, in Benares. 167. Until you have finished the commentary we wish you would joyfully remain here with us." Thus the *sannyāsis* pled with Eknāth. 168. "I will do so," said Eknāth, bowing his head to their request. He then started to finish the book, rejoicing in his heart. 169. As much of the commentary as he composed each day, the *Sannyāsi* would examine it, bearing in mind the meaning of the Sanskrit original, but he found not the slightest inaccuracy.

170. Six months passed and the book was finished, and because it was replete with the mystery of *bhakti,* all listeners were made joyous. 171. All were accustomed to take their seats and the head of the monastery would have the book read aloud again and again. At night when it was read, joy and satisfaction would come with a rush. The hearts of all became full of happiness. 172. As soon as the book was completed the thought came into the Mahant's mind to make a great celebration in the monastery, and worship Sarasvati. 173. With this happy inspiration he made all needed preparations, and hastened to send invitations to the other paṇdits who were in the sacred city. 174. He said, "Eknāth has written a *Prākrit* commentary on the Eleventh chapter of the Bhāgavata. I have examined carefully its contents and have experienced loving joy. 175. The book is at last finished. To-morrow there will be a celebration of the event at the monastery. I invite all of you Brāhmaṇs, great and small to come."

THE BRĀHMAṆS REVILE EKNĀTH.

176. When the earth-gods heard this invitation they all began to revile, "What! A *Prākrit* commentary on the Bhāgavata. This is an impossible idea! 177. In this beginning of the *Kali Yuga* heresy has spread to a marvellous degree. How is it that the *Svāmi* has been deluded! Why did he not at once stop his attempt! 178. In this great sacred city he is giving his cordial approval to this Prākrit version. This is one of the wonders of the Vaishṇava Māyā. The Svāmi has evidently fallen under Eknāth's spell. 179. Let us, however, hasten to go and

acquaint him with the injunction of the *śāstras*. We must certainly sink his book (in the river)." Such was the fixed determination of the Paṇdits. 180. Thus all the Brāhman Pandits, learned in the Vedic *śāstras*, and all the Vedanta propagandists, arrived at the monastery of the Svāmi, and made him a *sāshtāṅga namaskār*. 181. Then taking the *sannyāsi* aside, they said to him, "*Svāmi*, you are the chief of all. All of us Brāhmaṇs are your disciples in every respect. 182. You are the chief seat of all wisdom. You are our *Sadguru*, worshipful and great. Over and above this you belong to the noblest of all the four *āśramas*. As to worthiness of reverence you are supreme over all. 183. This being so, it seems to us altogether wrong that you, *Svāmi*, have given your approval to the *Prākrit* commentary on the Bhāgavata made by Eknāth of Pratishṭhāna. 184. That which has been evolved out of the churning of the Vedic *śāstras* is the Bhāgavata. On it Eknāth has made a Prākrit commentary. It deserves to be sunk in the Maṇikarṇikā. 185. Just as long ago Dvaipāyana sank the Bhārata, composed by Jaimini, and received renown thereby. 186. Or as the Achārya threw into the water the great book of the Jains, so the Prākrit Bhāgavata should be sunk in Maṇikarṇikā. 187. By doing this all the Brāhmaṇs will be made happy, and the fame of this sacred city will increase." Thus all the Paṇdits pled with the *Svāmi*. 188. The *Sannyāsi* replied, "I persecuted Eknāth severely, but he is not a human being. He is an *avatār* of Vishṇu in visible form. 189. All of you should indeed worship his book with *mantric rites*." Although thus exhorted by the *sannyāsi*, the Paṇdits would not at all listen.

THE BRĀHMAṆS THROW EKNĀTH'S MANUSCRIPT INTO THE RIVER.

190. The Paṇdits asked Śrī Eknāth for his Bhāga vata, and taking it from him, hastily rising, they went and tossed it into the Maṇikarṇikā. 191. Suddenly a miraculous event took place. Listen to it ye fortunate hearers. The Bhāgirathi river lifted up both her arms and caught the book in her hands. 192. On her arms were jewelled bracelets, beautiful, divinely marked. And as she held the book up in her hands all were amazed at the sight. 193. With cries of, "Victory, Victory," the assembled crowd clapped their hands and rejoiced. The *sannyāsi* exclaimed, "Chandramauli (Śiva) has manifested himself to me." 194. The chief of all the *sannyāsis* then leaped into the Maṇikarṇikā, and, grasping the book with his hands, lovingly held it on his head. 195. He brought it to the Paṇdits, and they looked at it with downcast countenance. The *sannyāsi* said to them, "Take warning, and go now as suppliants to Eknāth." 196. They listened and then placed their foreheads at the Svāmi's feet. "We are in every way at fault in not listening to you," they said. 197. "Eknāth is God visible. The truth we now know." All the Paṇdits then entered the Monastery and reverently greeted Eknāth. 198. They placed the book before him and said, "This is your gracious voice. Śrī Bhāgirathi put forth her hands and lovingly protected it." 199. And Śrī Nāth, as he saw the Paṇdits and the *sannyāsi* before him, made them a *namaskār*. The *Svāmi* then requested the Brāhmaṇs that they should lovingly worship Eknāth. 200. "Allow us," they said to him, "some service to a saint, that we may be saved from the

sea of this worldly life." And Śrī Nāth, on his side, bowed at their feet and said, "I beg you not to do anything so unseemly."

201. In the next chapter is a delightful story by the mere hearing of which the pious become freed from worldly desires. 202. *Svāsti.* This book is the Śrī Bhaktalilamrita. By merely listening to it one's desires are fulfilled. Listen then to it, ye pious loving *bhaktas.* This is the twenty-first delightful chapter. Chapter 21, verses 202.

CHAPTER 22.

BHAKTALĪLAMṚITA.

Mahipati's Invocation.

Obeisance to Gaṇeśa.

1. Victory to Thee, Guru-of-the-World, Lord-of-Paṇḍhari. Your Vaishṇava *Māyā* is unfathomable, impossible even for Brahmadeva and the other gods to understand. These are matters of experience. 2. If I should attempt to describe Thy greatness, why! even the Vedas do not know Thy extent! And what am I but one of little intellect, a mere servant, of humble life, a sinner, and stupid-minded. 3. I cannot use words correctly. The Sanskrit language with its abundant forms has not made itself intelligible to my mind. I speak at random and irrelevantly. 4. O Thou Merciful-to-the-lowly, Husband-of-Rukmiṇi, this is the witness of my own soul, and I do not know what this my poetic composition will finally be like. 5. But

Thou, Internal-witness and Intelligence, hast caused my mind tc remember, and hast committed to my keeping the secret store of Thy deeds. 6. Of all ignorant men I, stupid-minded, am the most ignorant, and that Thou, O Pāṇḍuraṅg, shouldst relate to me Thy deeds is most strange. 7. Formerly, in order to take away the pride of Nārada Thou didst cause a bear to sing. The impossible takes place through Thy will, O Śrī Hari.

THE MIRACULOUSLY RESCUED MANUSCRIPT IS WORSHIPPED.

8. In the last Chapter it was related how the Paṇdits threw into the water the Bhāgavata, composed by Śrī Nāth, and how the Bhāgirathi river held it aloft in her hands. 9. And then how the chief *sannyāsi* sprang into the Gaṅgā and seized the book in his hands; and how, when all came back to the monastery, Śrī Nāth came to meet them. 10. And how reverently he bowed to the *Sannyāsi* and Brāhmaṇa Paṇdits, and how the Svāmi, abashed, exclaimed, "By your nobleness you have sunk our pride." 11. The *sannyāsi* then quickly collected all the materials for worship, and commanded the Paṇdits to worship Śrī Nāth, as he ought to be, with reverence in their hearts. 12. The Paṇdits did not have real reverence in their hearts, but they fell at his feet because of the miracle they had seen. Eknāth begged of them that they should not do anything so improper. 13. "I am but a servant of the servants of Brāhmaṇs, holding the hope of your favor. Rather by reverently worshipping this book you will give me joy."

14. They listened to Eknāth's proposal and all approved. The *sannyāsis* had an elephant brought with a canopied seat. 15. The elephant was caperisoned with cloth studded with gems, and marked with *śendur*. And over all were spread embroideries in gold and silver thread, and other adornments. Thus beautifully adorned the elephant was quickly brought. 16. The *sannyāsi* begged Eknāth to sit on the canopied seat with the book. Śrī Nāth replied, "I will not do so wrong a thing." 17. The only right thing is to place the book on the canopied seat, and take it around in procession. I am in every way but a suppliant, desiring only the dust of your feet." 18. There were seven rich paṇdits, and the *sannyāsi* commanded them to make all the necessary preparations for feasting, each one providing for one day. 19. What the *svāmi* proposed was acceptable to all, for who could slight his wish? All the Brāhmaṇs of Benares were his suppliants. 20. So worshipping the book with due rites they placed it on the canopied seat, and a great crowd assembling marched in enthusiastic procession. 21. There were emblems and banners. The cymbal and drum gave sweet music. The Vaishṇavas sang lovingly and reverently, and with shouts of "Victory, Victory," they repeated aloud the names of God. 22. By the sound of the drum, and the kettle-drum the air was dense with sound. In great crowds men and women watched the novel sight. 23. Thus the procession marched until night, and then there were let off many kinds of fireworks, rockets, and moon-lights were fired off each step of the way. 24. Fragrant powders, many kinds of flowers, and perfumed substances were thrown into the air. A great festival was celebrated in the city of Benares. 25. Wherever the procession halted,

there the Pandits made preparations and fed the *sannyāsis* and Brāhmaṇs who had assembled in great crowds. 26. For seven days the festival was joyfully celebrated. By day and by night the book procession marched, and all praised the greatness of Eknāth. 27. On the eighth day the procession came back to its starting point. Here a great celebration was carried on, and observed with joy. 28. The *sannyāsi* then commanded the paṇdits, saying, "Collect all the chief Brāhmaṇs and lovingly listen to a *kīrtan* from Eknāth's lips." 29. Thus enjoined by the chief *sannyāsi* all were naturally gratified. "Call to day," he said, "an assembly of Brāhmaṇs, and listen to the kīrtan." 30. The learned pandits, the Vaishṇava *bhaktas,* the Vedic Brāhmaṇs, the saints and *mahants,* and all the pious men and women assembled in the monastery. 31. With the loud noise of the cymbal, the drum and the *vinā,* the sound took the very form of Brahma, and as Eknāth performed the *kīrtan* his heart rejoiced exceedingly. 32. The people shouted aloud the names of Viṭṭhal and clapped their hands. The air became dense with the sound as they cried, "Victory, Victory." 33. Eknāth strung together stories, whose contents were replete with *bhakti.* Among them were some that were philosophic, yet such as increased the glory of *bhakti.* 34. In this *Kali Yuga* it is the name of God that has saving power. Illustrative proofs are found in the *ślokas* of the Bhāgavata. Besides this, the *Sadguru* praised with his own lips the glory of *bhakti.* 35. As Śrī Nāth's words of grace were listened to, the assembled people became transfixed. The Paṇdits lost all consciousness of body. They became lost in contemplation. 36. The Brāhmaṇs said to one another, "There are many who perform *Hari kīrtans,* but truly there is no one who performs them with such extraordinary love." 37. And all the men and women declared, "What philosophic knowledge, and gracious poetry, and yet withal with what deep humility! Blessed are his mother and father." 38. The performance of the *kīrtans* lasted for four days. On the fifth day was celebrated the Gopālkālā. The playful acts of Śrī Hari were acted, and sweetmeats were distributed, to all. 39. All the twice-born of the city of Benares, from the child to the aged, great and small, cried, "Blessed, Blessed. He is an *avatār* in visible form." 40. The *sannyāsis* also exclaimed, "The deeds of Śrī Krishṇa at the time of his being an *avatār* we have seen with our eyes. Blessed are today's festive rites." 41. The *Sannyāsi* now said to all the paṇdits, "Let all of you assemble together and with your own hands make a copy of Eknāth's book, the Eleventh chapter of the Bhagavata." 42. "We will certainly do so," they said, and they took a chapter at a time to copy. In the mean time Eknāth began composing the Rukmiṇi Svayamvara. 43. Sitting on the bank of the Maṇikarṇikā the paṇdits, with minds fixed on the object, completed fully the book, on Rām's birthday. 44. When the copy of the Eleventh Chapter was completed, the Paṇdits lovingly brought it to the monastery, where the Svāmi lovingly read it each day.

EKNĀTH STARTS TO RETURN TO PRATISHṬHĀNA.

45. Eknāth now took leave of the *sannyāsi* and started to return to his own country. All the *sannyāsis* and paṇdits assembled and saw him off. 46. Śrī Nāth

reverently made a *sāshtāng namaskār* to the citizens of that sacred city. They embraced each other and said loving farewell. 47. After accompanying Eknāth for a short distance the citizens returned to the city, and always, day and night, held in memory the noble character of Eknāth.

EKNĀTH MEETS DĀSOPANT IN HIS WAY.

48. As Eknāth journeyed on, his heart always full of joy, he unexpectedly met Dāsopant* in his path. 49. From childhood Dāsopant had cherished the desire for a visible manifestation of Śrī Dattātreya. He had, therefore, undertaken severe austerities in this loving service. 50. You may ask how he performed them. Listen, ye fortunate hearers. He abandoned all his friends and went alone into the forest. 51. He lived on fallen leaves. He took not the least care of his body. He slept on the bare rock, enduring cold and heat. 52. If any human being unexpectedly appeared, he would run away from him. Without ceasing he kept Śrī Dattātreya in his mind. 53. From these austerities lovingly carried on, he finally lost all consciousness of body, and because he slept on

---

* *Note.*—Dasopant Digambar was born in 1551 and died in 1615. His tomb is at Ambā Jogāi, also known as Mominābād in the Hāidarābād State. The interesting story of his youth, how God took the form of a Mahār and brought the necessary ransom for his deliverance from the tyranny of the Mahomedan king is one well known. For a translation of this story, together with a collection of all the information available, regarding this poet-saint, who was a voluminous writer, see an article in the Journal of the American Oriental Society, Vol 42, pages 251-279, by Justin E. Abbott.

rocks his body was covered with sores. 54. For twenty years he carried on austerities in this way. Then finally, Dattātreya gave him a visible manifestation of Himself. 55. As Dattātreya embraced him, his body became divine, and through the blessing bestowed upon him he became a prolific poet. 56. And through the grace of the *sadguru*, and his good fortune, there came to him great wealth, and the respect of great men, as they recognized his great intelligence. 57. Dāsopant had placed his abode in Ambā Jogāi. He had heard of Śrī Eknāth's good fame from every one's lips. 58. As Eknāth was returning from the great Pilgrimage the two unexpectedly met. They embraced one another with great joy in their hearts. 59. They embraced one another's feet. They conversed together about their joy and happiness. Eknāth, full of joy, said to Dāsopant, "This is a fortunate meeting." 60 After much solicitation Dāsopant took Eknāth to his home. Waves of joy and happiness arose in his soul, and with pure reverence he paid him respect. 61. They dined on daintily cooked food. Then came the listening to the reading of the Bhāgavata, and at night Hari *kīrtans* took place, that deeply moved all, as they listened. 62. A month thus passed, and then Eknāth asked leave to go on. Dāsopant pleaded with him to accept horses and money for the journey and its expenses. 63. Śrī Eknāth, however, had a mind indifferent to worldly things, and would take none of Dāsopant's wealth. Nor would he even take a horse, "because," said he, "the way is difficult." 64. In leaving, Eknāth said to Dāsopant: "I am to celebrate at my home the festival of the birthday of Krishṇa. Come to the sacred city of Pratishṭhāna at that time." 65. "I certainly will come," he replied. They made one another *namaskār*, and Śrī Eknāth then hastened on his journey, and arrived at the sacred city of Pratishṭhāna.

EKNĀTH WELCOMED BACK TO PRATISHṬHĀNA.

66. As he approached the city the news reached Uddhava. He felt supreme joy, just as the earth does at the approach of the rain in time of drought. 67. He took with him emblems and banners, cymbals, *vināṣ*, and drums, fragrant powders, the *tulsi*, garlands of flowers, and all other needed things. 68. And the people of the sacred city, men and women, and the pious loving distinguished Vaishṇavas, singing and dancing with shouts of loving welcome, went out to meet Eknāth.69. And as they saw Śrī Nāth's form with their eyes, all were filled with joy. With shoutings of the name of Viṭṭhal, they fell prostrate before him. 70. Uddhava, with overflowing love, touched his forehead to his feet. Eknāth embraced him with both arms, unable to contain his love. 71. And so the other inhabitants of the sacred city greeted Eknāth. Uddhava then offered him the fragrant powder and the *tulsi*, and put on him the garland of flowers. 72. And, shouting aloud the name of Viṭṭhal, the Vaishṇavas sang with joy, exclaiming, " Blessed is this day on which the people have come to welcome you back." 73. Singing of the goodness of Śrī Hari, and dancing, Śrī Nāth entered the city. Sweet sounding instruments were played before him. The air overflowed with the sound. 74. They filled their hands with fragrant powders and flowers, and threw them over him. Thus honoured, he entered his

house, and at once his eyes fell on Pāṇḍuraṅg. 75. Śrī Nāth made a *sāshtāṅg namaskār* before the God and singing sweet songs of invocation waved offerings before the Husband-of-Rukmiṇi. 76. He gave everyone favors of sweetmeats to their great satisfaction. They asked him about his welfare on his journey. He told them of it lovingly as he sat on his accustomed seat. 77. It was now the fourth *ghatikā* of the night when all the people returned to their homes, and Girjābāi then with her own hands gave Eknāth a light refreshment. 78. After thus performing a *kīrtan* he paid his respects to Sleep. Then began the usual worship of Vishṇu, and the distribution of food to the hungry.

CELEBRATION OF KRISHṆA'S BIRTHDAY, AND ARRIVAL OF DĀSOPANT.

79. Two months passed in this way, and then came the festival of Krishṇa's birth. Uddhava, according to his custom, began to make all the necessary preparations. 80. He collected in the house an abundance of things needed for the dinner. He besmeared the walls within and without, and painted pictures upon them. 81. Suddenly, on the day of the full moon, Dāsopant arrived for the festival. Eknāth had not heard that he had arrived, when unexpectedly he appeared at the main door. 82. A strange sight was now seen. Śrī Datta, with his trident in his hands, stood watching at the entrance, as a doorkeeper. 83. Dāsopant saw him, and was supremely amazed. He leaped from his palanquin and made him a *sāshtāṅga namaskār*. 84. He embraced Datta and exclaimed,

"Why have you come here?" The Son-of-Anasuyā listened to the question, and replied. 85. "Eknāth is not a human *bhakta,* but a visible *avatār* of Śri Pāṇḍuraṅg. For the salvation of the world he has become an *avatār* in this *Kali Yuga.* 86. Only if by good fortune there exists the richness of a *punya,* performed in a former birth, can one have the opportunity of serving him. Know this fact for a truth. 87. I hold this trident in my hand, and guard securely the door. I will go in and inform Eknāth of your presence. Until then do not enter in." 88. As Avadhuta thus spoke, Dāsopant was overcome with astonishment, and extolling Eknāth's glory, said, "I did not recognize his extraordinary greatness." 89. Śrī Datta informed Eknāth that Dāsopant had come to see him, and Eknāth with Uddhava came out to welcome him and lovingly made him a *namaskār.* 90. They fell at one another's feet, and embraced one another. Eknāth took Dāsopant by the hand and led him into the house. 91. Uddhava made the needed arrangements for Dāsopant's palanquins and carriages. He gave his men the materials and the necessary equipment for cooking. Nothing was lacking. 92. Formerly in the time of Śrī Krishṇa's avatārship, Uddhava was greatly loved by God. The desire of Uddhava to serve God was not then fully satisfied. 93. In the former birth they were friends and so now the opportunity arrived for the unselfish service of Eknāth. 94. Dāsopant performed his bath, and finished his meal with Eknāth. All night he sat listening to the Hari kīrtan, until the sun began to rise. 95. He then performed the image of Pāṇḍuraṅg, anointing him and worshipping him with the various ceremonies, experiencing the while loving joy. 96. Festal instruments were played at the door. Festal invocations were sung. The Brāhmaṇs recited aloud from the Vedas, and finally handsful of flowers were offered. 97. The days were spent in feeding the Brāhmaṇs, the nights in Hari *kīrtans*. From the first day of the fortnight to the ninth, the festival was at its full. 98. On the tenth the Gopālkālā was excellently dramatised. Dāsopant saw it all with joy in his heart. 99. And exclaimed, " I have seen with my own eyes Śrī Eknāth with his unprecedented gracious voice, his make up, his dramatic power, and his mine of philosophic knowledge. 100. I thought myself to be a worshipper of Datta in visible form, but since seeing the glory of Eknāth with my own eyes, I have become one who recognizes no duality. 101. The great festival being ended, there was feasting on the twelfth day. Dāsopant then took leave and returned to his own home.

EKNĀTH'S INFLUENCE FOR GOOD.

102. There are many good men who give salvation to pious men, and send the impious, and haters of good, to Hell. 103. Not so in truth is the story of Eknāth's life as a deedful *avatār*. He saved very many haters of the good, and many evil minded. For this reason he is the great Jagadguru. 104. The *sannyāsi* and paṇdits who persecuted him at Benares, he turned to *bhakti* by showing them a miracle. 105. Knowledge and humility, with compassion for every creature characterized him to a degree extraordinarily strange. 106. Eknāth's pity for every creature, and his great zeal at the feet of Brāhmaṇs became a burden to Lord Śrī Krishṇa. He became in fact a debtor of Eknāth's because of that service. 107. And

so Chakrapāṇi became a Brāhmaṇ, (as we have already seen) and used to fill the vessels of the Kāvaḍi with the water of the Gaṅga and bring it to Eknāth, no one recognizing his miraculous deed.

EKNĀTH FORGIVES INSOLENT MAHOMEDAN.

108. There are still other interesting and deeply suggestive stories about Eknāth. Listen to them, ye pious people. Eknāth had finished his bath in the Gaṅgā and was returning to his home. 109. There was an insolent Mahommedan sitting by the city gate. Just as he was about to spit on the ground, Eknāth came by on the street. 110. As the Mahommedan spat toward the ground the spittle fell on Eknāth's person, but this did not excite him to the least anger. His feelings could not be hurt. 111. Just as the Earth is absolutely forgiving, so was Śrī Nāth in his character. There are some who worship the Earth, others throw the vilest filth upon it. 112. Just as the Earth keeps her joy or pain to herself, and has the characteristic of neither showing her affection nor her anger. 113. So when this ignorant man unwittingly spat on Eknāth's person he did not burst into rage, but rather greatly pitied the man. 114. "This fellow has certainly committed a wrong," he said, "and will go to Hell. I must therefore now think of some means by which he will repent." 115.,With this thought in mind he again bathed in the Gaṅgā, and, returning to his home, worshipped Vishṇu. 116. First offering the food to the gods and fire, the dinner with the Brāhmans was continued and finished. He then placed in a vessel food enough for two

men. 117. He took it to he house of the Mahommedan, who had spitten on him. And bowing reverently to the man Eknāth said, "Kindly accept this favor." 118. As the Mohammedan removed the cover he saw that it was divine food, and remembering his fault he repented, 119, "I, an insolent fellow, a supreme villain, a hater of Brāhmaṇs, the lowest of the vile, spat upon you without giving the least thought to what I was doing. 120. You are in this city a man of goodness, honored by all. Your Greatness, forgive me the wrong." And with this he prostrated himself on the ground. 121. Śrī Nāth lifted him up and lovingly embraced him, and said, "If I had watched my steps more carefully, you would not have been guilty of this fault. 122. This fault committed unwittingly and suddenly belongs to you only in the slightest degree. And now that you have repented of it in your heart, there is no other penance needed other than this repentance. 123. And now remember that the offense of having spitten upon me no longer exists." With this Eknāth returned to his home.

EKNĀTH'S KINDNESS TO A MAHĀR BOY.

124. One day at the time of noon Eknāth came down to the Gaṅgā. After finishing the Brahmayadnya he was about to hurry home. 125. It was in the month of Vaiśākha, when the sun was scorching hot, and the sand bank of the Gaṅgā was intensely heated. On the sand a little boy was crying loudly. 126. When Eknāth saw the sight his heart melted with pity. "He will lose his life at once," thought he, and so lifted him up, carrying him

on his hip. 127. Eknāth wiped the boy's eyes with his garment, and spoke comfortingly to him. "Tell me where your home is," he said. 128. The small child was unable to speak, but with its hand pointed to where it lived. As they came near the hovel the child's mother approached. 129. When the child saw her, it cried out, "Mother, Mother," Eknāth then realized the situation. "She appears to be a Mahār woman," he said to himself. 130. The moment Eknāth put the boy down he ran quickly to his mother. Eknāth returned to the Gaṅgā, and bathed with all his clothes on. 131. This Mercy-in-visible-form dried his *dhotar*, and marked his forehead with Dvārkā earth. Then returning to his home finished his meal with joy. 132. That Eknāth had placed the child of the Mahār woman on his shoulder was absolutely unknown to the Brāhmaṇ inhabitants of the city. 133. But it was Pāṇḍuraṅg's wish to make the fame of Eknāth widely known. So the God laid a plan. Let the hearers listen reverently to it.

EKNĀTH CLEANSES A LEPER.

134. There was a learned Brāhmaṇ who was afflicted with a wasting leprosy. He was repentant in heart, and was performing austerities before Tryambakeśvara. 135. It was because he had committed a great sin that this horrible disease had attacked his body. In order to regain health he was performing austerities that had this desire for its purpose. 136. He refused all cooked food and lived on bulbs and roots. According to prescribed rules he performed these austerities for twelve years. 137. Suddenly Tryambakeśvara appeared to him in a dream,

and said to him, "Go at once to Pratishṭhāna on the bank of the Godāvari. 138. There lives there one Eknāth, a Vaishṇava bhaktā devoted to the service of Brāhmaṇs and compassionate to all creatures. He has performed a special act of goodness. 139. Once when the sand was scorching to the feet, a little Unmentionable boy was lying on it. Eknāth soothed him, and taking him on his shoulder, 140. Carried him to his mother. This is the great deed that he performed. If he will give you that good deed, you will at once become whole." 141. After seeing the vision the Brāhmaṇ awakened with astonishment in his heart. He came to Pratishṭhāna and began enquiring of the people. 142. "There is one Eknāth here, a Vaishṇava *bhakta*. Where does he live?" Eknāth was just then bathing in the Gaṅgā, and the people pointed him out to the man. 143. The Brāhmaṇ plunged at once into the water and told Eknāth his story, adding, "You took an Unmentionable boy on your shoulder. That good deed is in your possession. 144. Śrī Tryambakarāja, the Husband-of-Umā has told me of it." With a smile on his face Eknāth replied. 145. "I will give you all the good deeds I have ever performed from my birth until now." The Brāhmaṇ replied, "I am not worthy of so much. 146. Give me only as much as Tryambakeśvara has informed me of." Eknāth then took water and placed it in the leper's hand. 147. The wasting leprosy immediately left him and his body became beautiful. He made a *namaskār* to Eknāth, and all the people witnessed the event. 148. The men and women of the sacred city then made their *namaskār*, so also did the great and distinguished twice-born, remarking to themselves. 149. "Eknāth's manner of doing things is most extraordinary. He turns the evil of evil men into righteousness." Thus speaking all the Twice-born became amazed in their hearts.

THE GODDESS OF THE RIVER.

150. One day the pious *bhaktas,* together with Uddhava made a request of Eknāth. "You *Svāmi,* have made a *prākrit* commentary on the Eleventh Chapter of the Bhāgavata. 151. We have the earnest desire to listen to it from your lips." Eknāth saw the mind of his hearers and assented. 152. Choosing a good auspicious day he began the reading of the Bhāgavata. All the pious and loving inhabitants of the city came to listen. 153. He began to read the Purāṇa at the third watch of each day. In the steady flow of Eknāth's voice the hearers were lost in attention. 154. But a very strange event now occured. Listen to it reverently, ye pious, and wise. The Gaṅgā river taking the form of a beautiful woman came to listen. 155. Lovely, charming, delicate in feature, adorned with garments and ornaments. So lovely and beautiful a woman had never before been seen there. 156. Possessed with this form this daughter of Vishṇu began to come and sit before Eknāth, listening. There were other women present, but none equalled her. 157. She listened intently to the delightful words from Eknāth's lips. She did not allow her mind to wander in the least, and in the meantime she lost all consciousness of body. 158. Whenever he came to a story, illustrating the mystery of *bhakti,* feelings of intense love filled her. Tears would flow from her eyes, all the people looking on. 159. There were among the listeners some of evil mind, and a suspicion

came into their thoughts. "Where does this beautiful young woman come from? We do not understand. 160. We never saw her before in this sacred city of Pratishṭhāna. Yet, she is coming regularly at the time for the reading and listens with ardor in her soul. 161. She avoids the crowd of other women, and places her seat away from them. She appears to be a married woman, young in years, but she speaks with no one. 162. She looks steadily at Eknāth, and gives loving attention." These evil minded men, thus suspecting her, spread the story of her in the town. 163. There were some, who wanting to see her wih their own eyes, what sort of a beautiful woman she might be, came with the pretext of being listeners. 164. Thus many days passed, and the reading of the book came near its end. It then came into the minds of these persons to find out where she lived. 165. They said, "As soon as the Purāṇa is finished, let us follow her, and from a distance find cut where she belongs. 166. Is she mistress of her own home, or is this young woman at her mother's home, or is she living at her mother-in-law's, that she comes here without asking the leave of anyone." 167. While these evil minded men were deciding what to do, the reading of the Purāṇa was completed. The Gaṅgā then made a loving affectionate *namaskār* to Eknāth. 168. She impressed upon her mind the form of Śrī Nāth, and immediately left. The evil minded men followed her, winking at one another. 169. Some walked before her, some behind, taking in her strange conduct. In the meantime this daughter of Vishṇu, of beautiful form, and character, arrived happily at the bank of the Gaṅgā. 170. She stood for a moment where the water was up to her ankles. She took up some water in her hand, sipped it, and immediately became invisible. 171. Just as the lightening flashes among the clouds and vanishes in a moment, in the same manner she manifested her lustre and disappeared. 172. The evil minded men now understood and exclaimed, "The Godā, flowing to the ocean, has been taking the visible form of a woman, and has been coming to listen to the Bhāgavata. 173. We truly have been dull of understanding. Our hearts have been defiled by suspicion. Śrī Nāth is an *avatār* of Vishṇu. We certainly must not call him human. 174. Imagine nectar in a glass bottle, and one looking carefully at it mistakes it for an intoxicating liquor. That is what has happened to us." 175. Thus repentant, they performed their devotions and worship and astonished in mind, returned to their several homes. 176. On the next day at the third watch they came again to Eknāth's house to listen. They made their *namaskār* to the *Svāmi* at once and took their seat. 177. Eknāth undid the book from its cloth and waited for a moment, saying, "One of our listeners has not yet come. She is very late." 178. Those who had been suspicious now came forward and fell at Eknāth's feet. Repentant in heart, they confessed the whole affair. 179. "The river, beautiful and lovely, has been coming here regularly to listen. Entertaining suspicions in our heart, we followed her out of curiosity. 180. She stepped into the Gaṅgā, and then and there became invisible, and we then understood that she was actually the Gaṅgā. 181. We have been of evil mind, and lacking in good, therefore, we were suspicious in our hearts. In this we have committed a great sin. Forgive us our wrong." 182. Śrī Nāth, full of joy in his heart, replied, "In your possession now is a full righteousness. You saw

Godā in visible form. By this your sin is shattered to pieces. 183. And now without doubt in your hearts listen to the Bhāgavata. I cannot now praise enough your greatness, for you have seen a miracle." 184. Thus reassuring them, he began reading the Purāṇa. And the people who saw the miraculous deeds of Eknāth rejoiced.

185. In this book I, Mahipati, am writing of the good renown of him, to listen to whom, the Godā, in visible form, came to Eknāth with a desire to hear the Bhāgavata. 186. Svasti. This book is the Śrī Bhaktalīlāmṛita. By merely listening to it one's desires are fulfilled. Listen then to it, ye pious, loving *bhaktas*. This is the twenty-second delightful chapter. Chapter 22. Verses 186.

CHAPTER 23.

BHAKTALĪLĀMṚITA.

Mahipati's Invocation.

Obeisance to Śrī Gaṇeśa.

1. Great sins are washed away by listening to the lives of the saints. Blessed are the *jivanmukta* (released while living) who sit down to listen with fixed attention. 2. One who listens in truth to the story of one's own special *bhakta,* attains to great righteousness. He will continue to enjoy the fruit of his righteousness in many ways, and it will never pass away. 3. There are austrities and rites belonging to the system of Works (*karma*). If these are performed one also attains righteousness (*puṇya*) but

after enjoying its fruit of happiness it passes away in a moment. 4. If one listens with fondness to the stories of the Bhāgavata, that good act never passes away. That person finally enjoys *Sāyujyatā.* (Final absorption in Brahma.) 5. He, who, having great fondness for the stories of the saints, listens with all his ears, even if he should fall into some great calamity, God will protect him. 6. In the last chapter, you fortunate ones, you listened to the story of how the Gaṅgā, assuming the form of a woman, listened attentively to the Bhāgavata. 7. How there were men of suspicion and hatred by whom the miracle was seen, and how their souls melted with repentance, and how they made their *namaskār* to Eknāth.

CONVERSION OF THE IMPIOUS MERCHANT.

8. Now let the wise listen to another story. There was a merchant living near to Eknāth, who was impious and wicked. He never went to Eknāth's house. 9. He would never listen anywhere to the reading of the Purāṇas. He would never go to hear Hari *kīrtans,* and although the river Gaṅgā was near him, he preferred to bathe at home with hot water. 10. He never performed morning and evening devotions, nor gave offerings to ancestors. He dined twice in the day, and cared only for his own family. 11. When Eknāth saw the manner of his life, great pity for him was aroused in his heart. "This man," he said to himself, "has acquired a human birth, but he will needlessly go to Hell. 12. I must adopt some means whereby, through being my neighbour, good desires may spring up in his heart and he may seek after the Supreme attainment." 13. Thus thinking, he went out into the street, and sought

to meet him. They exchanged salutations by word of mouth. 14. Out of respect for Eknāth, the man stood still for a moment, and Śrī Eknāth began to question him. "Who are your dependents? 15. What business are you engaged in? How do you care for your family." The merchant listened and then replied. 16. "I have sons and wife at home. I live near you. I am in the service of a business man who lends money. 17. He pays me wages, and on it I spend my days." To this Śrī Nāth replied, "I have now a request to make of you." 18. Great fear sprang into the mind of the man, blinded by his attachment to objects of sense, and a great miser withal, and so he made no answer. Eknāth, however, understood his mind and said. 19. "I have no desire to obtain from you any money, or any substance of any kind. I ask you only to take a moment's time to come to my house for the *kīrtans.*" 20. The man replied, "I have no leisure time, because of my concern for our daily necessities." Eknāth responded to this, "Listen to what I tell you. 21. I will repeat to you a śloka from Śrī Vishṇu sahasranāma. Commit that much to memory. That will fully satisfy me." 22. As he listened to Eknāth's voice a reverential feeling filled his mind. Eknāth wrote the words on a bit of paper and had him read them. 23. And as Eknāth gently caressed him with his lotus hand his heart was at once changed. He took the words of the *Śloka* to heart, and quickly committed them to memory. 24. On the next day he came and asked Eknāth for another śloka. After a few days had passed he had committed to memory the whole of the Sahasranāma. 25. Śrī Nāth then told him still further, that after his bath he should sit in fixed contemplation. 26. Speaking to no one, and repeating the Sahasranāma.

The man listened and assented. He now began to do that. 27. His heart now somewhat changed by all this, he began to come to Eknāth's house to see God. At the same time he would bow at Eknāth's feet, and then hasten back to his home to attend to his business affairs. 28. Many days thus passed, when suddenly he was taken with a nine-day fever. As his life was passing away the servants of Yama came to take him to Hell. 29. His voice was already choked and so the relatives gave him the penance. And as they were giving him the bath he suddenly remembered. 30. And began to repeat loudly the Vishṇu sahasranāma. All were greatly pleased and exclaimed, "Blessed is his fortune." 31. The angels of Yama, as they heard the sound of his voice repeating the names of Vishṇu, ran away. The angels of Vishṇu then came and paying their respects to him took him with them to Heaven (Vaikuṇṭha). 32. If Śrī Nāth had not taken pity on him, he would have gone to Hell. It is for this purpose that the saint became an *avatār* in this *Kali Yuga.* 33. The men and women of the sacred city said to one another, "It is because this man lived as a neighbour near to the Saint, that he received the visible manifestation of God. 34. Saints are indeed God of Gods. They are in no way different from Him. For a short time they take the guise of men, and manifest themselves through extraordinary miraculous deeds. 35. Śrī Eknāth has turned many men to *bhakti*, both, those co-operating with him, and those opposing him. He has thereby driven heretical beliefs away and increased the glory of the Name of God."

EKNĀTH AND GIRJĀBĀI'S CHILDREN.

36. Girjābāi, Eknāth's good wife, at first gave birth to a jewel of a daughter. She was named Godūbāi. 37. After her a son was born. He was named Hari. As his years increased he was invested with the sacred thread, and began studying in a Brāhmaṇa school. 38. After him there was another daughter born, and she was named Gaṅgābāi. Listen also to the story relating to whom they were given in marriage. 39. There was a gentleman in the sacred city of Pratishṭhana by name of Chintopant. Godubāi, the eldest daughter, was given in marriage into his family. 40. In the Karṇātak country, there lived one who was an old relative of his. To his son Gaṅgābāi was betrothed, and soon married. 41. Gaṅgābāi had a son by name of Puṇḍāji. He also became a loving worshipper of Vishṇu.

EKNĀTH'S SON, HARI, BECOMES A LEARNED PAṆḌIT.

42. As to Eknāth's son, Hari, he was very intelligent. He studied all the sciences. 43. He became proficient in the six *śāstras*. The highest Brāhmaṇs paid him respect, and called him Hari Paṇḍit. 44. The Brāhmaṇs of distinction in Pratishṭhāna continually praised him. "His intelligence is greater even than that of his father," they said. 45. "Eknāth, becoming a saint, sings his songs in the Marāthi language. Women and Śudras, listening with all their hearts, become wholly absorbed in them. 46. Eknāth, by singing in the Prākrit has captivated all the pious people, and thereby the reading of the Purāṇa in

the Sanskrit has disappeared. Haripant has resuscitated its reading. 47. Gold comes out of the earth, and the rich make of it ornaments. So Haripaṇḍit, be it known, has become a greater man than his father. 48. Or just as a lustrous diamond comes out of a rock, so it is true of Hari Paṇḍit. Our minds realize this now. 49. Viewed from the point of depth a large body of water is called an ocean, but its water is salty. The son of the ocean, the brilliant moon, sprays nectar. 50. So from Eknāth's loins there has come forth this jewel, Haripaṇḍit, a Brāhman, proficient in the six *śāstras,* and he is in every way acceptable to us." 51. Thus these distinguished Twice-born, using high sounding similes frequently insulted Eknāth in praising his son.

HARIPANT'S CONCEIT, ASHAMED OF HIS FATHER, GOES TO BENARES.

52. To begin with, Haripānt's heart was filled with the pride of knowledge, and in addition to this there was his association with scoffers. Thus his heart was defiled with wrong thoughts, and he said to himself, "How long shall I continue to listen to my father?" 53. "I am a paṇḍit, proficient in the six *śāstras,* but my father reads aloud the books in Prākrit. I feel ashamed among the distinguished Brāhmaṇs of this city." 54. Thus thinking in his mind, he said to himself, "I will abandon at once my country, and go and live in the city of Kāśi (Benares)." And this he decided to do. 55. Haripandit had three sons. Two of them he took with him, along with his wife, and arrived at Kāśi.

EKNĀTH'S GRANDSON RĀGHOBĀ.

56. The youngest son, of beautiful character, by name of Rāghobā, remained lovingly with Eknāth. 57. He did not sorrow for his mother and father. He remained with his grandparents day and night, lovingly performing his little acts, his heart full of happiness. 58. When a *kirtan* was being performed at Eknāth's house, he would take the cymbals in his hands, and sing with all his might to the astonishment of all the people. 59. At the Gopāl festival he would act out the scenes with gestures and movements, and repeat aloud without hesitating the words sung by Eknāth. 60. One day, watching for a time when Eknāth was alone, he humbly placed his forehead on Eknāth's feet and thus in his very childhood he received in his ear Eknāth's *anugraha* (mystic formula). 61. Seeing his good qualities, shown in these ways, people praised him, saying, " He certainly will draw to himself the greatness of Śrī Nāth. 62. He is worthy of taking Eknāth's place. His character appears so noble. His father, because of his pride of knowledge, devotes himself to a paṇḍit's profession." 63. Thus the pious discussed the matter among themselves. Now as to Hari paṇḍit. He, with all his dependents, continued to live at Kaśipuri (Benares). 64. As Hari paṇḍit was proficient in the six *śastras,* and had the gift of speech, he amassed great wealth. He built a residence in the great sacred city, and made Kāśi his permanent abode.

EKNĀTH LONGS FOR HIS SON HARI.

65. On the other hand in the sacred city of Pratishṭhāna Eknāth continued performing regularly the Hari

kīrtans, turning every one to *Bhakti,* and to the praising of his teachings. 66. One day Eknāth sat alone and thought thus, " In this sacred city all its inhabitants now worship Śrī Krishṇa. 67. But my son Hari still takes great pride in his scrupulous observance of rites and ceremonies. The adage is true of him, "Under the lamp the darkness is greatest." 68. So, I will go to Benares personally, and bring him back. It is my fixed purpose to complete with this act my life as an *avatār*. 69. Just as if a hail stone should remain solid in water, so I think of my son. I must show him some miracle to turn my son to *bhakti*. 70. Thus determined in mind, Śrī Nāth went to Kāśipuri. (Benares.) First he bathed in the Maṇikarṇikā, and then went to meet Viśvéśvara (Lord-of-Universe). 71. As he was walking along to Haripaṇḍit's house, his son came forward to greet him. He made him a *namaskār,* and embraced him with exceeding love. 72. He prepared a seat for his father, and seated him upon it. He performed all the rites of worship, and his heart was full of happiness. 73. He enquired of his father all the news. They then finished their meal. And because Eknāth had made this journey to his home, the son was greatly gratified. 74. Eknāth remained there many days, during which his son ministered to him. And people everywhere related the story of how formerly the *prākrit* Bhāgavata had been written there by Eknāth. 75. The *mahant,* and the *sannyāsis* of the monastery exhorted Hari paṇḍit thus, "Conduct yourself without fail according to the injunctions of Śrī Nāth. 76. Know this that he is not a human being, but the visible *avatār* of Vishṇu. I also persecuted him greatly, but his miraculous deeds are limitless." 77. To this Hari paṇḍit replied, " What! Do you mean to say that I act outside of his wishes." And with this remark, Haripandit hastened back to his home. 78. After many days spent there Śrī Nāth said aside to his son, "My declining age nears its completion. The time of my departure is at hand. 79. The wish of my heart is to spend the rest of my life with you. I cannot bear to live without you. My heart pines for you. 80. You are my good son, my only begotten. I have no other close relation. If you will come now to Pratishṭhāna, your fame will greatly increase thereby. 81. You have built here in this sacred city a great residence. Leave here your two sons, and take to yourself permanently my place at Pratishthāna."

EKNĀTH ACCEPTS HARI PANDIT'S TWO CONDITIONS FOR HIS RETURN.

82. Hari paṇdit listened to the words of Śrī Nāth and then replied as follows, "I have one request to make of you, my *Svāmi,* but you will not be willing to grant it. 83. Do not eat food prepared by others outside of our home, and do not read the Purāṇa in the Prākrit. If you will accept these two conditions, I will go back with you." 84. Śrī Nāth, now filled with joy, made no protest whatever against this and replied, "I will conduct myself as you may desire." 85. With this promise his son was satisfied, and the two lovingly started to return. 86. They journeyed along as it pleased their fancy, and finally reached the sacred city of Pratishṭhāna. The people were very glad, and went out from the city to greet them. 87. Eknāth's returning was to the lotus eyes of the pious like the festival of lights. They made *namaskār* to him, and embraced him joyfully.

EKNĀTH'S KĪRTANS CEASE AND HARI PERFORMS.

88. Thus Eknāth entered his home. The pious cherished a hope in their hearts. "To-day there will be a *kīrtan,*" they thought, but Eknāth sat still on his accustomed seat. 89. On the next day Hari paṇdit read aloud the Purāṇa in Sanskrit. On the day he began it many of the intelligent people assembled. 90. Śrī Nāth quietly placed his seat and sat lovingly listening, but all the people had the desire to listen to words from Eknāth's lips. 91. The news now spread in the city that Eknāth had abandoned the reading of the *prākrit* books, and the Hari *kīrtans,* and had brought back Hari paṇdit to conduct the *kīrtans.* And also that he had agreed to eat no longer at another's house. 92. The pious took this very seriously to heart. "Our good fortune is broken and lost," they said, "and therefore Eknāth has given up reading the Prākrit books, and he himself listens to the *Purāṇs* in Sanskrit." 93. The women, śudras and those of other castes could not understand the Sanskrit, and so while the Purāṇa was being read they would get up and leave, abandoning the habit of regularly listening. 94. When Śrī Nāth used to read the Purāṇa the *wādā* (house) was more than filled. Five or ten had to remain outside regularly. The place simply swarmed with men. 95. Eknāth understood the inner feelings of all, and said to himself, "There has been a great falling off in *bhakti*" There now occurred another event. Listen to it, ye pious *bhaktas.*

HARIPANT'S CONVERSION THROUGH A MIRACLE.

96. There lived in the sacred city of Pratishṭhāna a rich Twice-born. His wife made a vow to the Husband-of-Rukmiṇi. 97. "If Thou, O Life-of-the-World, wilt grant my request, I will feast a thousand (Brāhmaṇs). She had no sooner expressed this thought, when the King-of-Heaven granted her request. 98. Later through destiny because of deeds in a former birth, his wealth was scattered. Her husband also died, and she became poverty stricken. 99. Of course to care for her body she needed daily food and clothing, so by carrying water from house to house she earned a few pice each day. 100. In this way this Brāhmaṇ woman of Pratishṭhāna passed her days. She was accustomed to come regularly to Nāth's house to listen to the Purāṇa. 101. It now happened that she mentioned to a wise and pious Brāhmaṇ the matter nearest to her heart. "I made a vow once," she said, "that I would feed a thousand (Brāhmaṇs). 102. But through the strange vagaries of destiny all my wealth has been scattered, and on top of this finally came widowhood, and I have been unable to earn sufficiently for food and clothing. 103. By delivering water from house to house I have thus far been able to pass my days, but I continually remember my debt to God. How can I pay it?" 104. Listening to her words, the Twice-born replied, "If one gives a meal to one who is absorbed in Brahma, there is no limit to the result of that good deed. 105. To feast a hundred Brāhmaṇs who cannot read the Vedas, and who have merely learned to repeat the Gāyatri *mantra,* and to feast one Brāhman who reads the Vedas, is the same in

value. 106. To feast a hundred Brāhmaṇs whose knowledge comprises merely the three Vedic books, and to feast one great paṇdit, who understands the Vedanta philosophy, is of the same value. 107. And to feast one who in his practice of life acts as he talks, at the sight of whom guilt disappears, has a hundred times more value than to feast a Vedantic scholar. 108. To worship one who has his passions under control, who uses the means that produce the subjugation and the guiding of the organs of sense, and always pure in heart, has a hundred times more value than the worship of a Vedantic scholar. 109. The good deed of feeding at one's home a hundred of such who control their passions, is equal to feasting one Vishṇu *Bhakta,* who is without envy and hate. 110. He, who, therefore, serves a meal to Eknāth, to whom enemy and friend are alike, and who appears to be Janārdan in visible form, feeds a hundred thousand Brāhmaṇs." 111. With these loving words of the gentleman, the Brāhmaṇ widow experienced joy of heart, and going to her home began collecting materials for a feast. 112. She entertained the desire of bringing Eknāth, the deedful *avatār,* to her home for a feast, and of serving him with many kinds of daintily cooked food. 113. Poor in worldly things was this poor Brāhmaṇ widow. No money or grain was to be found in her house. Only by carrying water to the houses of people could she daily save up some money. 114. She began to purchase, and store in her house wheat, rice, *dāl* and *ghi.* And with her own hands she prepared vaḍe, pāpad, and vaḷavate. 115. She also collected such materials as vegetables, greens and sugar. Then taking the gentleman along with her she went to give her invitation to Eknāth. 116. At that moment Hari Paṇdit was reading the Purāṇa, and Śrī Nāth was listening to him. So they sat quietly until the reading was ended. 117. When the reading of the Purāṇa was completed, Haribā arose and went into the house, and the gentleman, along with the Brāhmaṇ widow made their request to Śrī Nāth. 118. Her story was told from beginning to end. "Her feasting a thousand (Brāhmaṇs) still remains to be done. If you will so much as eat a mere handful, a hundred thousand Brāhmaṇs will have been fed." 119. Appreciating the reason why she felt as she did, Śrī Nāth replied with a request, "Haribā has just gone into the house. Go and ask him." 120. They listened to this request and both went in, but in great fear. Hari Paṇdit was sitting in the house, and they told him their story. 121. Hari Paṇdit became enraged, and turned on the Brāhmaṇ widow with scorn. "Eknāth has been on the Great Pilgrimage," he said, "and since then has given up taking food at another's house." 122. As the widow listened to these harsh words, she felt helpless, and coming back to Eknāth, she stood before him with hands palm to palm. 123. She murmurred, "Hari Pandit does not approve, but my desire is still very great," and tears of love flowed, and her voice became choked with emotion. 124. Śrī Nāth was greatly troubled, and the widow's desire was so full of love, that he hastened within to his son and said, "Fulfil her wish." 125. Hari paṇdit replied, "Father, keep the promise you gave me. I have followed you back to this sacred city, because I know how your heart works." 126. Śrī Nāth then proposed to his son, "You prepare the cooked food with your own hands, and then both of us will go and dine there. This will meet her desire. 127. In this way the promise I gave you will not be broken, and at the same time her vow will be fulfilled, the poor, helpless, old widow!" 128. Out of respect for his father Haripaṇḍit consented, and Eknāth came outside and sat down. The Brāhmaṇ widow continued to plead. 129. "The vaḍe, the pāpad and the valvate, which I have prepared with my own hands, and which I have been keeping for the last six months will be in vain, after all the pains I have taken. 130. You are indeed one who hungers for devotion, you a deedful *avatār*. Propose O svāmi, some plan whereby my wish may be fulfilled." 131. Hearing her loving pleading Eknāth rejoiced in heart and said, "You have with love prepared the vaḷavate. Now fry it with your own hand. 132. After I have taken the morsel addressed to the five vital airs, then you may serve whatever you have prepared at home." When she heard Śrī Nāth's reply she was exceedingly happy. 133. Eknāth added also, "Whatever you yourself are fond of that will seem delicious to me. I have no other craving." 134. Listening to his nectar voice, her heart became full of happiness, and returning to her home she began to prepare the vegetables. 135. She arose at dawn the next day, swept and garnished her house, cleansed and polished the vessels, and then bathed by the bank of the Gaṅgā. 136. This poor old woman fetched water and placed it in her house pulling the door after her. Then she went to Eknāth's house. 137. She bowed to Hari paṇḍit, and said, "I have collected all the necessary materials, now come to my house, and fulfil the desire of my heart." 138. Śrī Nāth then requested his son, saying "Go and cook the food, I will soon follow." 139. Hari paṇḍit then went with the Brāhmaṇ widow. He first bathed, and then cooked the meal. 140. The widow lovingly brought him whatever materials he needed, for whatever he knew how to cook. 141. After giving him what he required for his purpose she left him to do her own cooking. Now Eknāth, who understood the widow's inner feelings, said to himself. "She has no one to send and summon me." 142. So just as Śrī Hari went to the house of Vidur without being called, so on this occasion Eknāth arrived at her home unsummoned. 143. She gave him water for his bath. Haripaṇdit then made the offering to fire, and with his own hands served two dishes. 144. And as Śrī Nāth was served freshly heated *ghi* he called to the Brāhmaṇ widow and said, "Janārdan is the enjoyer of this," and with this mantra poured water on her hands. 145. Then bringing the image of Pāṇḍuraṅg into his mind, he lovingly made an offering to Him. Eknāth then took a sip of water, and morsels of food in the name of the vital airs. 146. Father and son then sat down to eat, and the old woman went back and forth into the kitchen, and brought out the food. 147. She brought a tray full of food, and placed it before Śrī Nāth, and served with her own hands light puranpolis. 148. With her own hands she served the *vaḍe,* the cakes fried in oil and the nine preparations of milk and sugar. Śrī Nāth refused nothing. He ate rapidly and eagerly. 149. Seeing this strange sight she was greatly pleased. The same was happening now as when Rāma ate the bor fruit belonging to the Bhil woman. 150. But when Haripaṇdit saw the strange sight he was angry. He rolled his red eyes, and gnashed with his teeth. 151. The old woman, however, stood before Eknāth with hands palm to palm, saying, "You have had mercy on a helpless one and fulfilled my desire." 152. Haripaṇdit, on the other hand, thought to himself, " If such was his intention, why did he let my hands be scorched (in cooking), " and he was unable to control his rage. 153. He stared at the old woman, rolling his reddened eyes, savagely biting his lips, and his whole body trembling. 154. God is fond of the sweet food of *bhakti,* and the *bhakta* is closely bound to God through love. The desires of each are sweet, but who cares? 155. Anger is a mad elephant, whom you would control, but cannot. The paṇdit, however, used his reason as his elephant goad, and restrained himself. 156. He thought to himself, " If I treat my father with disrespect a great sin will rest on my head." With this consideration in mind, he joined in the meal with loving thoughts. 157. Eknāth enjoyed to the full the juices of happiness. He then drank Gaṅgā water and washed hands and mouth. 158. The old woman had already provided a special seat for Eknāth, and had prepared two *vidās, tulsi* leaves and Vishṇu water. 159. After Eknāth had rinsed out his mouth, he said to his son, " Take away now at once our two used leaf plates. 160. This old woman is entirely alone here. She has no one with her. Unhelped, it will be very difficult for her later to take her bath." 161. Śrī Nāth made this request and Haripaṇdit paid respect to his father's suggestion. He tucked up his *dhotar,* and began taking up the leaf plates. 162. He took up Eknāth's plate and put it on his own plate, when behold, to his great amazement he saw another plate. 163. He thought to himself, " The old woman must have brought him another from the kitchen with food." So he took that plate away also. 164. When behold, he saw a third leaf plate, and so one after the other. His lotus heart, full of astonishment, he excitedly took them up. 165. He took up more than a thousand, but still they did not end, and Haripaṇdit, now full of repentance, made a *sāshtāṅga namaskār* to Eknāth. 166. He stood before him with hands palm to palm. Tears rushed to his lotus eyes, and the eight emotions filled him. 167. He exclaimed, "Victory, Victory to Thee, Thou Eternal being, Unmanifested, Void-of-darkness, Imperishable, deedful *avatār*, Lord-of-all, King-of-Heaven, Guru-of-the-World. 168. I, a sinner, was ignorant of your greatness. I have greatly transgressed. You are a visible Vishṇu *avatār*. This conviction has now permeated my soul. 169. Cease your miraculous deeds now, and have mercy upon me, father." Thus repenting in heart, he placed his head at Eknāth's feet. 170. Śrī Nāth, in great pity comforted his son, caressing him with his hand. "You have been put to much trouble darling," he said, "but there will be no more leaf-plates to be taken up." 171. With this assurance of Eknāth's Haripaṇdit removed all the plates. He had taken up and collected a thousand plates. He then said to the Brāhmaṇ widow. 172. "Your good fortune is extraordinary. In inviting Śrī Nāth you have truly fed a hundred thousand Brāhmaṇs. I am convinced of this now by experience to the full." 173. The eight emotions now crowded the old woman's heart. She reverently made her *namaskār* to Eknāth. "You have had pity on me, a helpless one," she cried, "and have saved me." 174. Haripaṇdit said to his father, "I have become proficient in the six *śāstras*. On account of my pride of that knowledge I did not recognize your greatness. 175. Now, O *Svāmi*, wherever thy purpose is a pure one, there eat, and also read aloud the *prākrit* books." 176. Thus conversing, the two returned to their home, and the old woman took the food left on Eknāth's plate and sat down to eat. 177. Blessed, Blessed was her *bhakti,* where Eknāth ate and was satisfied. It is what Eknāth left on his plate that Mahipati herewith lovingly serves (to you listeners). 178. Svasti. This book is the Śrī Bhakṭalīlāmṛiṭa. By merely listening to it one's desires are fulfilled. Listen then, ye, pious, loving *bhaktas.* This is the twenty-third delightful chapter. Chapter 23, verses 178.

CHAPTER 24.

BHAKTALILĀMRITA.

Mahipati's Invocation.

Obeisance to Śrī Gaṇeśa.

1. Victory to Thee Līlāvigrahi, Noblest-being, *Saguṇ* being, dark-complexioned-one, Glorious-Guru-of-the-World, Āṭmārāma. Thy greatness is unknowable. 2. In the family of Bhānudās at Pratishṭhāna Thou didst become an *avatār.* Thou didst manifest Thyself in many acts and show miracles to the wicked. 3. Thou Thyself didst become a *bhakta* of God, and wonderfully magnified Thine own name. Both by the hatred of some, and by the devotion of others, Thou hast saved many. 4. O King-of-Heaven, Thy incomparable miraculous acts cannot be described, and where the Serpent's tongue split in its effort to describe Thee, where am I a mere mosquito. 5. Praising Thee with uncouth words, somehow or other, I write them in this book. Accept them in Thy mercy, and in Thy supreme pity. 6. I speak of my gift of speech, but

this is my transgression. O Paṇḍharināth, Thou art the true mover of the mind. No one else has that power. 7. If my mind is the least disturbed, I cannot think of a single word, but Thou dost give me remembrance, and therefore this length to this book. 8. Using me as a pretext, O glorious-Lord, Thou dost publish Thine own good fame. This conviction has impressed my mind. I have no other thought. 9. Among all versifiers I am the one and only ignorant one, and every one knows this. But Thou Pāṇḍuraṅg dost perform strange thing. 10. When an infant speaks with a lisping tongue its mother regards it happily. So Thou, giver of absorption into Brahma, comfort and glorify me.

EKNĀTH RESUMES HIS KIRTANS.

11. In the last chapter was the extraordinary story, how the knowledge-proud Haripaṇḍit began removing Śrī Nāth's leaf-plates, until more than a thousand were removed. 12. How he became supremely ashamed, how perspiration covered his body and how becoming humble, he made Eknāth a *sāshtaṅg namaskār*. 13. With hands palm to palm he pleaded with Eknāth, "You are an *avatār* of Vishṇu in visible form. Wherever you have a purpose, that is pure, go there and dine, O *Svāmi*. 14. And the *prākrit* books, which you have yourself written, and have read aloud, continue to read them each day." And with this he fell at Eknāth's feet. 15. While his son was thus speaking to him, Eknāth reached his home. Aside from these two, no third person knew of the above events. 16. In the meantime the Brāhmaṇ widow ate her meal in her kitchen, and then fastening together the thousand and more

used leaf-plates, she placed them on her head, and came to the bank of the Gaṅgā. 17. And there to the people of Pratishṭhāna she related the events. With her own hands she committed the leaf-plates to the flowing stream of the Gaṅgā. 18. And the pious *bhaktas*, to whose hearts came great joy, said to themselves "Now Eknāth will give readings of the Purāṇa, and we shall listen to his *kirtans* to our heart's content. 19. Thus people spoke to one another, and the story spread in the city. Haripaṇdit changed to one of reverent spirit, became a *bhakta* of his father's 20. And with fixed attention would sit listening to the reading of the Purāṇa from the lips of Śrī Nāth. Many pious people now gathered to listen to the Hari *kirtans*. 21. With shouts of "Victory, Victory" the assembled *bhaktas* clapped their hands and rejoiced. Tears filled Haribā's lotus eyes. 22. The loud noise of the cymbals, the *viṇā*, and drum, came in reverberating waves. Especially did they proclaim the greatness of God's name. The mere listening to His names made their minds happy. 23. Haripaṇdit thought in his heart, "When the former events happened in Paiṭhaṇ, I was in the ignorance of childhood, but the *Svāmi* has today had pity on me. 24. I did not recognize Śrī Nāth's great glory. I was greatly misled by my pride of knowledge. I deserted this Guru-of-the-world and went to live in Kāśi. 25. As in the Dvāpārayuga the *bhakta* Arjuna was accustomed to regard Śrī Krishṇa as a close relative, but after he had manifested himself in the form of the universe, he seemed to him to be the soul of the universe." 26. So in fact did it happen to Haribā. He now sat attentively at the *kirtans*, and understanding Eknāth's wishes served him for his own good.

EKNĀTH CARES FOR AN IDIOT BOY, GĀVABĀ.

27. There are other stories, delightful and deeply suggestive. Listen reverently to them, ye pious folk. On the bank of the Gaṅgā there was a very humble village. In it there was a Brāhmaṇ. 28. His occupation was that of town-clerk, but he was very poor in every respect. He was, however, father to a large number of children, but with no food for them to eat. 29. The last to be born was a boy, an idiot, and dumb. The women called him Gāvabā. But listen to his story. 30. Gradually he grew to be a big boy, and was always playing with little boys. He became eight years of age and still could not speak distinctly. 31. His father regarded him as of no account, but the ceremony of the sacred thread, however, was performed. The boy could not even say, "Keśava Nārāyaṇ," much less repeat the Gāyatri *mantra*. 32. The father said, "This is indeed destiny, from deeds laid up in a former birth, that my last son should be dumb. He eats a stomach full, but speaks not a word. 33. I must have in my possession ten million sins, as a consequence of which I have had born to me this demon. Who will in the end care for him?" Thus the father and mother were troubled about him. 34. Because of sin in a former birth a foolish son is born. How can he give happiness to his parents? He is a giver of pain. 35. It happened that on a certain day the Brāhmaṇ celebrated a festival at his home. The boy was given some *puraṇpoḷi*, of which he ate a stomach full. 36. On the next day, at the same time of day Gāvaji asked his mother for some more *puraṇpoli*. She had laid some stale *puraṇpoḷi* aside. She brought it out and gave it to him. 37. After that night

had passed, Gāvaji would not eat the usual bread and greens. With his hand he made a sign that said, "Give me some more *puraṇpoḷi.*" 38. The mother became angry, and slapped her son. "You wretch," she cried, "Is this why you have been born, to ask for dainty food?" 39. Gāvaji cried and rolled on the ground. He then got up and again running to his mother with signs asked for *puraṇpoḷi.* 40. His mother now felt pity for him, "What shall I do with this craving of his", she thought. Then taking him by the hand she led him quickly to Paiṭhaṇ. 41. She went to Eknāth's house, and reverently made *namaskār* to the *Svāmi.* She placed Gāvaji at his feet, and said, "Merciful One, accept him. 42. He is nine years old, as you see, but he cannot speak one single word. Yet he asks for dainty food. What am I to do? 43. We are weak and helpless Brāhmaṇs. We live in a humble village, but here with you, there daily takes place a feast where Brāhmaṇs eat dainty food. 44. My ears have heard of your compassion, and so I have brought him here." Śrī Nāth replied with these nectar words, "Let him remain here in my home." 45. Eknāth then spoke to Girjābāi, and asked her to care regularly for the boy with feelings of love. 46. In accordance with Śrī Nāth's request she gave Gāvaji water to bathe with, a serving dish, and seated him to eat. 47. Gāvaji's mother was now filled with joy. She took her leave of Eknāth and hastened back to her village. 48. She told her husband that she had come back from committing her dumb boy to Eknāth's keeping. "Now let us put aside feelings of affection for him, and empty love. 49. It was evidently well with him in a former birth, and therefore he has now found an excellent home." Thus father and mother felt great satisfaction. 50. Now as to Gāvaji, Eknāth, with his own hands supplied him with clothes. He ate both the morning and evening meals, and was always playing with other boys. 51. He no longer remembered his parents. His heart was full of happiness here. He received daintily cooked food, such as he had not received before, and his physical frame became well nourished. 52. It happened that one day Eknāth was sitting alone in the God-room. Eknāth called Gāvaji to him there, and tried to have him repeat a formula with the name of Rāma. 53. But that dumb boy was very stupid and could not repeat a single syllable. Eknāth then questioned him. "What is my name?" 54. Suddenly the power of speech developed. "Eknāth," he cried. Then Eknāth, in his kindness, gave him that name as a formula for continual repeating. 55. He took a cord and with his hands tied many knots in it, saying to the boy "I want you to constantly repeat my name on this rosary." 56. From that time Gāvaji met his dear *sadguru*. He became deeply interested. He forgot to play, and enjoyed the happiness that comes from love. 57. He would not repeat any other word. To all others he was dumb, but affection for Eknāth touched the depths of his heart. 58. He conquered his craving for sweet things. Taking but little food, day and night he spent in worship. 59. When the people of the town saw the manner of his life, they were amazed, and said, "No sooner did he experience Eknāth's compassion than his conduct changed. 60. Gāvaji's father and mother once came to visit him, but he showed no love or affection for them. He would not even look at them.

GOD RĀM TELLS EKNĀTH TO COMPOSE A PRĀKRIT RĀMĀYAṆA.

61. After some days passed in this way a notable event took place. Eknāth was in deep contemplation in his God-room. 62. Śrī Rāma revealed himself there to him, and taking Eknāth by the hand awoke him. As Eknāth opened his eyes he beheld the Husband-of-Jānaki. 63. Eknāth overflowed with the eight emotions. With love he embraced his feet. Raghupaṭi drew Eknāth to his heart in his embrace, full of love. 64. Raghunandana then gave this command, "Compose with your own lips a Prakrit commentary on the Rāmāyaṇa by Śrī Vālmiki." 65. Thus commanded by the Lord-of-Ayodhyā, Eknāth made this answer, "My mind cannot comprehend the seven chapters that describe your good fame. 66. And though I attempted it in my uncouth words, yet there is little left of the limit of my life. I doubt in my mind whether the book can be completed. 67. Raghunandana replied to this, "Perform your devotions and your regular religious duties moderately and to a less extent, and give all your time to the composing of the Rāmāyaṇa. 68. Your noble emotions and love are wonderful. I am truly fond of your writings, and so I wish you to name the book the Bhāvārtha Rāmāyaṇa. 69. I, the Dark-complexioned one, will abide in your heart, and at all times give you remembrance. The Kaliyuga and Death are under your sway; do not be in the least troubled." 70. Thus spoke Raghunandana, and Eknāth worshipping his feet said, "Your command is my authority. I can plan nothing otherwise." 71.

Thus much spoke the Lord-of-Ayodhyā, and at once became invisible, or rather Rāmchandra took up his abode in Eknāth's heart.

EKNĀTH COMPOSES THE BHĀVĀRTHA RĀMĀYAṆA.

72. After this Eknāth chose a very auspicious day and began the Rāmāyaṇa in Prākrit. Because of this the loving pious *bhaktas* felt great joy. 73. Each day they listened to as much of the book as he composed. From it sprang sweetness, sweeter than nectar. As men listened to it they lost all consciousness of body. 74. On the ślokas of the book composed by Vālmiki, Eknāth wrote a Mahārāshṭra commentary. As men listened to it they became absorbed in contemplation, and the dull and stupid became full of love. 75. Eknāth began with the Bālakānḍa, and completed it. He then began the Ayodhyākāṇḍa, and brought that also to completion. 76. After this the Araṇyākāṇḍa where Raghunandan went into the forest. Then he completed the whole chapter of the Kishkindhākāṇḍa. 77. Then came the Sundarakāṇḍa, where Hanumant performed wonderful deeds accomplishing the search for Sitā, and in which Raghupaṭi goes to Laṅkā. 78. Then Eknāth began the Yuddhakāṇḍa and himself completed forty-four chapters of it. But the time of his departure was now near at hand. 79. And when the pious heard Eknāth say, " The time of my departure is now truly near at hand," they became greatly troubled. 80. They said " We hoped that from the Svāmi's own lips the whole of the Rāmāyaṇa would be completed. He

has not yet fully completed the Yuddhakāṇḍa. 81. The whole of the Uttarakāṇḍa yet remains to be done. Therefore we are very anxious. First bring the book to full completion and then name the time of your departure." 82. To this plea of the good *bhaktas* Śrī Nāth made a reply, "If Death has appointed his abode in any particular body, he cannot be avoided." 83. The hearers returned answer, "When Krishṇadās Loḷyā came supplicating you, you caused him to escape Death for eleven days, and let him finish the whole of the Yuddhakāṇḍa. 84. So now stop Death, and let us see the joyous occasion of the completion of the book. As we shall listen to the Svâmi's loving poetic skill we shall all rejoice." 85. Śrī Nāth replied, "Listen to my words. To punish Death so as to bring my poetry to completion seems to me unworthy.

EKNĀTH ASSIGNS GĀVAJI THE TASK OF FINISHING THE RĀMĀYAṆA.

86. Gāvji will now bring the Yuddhakāṇḍa to its completion, and also the Uttarakāṇḍa. There is no other way." 87. As Śrī Nāth made this statement the people were astonished, "What Gāvaji," they cried," that lifelong mute, who speaks to no one! 88. How can he compose the Rāmāyaṇa! This seems untrue to us." But Śrī Nāth called Gāvaji to him and bestowed his grace upon him. 89. He lovingly placed his hand on Gāvaji's head, and gave him his pen, saying, "May the poetic inspiration in me pass to you." 90. With this boon of Eknāth's grace Gāvji's mind immediately expanded and taking the paper in his hand began writing in the book. 91. His composition was exactly like that of Eknāth's *ovis*. When one

chapter was finished the pious people listened to it. 92. They remarked, "Through the kindness of Eknāth this mute has become gifted with the power of speech. His language is also exceedingly sweet. He will complete the whole book. 93. In the presence of Eknāth he wrote one chapter. The remainder of the book he carried to full completion later.

EKNĀTH ANNOUNCES HIS DEPARTURE FROM THIS LIFE.

94. In the month of Phalgun, on the night of the fifth day of the dark fortnight, Śrī Nāth performed a *kīrtan*. After distributing sweetmeats, he said, "Listen to my request. 95. To-morrow I am to depart. All of you, after bathing come as far as the Gaṅgā to see me off. And then return to your homes. 96. As the pious folk heard this request of Eknāth's they became very sorrowful, and said, "The life of this *avatār* now ends," and their hearts were in great distress. 97. On the next day, early in the morning, all his circle of friends gathered in his *wādā*. Śrī Nāth's relatives were in a fainting conditions. 98. When the pious people saw this state of affairs they became exceeding sorrowful. Their eyes filled with tears, as they looked at Śrī Nāth. 99. The revilers, the perverse, and the evil minded, however, made adverse remarks. They said, "He exhibited many wonderful acts, but the path of death is the same for him as for others. 100. He has shown in the past many miracles, but now Death has him in his mighty grasp. At the end Eknāth's body will be carried along on the shoulders of men." 101. As the

pious folk heard these remarks of the revilers, they were sad, but they recalled to mind the fame of Eknāth's deeds. 102. They said, "In order to save the world you, Eknāth, became an *avatar* with human qualities. We wish that your death could be different from that of ordinary men." 103. When Śrī Nāth heard this desire of the pious, he became conscious and sat up, like one awakened out of sleep. 104. At this sight all clapped their hands with shouts of, "Victory, Victory." The pious folk then shouted the name of Viṭṭhal and rejoiced. 105. Eknāth then asked Uddhava to bring water quickly for his bath, After bathing with the repetition of *mantras*, he with his own hands put on clean clothes. 106. Then taking his seat he made the twelve marks with clay, and lovingly placed the *tulsi* garland around his neck. 107. He then repeated the names of Janārdan, and pronounced the *tāraka mantra*. He meditated, and then loudly repeated the names of Viṭṭhal. 108. Eknāth took his *viṇā* on his shoulder, and praising the attributes of Śrī Hari, and making *namaskār* to *Pāṇḍuraṅg*, he held his form in his mind.

EKNĀTH GOES INTO THE RIVER AND ENDS HIS LIFE.

109. Loudly repeating God's names he left his *wāḍā*. The people lovingly worshipped him. "Blessed and holy is this earth," they cried. 110. Every step of the way men and women worshipped him, offering such things as fragrant powders, flowers and tulsi garlands. They sang various invocatory songs. 111. As they impressed Śrī Nāth's form on their minds, tears came to their eyes.

Thinking that they would never see him again, great numbers of people came from afar. 112. There was a great collection of banners and flags. Every now and then there was the shouting of God's names. The path became densely crowded. The dome of heaven was filled to overflowing with sounds. 113. People from the little hamlets outside the city came with their specially chosen forms of procession. Before and behind Eknāth there was a dense crowd, so that the sight of him was obstructed. 114. All marched in procession to a place in the Gaṅgā called Lakshmitirtha. The gods now came riding on their sky automobiles, and showered flowers on Eknāth. 115. Innumerable water lilies fell to the ground. These the people saw with their own eyes and clapped their hands shouting the names of Hari. 116. Blessed were the people of that time, who saw that wondrous scene. The Gods also unseen by men, viewed the scene. 117. As the crowd reached the sand bed of the Gaṅgā Śrī Nāth told all the people to quiet their minds, and listen to the attributes of Hari. 118. Listening to the request of Śrī Nāth, all felt great joy. All the men and women then seated themselves, looking intently at the form before them.

EKNĀTH'S FINAL MESSAGE.

119. With loud repeating of Viṭṭhal's names the Hari ***kīrtan*** was commenced, Eknāth wondrously described the greatness of ***bhakti***, and the power of repeating God's names. 120. "In this Kaliyuga there is no means of salvation other than that of His Name. Be kind to every creature. Keep this truth in your hearts. 121. I had to come here into this world of mortals for your good.

Otherwise I am above Māyā, the absolutely perfect, pure spirit." 122. As they were listening to Eknāth's ***kirtan,*** a good man put this question to him. "You, Svāmi, will have to become an *avatar* again sometime in the future, will you not? 123. Such is the hope of all. O image-of-compassion, tell this." Śrī Nāth listened to this question and replied in an *abhang* verse. 124. I will quote this in this book. Reverently listen ye, wise *bhaktas,* to these gracious words, to hear which bestows enlightenment on the soul.

1. 'When the path of righteousness is destroyed, and unrighteousness has lifted up its head, then ,I must return to this worldly existence. 2. Many, many kinds of beliefs, heresies, and scrupulous observance of rites, and ceremonies have risen in revolt, their faces must be smashed by the worship of Hari. 3. Whatever was Hari's deedful life that is also mine independently. But God and his *bhakta* are united. There is no difference between them. 4. Whatever avatār Hari assumes that I also assume. I proclaim aloud Hari's names, for the salvation of the world. 5. That in all creatures there may be the thought of God and that the blessing of *Dharma* may increase, is the real object of *Bhakti.* 6. It is the injunc ion of the Vedas that toward all creatures one should preserve pity and friendliness. It is this indeed that I came to do. 7. God when assuming a deedful body is called the ever-free. Am I indeed different from that? 8. Krishṇa showed Arjuṇa Himself in the form of the universe. One should never therefore so much as speak of various differences. 9. The story of his taking away the calves. Here the calves and herdsmen were different, but He Himself became

the musical instrument, the shoes and the waist cord. 10. Ekājanārdan says, "I regard Govinda in the form of the Universe. He who considers there is a difference is more contemptible than the most contemtible."

125. This *abhang* of Śrī Nāth, containing his gracious message on the occasion of his departure, Uddhava, taking paper in his hand, wrote it down at that very time. 126. Then under Viṭṭhal's name there was the shouting of the praise of Hari, and all clapped their hands. Invocatory hymns were sung. Listen to them all of you.

1. As one looks at men one sees Janārdan. Where there are differences there appears identity. Where there are many there appears perfect unity. Where the mind and intellect are insufficient to describe, how can there be such a thing as attributes and non-attributes? Chorus. Victory to God, Victory, Victory to Janārdan. This Invocatory Hymn we sing of wonderful meaning. 2. This *ārati* has been made brilliant by the light of the lights. As one looks at it, the state of difference, and the consciousness of body no longer remains. 3. When that light is lighted one experiences the fact that there is no state of difference. When the body is offered to body, quickly the difference of Jiva and Śiva vanishes. 4. No back and no front, all one dense mass. The one who sees is the one over all. Neither desired nor undesired, neither secret nor disclosed. The I fills all space. 5. Always seen but never comprehended by the mind. Whatever is seen is not kown by the sight. Non-existence has swallowed existence. This *ārati* is a strange one, O Ekājanārdana.

EKNĀTH'S DEATH.

127. This invocation Śrī Nāth sang with his own voice. He loudly repeated the names of God, and made a *namaskār*, prostrating himself on the ground. 128. After Śrī Nāth had thus prostrated himself he made a request of the people with his hands palm to palm. "Let the kindly thought of you all rest upon me," he said to them, and again bowed low to them. 129. As they thus listened to his voice tears came to their eyes, and crying, "Victory, Victory to Nāth, Victory to Eknāth," they made him a *namaskār*. 130. Eknāth then waded into the water of the Gaṅgā. When the water reached his navel he stood still. 131. He caused all to repeat aloud the names of Hari, during which his soul left its abode, the Gods showering flowers upon him. 132. All the people who had come to see the sight now mourned in their love. They then committed his body to the fire, according to the common practice. 133. After seeing the departure of Eknāth the people returned to their homes. All were on that occasion agitated by their sorrow.

THE MIRACULOUS AŚVATTHA TREE SPRINGS FROM HIS ASHES.

134. On the next day along with his son they came to collect Eknāth's ashes, when lo, they saw the Kṛishṇa *tulsi* plant sprouting out of the ashes, and also a young *aśvattha* tree. 135. When the people saw its tender and brilliant green leaves they rejoiced and cried out "He has indeed manifested himself in the form of the *aśvattha* tree. Śrī Nāth has already become an *avatār* in advance. 136.

Then keeping the *aśvattha* tree in the centre they built a stone platform around it, and in the shrine they installed Śrī Nāth's *pāduka*. To this day the place fulfils one's desires. 137. Many men and women, inhabitants of the sacred city, continually serve at that place, and the compassionate Śrī Nāth fulfils the desires of their hearts. 138. According to the faith of each one he obtains from the God-of-Gods. On the *shashṭhi* there takes place at Paiṭhaṇ a festival of great grandeur. 139. Śrī Eknāth gives a visible manifestation of himself in the form of the *aśvattha* tree. Many orther wonderful things take place there. Listen to them, ye pious *bhaktas*. 140. Lest the stone platform should be broken the *aśvattha* tree remains just as small as it has always been. Even Brahmadeva and the other Gods cannot know fully the miraculous deeds of Śrī Nāth. 141. Blessed are the inhabitants of the sacred city, who can always see this manifestation of Śrī Nāth. Innumerable sinners have been saved by the sight of his pādukā (sculptured foot prints.) 142. Those who hear of the death of Eknāth will have no agony at their death. Giving them happiness the King-of-Heaven takes them to his abode.

143. I have written this book in uncouth language but by the command of Śrī Pāṇḍuraṅg. Otherwise, I, a sinful stupid man, could never have completed the story of the saints. 144. In the next chapter is a pleasant story of the Vaishṇava *bhakta Tukārām*. His story is exceedingly long, but listen all of you to it. 145. He, who is merciful to the poor, the Husband-of-Rukmiṇi, Brother-of-the-help-

less, Ocean-of-mercy, He has given me, Mahipati, assurance; and causes me to write of these visible manifestations of Himself. 146. This book is the Śrī Bhaktalīlāmṛita. By merely listening to it one's desires are fulfilled. Listen then, ye pious loving Bhaktas. This is the twenty fourth delightful chapter. Chapter 24, verses 146.

THE WRITINGS OF EKNĀTH.

In his Mahārāshṭra Sārasvata (History of Marāṭhi Literature) first Edition page 553 Mr. V. L. Bhave gives a long list of works ascribed to Eknāth. Some of those listed as separate works are, however, but chapters or portions of his works under another title. I am acquainted with but ten of his works, as follows:—

Chatuśloki Bhāgavaṭa.
Abhaṅgs.
Hastāmalaka.
Śukāshṭaka.
Svātmasukha.
Ānāndalahari.
Anubhavānanda or.
Ānandānubhava.
Rukmiṇi Svayamvara.
Bhāgavata.
Bhāvārtha Rāmāyaṇa.

Of the remaining in Mr. Bhave's list which are chapters or portions of the above.

Bhikshugita is the 23rd chapter of the Eknāthi Bhāgavata. The following are titles of abhaṅgs to be found in the collection of his Abhaṅgs.

Ekādaśi Māhātmya.
Krishṇadānavrata.
Gitāmāhātmya.
Govardhanoddhāraṇa.
Chiranjivapada.
Pralhād Charitra.
Bhārud.
Sitāmandodari Samvāda.
Svātmabodh.
Pade.

The following in his list I have no knowledge of;

Ashtāvākra.
Kāliyāmardana.
Kausalyā Svayamvara.
Gajendramoksha.
Ganeshavilāsa.
Gitārthasāra.
Guhyapanchaka.
Nāmasāra.
Mudrāvilāsa.
Vedāntanirupaṇa.

The following brief summaries of ten of his works will, I trust, be of suggestive value to the student of Eknāth.

THE WRITINGS OF EKNĀTH.

CHATUŚLOKI BHĀGAVATA

The Chatuśloki Bhāgavata is a commentary on the Sanskrit text of the Bhāgavaṭa Purāṇa the ninth chapter of the second *skanḍha,* consisting of 44 verses in the original text, but appearing as 45 in the commentary.

Near the close of the work Eknāth adds an interesting historical note, explaining why he was led to its composition, and when this took place (verses 1016-1032). " Listen attentively. I will tell you how I came in possession of the Chatuśloki Bhāgavata, and the reason for my producing this commentary. On the Godāvari river, on its north bank, four *yojanas* away, is Mount Chanḍragiri. Śrī Janārdan in his pilgrimage naturally went there. It is a very long climb to the top of Mount Chanḍragiri, but at its base is the town of Chanḍrāvati. A distinguished Brāhmaṇ named Chandra (Chandrabhat) lived here, and it happened that we put up at his house. He was in the habit of expounding the Chatuśloki Bhāgavata and praised it highly. Janārdan was greatly pleased with Chandrabhat's exposition, and with loud exclamations of pleasure he told me to put the mystic teachings of the book into the common language of the people (the Marāṭhi). My education was mediocre. I did not know Sanskrit, its words, nor their meanings, but, because of the supremacy of his strict command I was inspired to carry out his wish." After citing examples of the wonders accomplished by obedience to the commands of a guru, and his own intense absorption in the work of composing the commentary, he ends by saying, " Thus this Chatuśloki Bhāgavata, compounded of knowledge, by the power, might and glory of my *guru's* command has been rendered in a Prakrit version."

This historical note should be compared with the traditional account of the meeting of Eknāth and Janārdan with Chandrabhat, the reasons leading to Eknāth's writing the commentary on the Chatuśloki Bhāgavata in Marāthi. (Bhaktalilāmṛita 14,123-176, and Keśavasvāmi's Eknāth charitra 5,1-57. A comparison of texts gives no suggestion that Keśava Svāmi followed by Mahipati in the Bhaktalilāmrita, obtained his information about Chandrabhat and the writing of the commentary on the Chatuśloki Bhāgavata, from this work of Eknāth's. The fact that this is an independant historical account, and that Kaśava's and Mahipati's Bhaktalilāmrita accounts agree with it, naturally leads one to stronger confidence in Keśava's and the Bhaktalilāmrita account, as truer to fact than the Bhaktavijaya account, and the unknown source from which Mahipati obtained it.

Contents of the Chatuśloki Bhāgavata. As Eknāth's work is a commentary of the Sanskrit text of the ninth chapter of the second *skandha* of the Bhāgavata Purāṇa, he naturally follows the contents of the original text. It is a philosophic work, and strictly Vedantic in all its conceptions. But while following the text in his explanations, he goes outside of the text in constantly emphasizing several points to which he seems to ascribe great importance.

1. The need of a guru, without whom the mysteries of true knowledge cannot be known. The characteristics

of a true guru, a *sadguru,* and a true disciple are emphasized.

2. The importance of *gurusevā,* or the faithful service to be rendered to a *guru* is emphaszed. A *sadguru* is really God manifest in human flesh, and reverence, obedience, and service should be rendered to him.

3. As fundamental to all benefits from Knowledge, religious acts, and devotion to God (*bhakti*) there must be a pure and sincere ethical life. There can be no such thing as true *tapa* (the outward religious life,) or true *bhakti* (the inner worship of the heart) without purity of life and heart. To this practical, ethical side Eknāth, again and again, calls attention with emphasis.

4. While Eknāth is willing to concede the Way of Knowledge (*dnyānamārga,*) the Way of Works (*karmamārga*), as ways of salvation (*mukti*); they are, however, difficult ways for the ordinary man. In their very success there is the danger of pride. The Way of *Bhakti,* has no such danger. Sincerity is needed, after that God himself comes to the rescue of the feeble and the sinful and saves them.

From verse 390 God Himself is represented as speaking and explaining the fundamentals of the Vedantic philosophy and the ways of Salvation, Knowledge, Works and *Bhakti,* in all of which ethical purity is represented as essential.

THE ABHAṄGS OF EKNĀTH.

There are two easily available collections of the *abhaṅgs* of Eknāth, one the Tukārām Tātyā edition of

1903, containing 2754 *abhaṅgs,* including 47 by Bhānudās; another, and a more recent edition by Tryambak Hari Avate in 1924, and consisting of 4001 *abhaṅgs.* All my references to the *Abhangs* of Eknāth will be from this Avate's edition. These two collections differ in their arrangement of the *abhangs,* as well as in their number. I am unaware as to the original manuscripts on which they be based. There are questions of textual criticism, and doubts connected with the authorship of some of the *abhaṅgs.* A discussion of this subject belongs however, to another place.

Contents of the 4001 abhaṅgs.

These *abhaṅgs* cover a great variety of subjects, mostly of course, of a strictly religious nature, but others are especially suited for use in worship, at festivals, and even games. A detailed analysis would be out of place here. In general, however, they are not philosophic, but have to do with the practical religious life, of relationship to God and man.

God, under whatever name, or manifestation, is a being very near to man. He is frequently addressed as, "Father and Mother." "His mercy is to all creatures." "He does not regard caste." "To him high and low are the same." "All castes can be saved."

"In man's relation to God he must be free from hypocrisy." "He must have true love for God." "Without love no one can meet with God." "Why go on pilgrimages to sacred places? One's mind should first be pure. Can one's mind be made pure by going to sacred places? Retire rather to some quiet spot. If the heart is pure, God is there in your own home. You can see Him where you are sitting, if your trust is in Him."

The need of a *sadguru* is, of course, frequently emphasized. To Eknāth the human *guru*, was a manifestation of God, "Guru is the Supreme Brahma." "Salvation comes through the favor of the *Sadguru*, all sins are destroyed through him." "In this life happiness is the gift of the Sadguru. O my soul, put all your trust in Him."

The *abhangs* contain frequent references to the saints of Mahārāshtra, from Dnyāneśvar to his own saintly *guru*, Janārdan. In his various lists 59 names appear, including a few outside of Mahārāshtra, such as Kabir and Rohidās. Connected with some are extended historical notes, such as those on Dnyāneśvar and Nāmdev. These notes show that many of the traditional stories recorded by later authors, such as Mahipati and others, existed at the time of Eknāth, and therefore have much historical value.

These *abhangs* of Eknāth, are well worth careful study, for they pertain to the many sides of man's relationship toward God and man, and if they can be trusted as really the work of Eknāth, they are through the light of his own personal life and character.

HASTĀMALAKA.

The Hastāmalaka is a philosophic work consisting of 674 verses. It is in the nature of a commentary on fourteen ślokas. On the Sanskrit original see Indian Antiquary

Vol. IX page 25, article by Professor E. B. Cowell M.A., Cambridge.

The story underlying the Sanskrit text and its commentary is that to a certain Brāhmaṇ there was born a son (32). The child exhibited unusual characteristics. It did not cry when born. So inactive did it appear that the neighbours, who gathered to see it, remarked, "One would call it a corpse, were it not for the signs of life." If it fell out of its cradle it would not cry, nor when bitten by ants. It refused to take nourishment from its mother. Up to eight years of age the boy seemed absolutely dumb. The parents tried to have him repeat the Gāyatri *mantra*, with no success. As at least that amount of knowledge was necessary for the investment of the sacred thread, they tried to force him even by depriving him of food. They were not successful, and he on the contrary, showed no resentful feelings towards them. It now happened that Shankarāchārya, came to that house on his begging errand. The āchārya at once understood the boy, as the parents had not, and began to question him. "Who are you? To whom do you belong? Where are you from? What is your name? What is your caste? Whence have you come, and whither are you going? To my friendly question you should give a friendly answer." To this the boy replied," I am not man, God, nor any other creature. I am not *Brāhmaṇ, Kshatriya, Vaiśya* or *Śudra.* I am pure Intelligence." To the āchārya's further questions the boy answers to the effect that he is pure *ātmā,* that all differences appearing in the universe, are but the forms in which the ātmā appears with names to those forms, just as the one sun has many reflections in the little pool rippled by the wind. In these answers the boy brings out the various catagories and definitions of the Vedantic philosophy. The Āchārya, being highly pleased with the wise answers of the boy, whose apparent lack of intelligence, was merely a cover to his profound wisdom, recognized his worthiness to be invested with the sacred thread.

The Hastāmalaka is a purely philosophic work, with the design of explaining the fundamental conception of the Vedantic philosophy of the absolute oneness of the ātmā, the one substance of which all apparent differences are but that one substance in various forms,. To understand these mysteries the need of a *guru* is stated; but that need is not emphasised. The work being purely philosophic, the practical side, namely, the ways of salvation, *dnyāna, karma* and *bhakti* are not emphasised, indeed the word *bhakti* even does not once occur.

The frequent quotations in the commentary from the Bhagavadgita and the Upanishads show that Eknāth was a student of those sacred books.

ŚUKĀSHṬAKA.*

The Śukāshṭaka is a commentary on eight Sanskrit śloks. They are the words of Śuka, hence Śukāshṭaka, the Eight sāyings of Śuka. This short commentary of Eknāth's consists of 447 verses.

In brief the contents are as follows.

1-9 Invocation.

---

*For text see Laghukāvyamālā Part four page 90.

10-19 References to Śuka and the eight Sanskrit verses.

20-129 Explanation of "Bheda" and "abheda," as applied to the idea of Ātmā, and how he, who experimentally reaches that condition of recognizing no differences, is outside of the law of *vidhi* and *nishedha*, (laws, prescribing, or forbidding).

130-156 The ātmā as one substance pervading all. Many illustrations are used to make the idea clear, as for example, as the waves of the sea are to the sea, so individual souls are to the ātmā. Waves gain form and name but the substance of the waves is the same as the ocean.

157-197 How the one substance, ātmā is seen from the point of view of name and form. One of the illustrations being that of the one substance gold, but, appearing in many ornamental forms.

198-220 The five elements, apparently showing variety, but really one substance.

221-256 When a soul realizes his oneness with the ātmā, it is like that of a river flowing into the sea. The form differs but the substance, water, is the same.

257-295 A *jivanmukta*, is one, who, while alive in this world, has gained the supreme knowledge. To such, there is consequently no prescribing or forbidding laws. No *vidhi*, no *nishedha*.

296-324 The life of a *Jivanmukta*. To him there are no differences, no high, no low, nothing desired, nothing undesired, hence he is not under prescribing or forbidding laws.

325-365 The idea of , "I," and "Thou," disappears in the one universal substance. To him, who realizes this, there are no prescribing or forbidding laws.

366-447 The fruit to be obtained from the study of this work. Life is likened to a forest in which the sensual appetites are the ferocious animals. The reading of these eight verses is a fire that burns up the forest, and with it, of necessity, the animals, the sensual appetites.

As in all of Eknāth's writings this work is full of illustrations and similes drawn from nature and human life.

In this work also mention is made of his Great grandfather Bhānudās (438).

SVĀTMASUKH.

The Svātmasukh is a philosophic poem of 511 verses. After an Invocation it begins with the usual Vedantic formulae and definitions, copiously illustrated by similes drawn from nature and human experiences. Eknāth then calls attention to the need of a *Guru,* a qualified teacher, to enable one to understand what would otherwise be unknowable. The favor of a Guru is essential. Hence the importance of a worshipful attitude towards a Guru. With the enlightenment obtained from a *sadguru,* comes joy, hence the name of this work, *svātmasukh,* or, The Joy of the Soul. It is to be noted that *bhakti* is not referred to, indeed the word *bhakti* does not once appear. It may, therefore, be called a treatise on the Dnyānamārga, the Way-of-Knowledge, thus differing from the Ānandalahari, a treatise on the Way-of-Bhakti.

The contents in the main are as follows. 1-16 Invocation. 17-103 Definition of Ātmā. Ātmā being defined as sat, chit, ānanda, these three phases are defined. Eknāth is careful to state that this trinity does not imply three substances, but is one only. Here he introduces the need of a Guru to enable one to grasp the mystery of the above (103). The terms Kāla (destruction), and Māyā are explained, and here again Eknāth pleads with the reader to seek a *sadguru,* that the evil effects of these may be overcome (142-218). From verse 230 *ātmasukh,* the joy of the soul, is dwelt upon. He gives his own personal experience, as he, through his *sadguru,* Janārdan, acquired the knowledge of the ātmā and felt the resultant joy. This joy is attainable by all (419), hence Eknāth again pleads for all to seek a *sadguru,* who holds the " key to the attainment of Brahma " (421). From 432 to 450 The importance of *bhāva,* or trust in one's *sadguru,* is stressed, and his own personal experience emphasized. " Without *bhāva* there cannot be attained the supreme end of existence " (445). Of himself he says, " (450-51) By holding to the feet of one's guru all ignorance entirely disappears. This praise of *bhāva* is not a matter for discussion; it is my personal experience. I have not performed cruel austerities, I have not depended on continual repetitions of God names, I have not taken the trouble to practise *yoga* or perform sacrifices, nor have I wandered to sacred places. For me the means of all means is the feet of my glorious *sadguru.*" In closing Eknāth calls attention to this work of his as "hard (472) for the superficial reader, but sweet for those who get its inner meaning." He closes with saying, "I have written this book for the soul's good. Merely by listening to it joy is aroused" "May the nectar of this book forever give happiness to reader and listener, as with one mouth they drink it in."

In 505 Eknāth pays tribute to his Great grandfather Bhanudās, as a poet likened to a vine, which has now the form of his great grandson developed into flower and fruit, for the happiness of the saints.

ĀNANDALAHARI.

The Ānandalahari is a small work consisting of 154 verses. In the concluding verses Eknāth explains why he calls the poem, Ānandalahari "Wave of Joy." Because when one has received salvation through the *Sadguru* there is happiness in the soul, and, "waves of joy."

In philosophy it is Vedantic, but concerns itself with the practical side of salvation through the way of *bhakti*, devotion to God. It begins with an invocation to God, using such epithets as Supreme being, Nirguṇ Life-of-the World, Primal-Cause, All-Pervader, Thou who carest for all, Invisible, Supreme-Brahma, Abode-of-Joy, The-Ruler of-all, Ocean-of-Knowledge, The Home-of-Salvation, The Sustainer-of-the-Universe. "The sight of Thee produces a joy that the Universe even cannot contain. It breaks the chain of births and deaths, and makes me fearless in heart."

Under the epithet of *Sadguru,* God is the Saviour of all who turn to Him in devotion, in true *bhakti.* "There is no salvation except through the Sadguru." "There is no necessity for Yoga, sacrifices, sacred places, austerities, abandoning the world, special religious acts, giving away of property. The one essential is the worship of the *Sadguru,*" "The worship of the Sadguru is the supreme means of salvation."

Eknāth mentions two notable examples of historic interest, king Bhartṛihari (95) and Nāmadeva (119) who gave up all to devote themselves to *bhakti.*

This small work is well worth close study as showing the emphasis that Eknāth placed on the duty and joy of intense, and true devotion to God.

ANUBHAVĀNANDA.

The Anubhavānanda is also known as Ānandānubhava. It has been published in the Kāvya-sangraha-Granth-Mālā series, Part 4, page 122, in 1903.

It consists of a dialogue between a *guru* and his disciple. The disciple asks, Who am I? The *Guru* answers his question, quoting first the Bhagavadgitā, and following it with explanations of the Vedāntic idea of the oneness of the *Parabrahma* and the individual ego. The *guru* makes full use of a play on words, and as the mystery of the philosophy deepens he has to remind the disciple frequently of the need of a *guru* to understand it. Near the close the *guru* speaks of the joy that comes through the knowledge of recognizing one's oneness with Brahma. The disciple asks the *Guru*, how he can repay him for the enlightenment that he has given him, since all earthly gifts are perishable things. The *guru* replies that the only recompense he wants is that the disciple should recognize that his oneness with Brahma means his own oneness with all creatures, and so that with enmity towards none he should live rightly and kindly with all (220, 221).

RUKMIṆISVAYAMVARA.

The Rukmiṇisvayamvara by Eknāth is based on the story as told in the Bhāgavata Purāṇa, in the Uttarārdha the 10th *skandha* and 52nd chapter. The Story is one that has attracted many Marāthi poets. In brief, it is that of Rukmiṇi, a king's daughter, hearing of the virtues and charms of Krishṇa, herself choses him to be her husband.

A very interesting historical note, supposedly by Eknāth himself, appears at the close of the work. " This book was completed in the great city of Benares, on the banks of the Maṇikarṇikā, during the celebration of the birth of Rāma in the *śaka* era, fourteen hundred and ninety-three (A.D. 1571), in the *samvatsara* Prajāpati, in the month of Chaitra, during the festival of the Rām-navami, the Rukminisvayamvara was completed."

THE EKNĀTHI BHĀGAVATA.

The Eknāthi Bhāgavata is the commentary made by Eknāth in the Marāthi language on the 31 chapters of the 11th *skandha* of the Bhāgavata Purāṇa. This and his

Rāmāyaṇa are his largest works. This is his most important work. At the close of this work he tells us where and when it was completed. "At Vārāṇaśi ((Benares), the great sacred place for salvation, in the Vikrama era in the varsha sanvatsara 1630 (A.D. 1573) this commentary was completed through the favor of Janārdan. It was in the auspicious month of Kārtika in the fortnight of the bright half of the moon, on the day of the full moon, on a Monday, this commentary of the eleventh *skandha* was completed. But listen to the date in the era and *san—vatsara* used in my own land at Pratishṭhāna, on the bank of the Godāvari river, in the Śri Rāma *kshetra,* and Danḍaka forest. In the Śalivahana era 1495 (A.D. 1573) in the Śrīmukha sanvatsara his commentary was completed." Chapter 31,552-555.

The full account of the writing of this commentary, and the persecution which it brought upon him, with however ultimate triumph, is found in the 22, 23, and 24th chapters of Keśavasvāmi's Eknātha charitra, and the same in the Bhaktalilāmrita Chapter 21, 37 to Chapter 22, 44. The Bhatavijaya and Bhimasvāmi's account are silent on the history of this commentary. According to the above accounts five chapters were written at Paiṭhaṇ and the remaining twenty-six at Benares.

Contents of the Eknāthi Bhāgavata

As the Eknāthi Bhāgavata is a commentary, it, of course, follows the original Sanskrit text. No particular system seems to govern the original text, and therefore none is to be found in the commentary. It, however, embraces almost every conceivable subject connected with the Vedāntic philosophy, with practical religion, theology, social relations, eschatology, sotericlogy, indeed the whole range of man's religious, social and ethical life.

In Mr. Pāngārkar's edition (Nirṇayasāgar Press 1915) Mr. Pāngārkar has inserted a very detailed table of contents. If Eknāth's point of view is desired on any particular subject it will not be found difficult to go through the Table of Contents with the subject in mind, noting the references for after study.

In studying the contents of the Eknāthi Bhāgavata, it is necessary to bear in mind that Eknāth was a firm believer in the divine inspiration of the Vedas, the Upnishads, the Mahābhārata, the Rāmāyaṇa, and Purāṇs. His philosophy was that of the Vedānta. He believed in the Indian social system of Caste, placing the Brāhmaṇ first. The ordinary social customs of the time in which he lived were the accepted customs of his own life. He was an idolater. He was a strict monotheist, however, in that the whole universe was but the manifestation of the One Supreme God, all Gods being manifestations or *avatārs* of the Supreme *saguṇ* God, and God in all creatures, Janijānārdan, is a conception that pervades his thought. Eknāth was not a Reformer, he had no new doctrines to preach, but what especially marks his Bhāgavata, and makes it unique in Marāthi literature is its emphasis on universal moral truths. Did he believe in Knowledge as a way of salvation? Yes, but it must be sincere, without hypocrisy. Did he believe in *Bhakti* as a way of salvation? Yes, but it must mean true love of God, and sincere. Did he believe the Brāhmaṇ held the first place in the social system? Yes, but a Brāhmaṇ, without true devotion to God, would go to Hell, and the

Śudra with true devotion would be found in Heaven. Did he believe in Caste? Yes, but his firm conception that God was in all men, Brāhmaṇa or Śudra, and even Mlenchha (foreigners) made him, if the traditional stories of him can be believed, disregard the rules of caste when the needs of humanity demanded it; as for example, the carrying of a suffering Mahār boy on his shoulder, giving refuge to a starving Mahār thief, feeding Mahārs at his own home, and even dining at the house of a pious Mahār couple, to whom he had preached the oneness of mankind, God being in all. His Comments on the Bhikshugita, the life of a converted miser, brings out very strongly how Eknāth was impressed by high moral ideals.

While the thoughts that Eknāth brings out in the Bhāgavata are based on his belief in the Scriptures, the Vedāntic philosophy, the three ways of salvation, and the then current religious and social life and customs, it is not a book with the purpose of teaching those doctrines. It is rather the thought of sincerity, absence of hypocrisy, true love of God and man, moral ideals of truth and honesty, purity of life, sacredness of marriage, condemnation of immorality, selfishness, avarice, drunkenness, and other forms of vice, in all phases of life, that runs through the book and gives it its distinction. In brief, Eknāth uses his opportunity of commenting on this passage in the Bhāgavata Purāṇa for impressing on his readers and hearers the absolute importance of high moral ideals and sincerity, in all their divine and human relationships.

The work is too large, the subjects too varied, for any detailed analysis here. But it is in Marāthi literature a unique book and worthy of study, for its presentation of moral ideals, as they appealed to that great religious teacher, to whom the trueness of the inner spirit was more than any outer form.

The edition of the Eknāthi Bhāgavata most useful to the student is that edited by Lakshmaṇa Rāmchandra Pāṅgārkar, and published by the Nirṇaya Sāgara Press, Bombay 1915. It contains a valuable table of contents and in foot notes a useful glossary of difficult words, and various readings.

BHĀVĀRTHA RĀMĀYAṆA.

According to tradition Eknāth's Marāthi version of the Vālmiki Rāmāyaṇa was his final work. Tradition ascribes the final chapters to a disciple, Gāvabā, Eknāth being an old man when he began the work, and his death prevented his completing it. This and the Eknāthi Bhāgavata, are Eknāth's great works.

As is well known to scholars, there are in India at least three recensions of the Sanskrit text of the Rāmāyaṇa, commonly known as the Bengal recension, the Bombay recension, and the Western recension. These differ considerably from one another. The sanskrit text that is imbedded in Eknāth's Rāmāyaṇa, as published at Paṇḍharpur by Gaṇeśa Supekar in 1914, follows, neither the Bengal nor the Bombay recension. The Western recension has only lately become available for scholars. I have not as yet had the opportunity of examining it, and hence cannot pronounce on the text which Eknāth presumably followed in composing his version of the Rāmāyana. That he did not have before him, either the Bengal or the Bombay recension is perfectly evident. I have no means of knowing the history of the Sanskrit text, that is printed in Eknāth's Rāmāyaṇa, presumably, however, it has come down from Eknāth's time in the various copies of manuscripts.

Eknāth's Rāmāyaṇa is a complete work, covering all the seven great divisions (Kāṇda). So far as the story of Rāma is concerned, Eknāth follows closely the Sanskrit text before him, but in details Eknāth uses his poetic liberty in expanding scenes, in adding vividness by skilful rhetorical touches, and thus creating a very readable Marāthi version of the great Indian epic.

For the traditional story of the inception of the work, and its completion by his disciple Gāvabā, see Keśavasvāmi's Eknāth charitra the 29th and 30th chapters, and the same only told in different words by Mahipati in the 24th chapter of the Bhaktalilāmrita. Eknāth is said to have cared for an apparently idiot boy, whose parents knew not what to do with him. Eknāth with his characteristic sympathy for any one in distress, received Gāvabā into his home, and little by little accomplished the miracle of stimulating his intelligence, and developing his moral character, so that he could complete the great work of his *guru,* when the *guru* from age, sickness and death had to lay down his pen. Eknāth is said to have composed his Rāmāyaṇa as far as the forty-fourth chapter of the Yuddhakāṇḍa. The remaining chapters of the Yuddhakāṇḍa, and the final Uttarakāṇḍa are ascribed to Gāvabā. (Bh. L. 24, 78) also (Ke. Ek. Ch. 29, 105).

NOTES ON THE LIFE OF EKNĀTH.

Sources of Information.

1. In Eknāth's own writings there are occasional references to himself and his family line from his Great-grandfather, Bhanudās. These references are very brief, and give us very little information, but their historic value is, of course, great.

2. Mukteśvara, grandson of Eknāth and in many ways considered the greatest poet of Mahārāshṭra, whose generally accepted dates are, born 1599 and died 1649, (M. S. page 145) is the author of Śri Khaṇḍyākhyāṇ, a story in the life of Eknāth, where Krishṇa, in the form of a Brāhmaṇa, serves Eknāth for twelve years, and his identity is finally revealed by the coming of a Brāhmaṇ from Dvārakā. (Ke. Ek. Ch. Chapter 19 and Bh. L Chapter 20, 61-150.)

3. Keśavasvāmi, whose date is uncertain, whose death is placed by Mr. Bhāve about 1684, is the author of an Eknāthcharitra. A comparison of this life of Eknāth, in its chapter on Śri Khaṇḍyā, with the same story as told by Mukteśvara, makes it perfectly evident that the two accounts are related to one another. The impression the comparison makes is very strong that Keśavasvāmi had Mukteśvara's version before his eyes when he wrote his own account, or that both drew from another account.

4. Mahipati, born 1715, died 1790, in his Bhaktavijaya, has a short and incomplete account of Eknāth, chapters 45 and 46. When compared with Mukteśvar's

chapter on Śrīkhaṇḍyā, and the same in Keśava's account, it would almost seem as though Mahapati had both before him as he wrote that story in his Bhaktavijaya, but as a whole the Bhaktavijaya differs in so many important points from Keśava's charitra, that one is rather forced to think that Mahipati depended on some other account than that of Keśava's. I cannot but ask the question whether there may not have been a complete life of Eknāth written by Mukteśvara, which is lost, only one chapter being now preserved, entitled the Śrīkhaṇḍyākhyāna, this fragment usually bears the name of Eknāth charitra. If not, such an account by Mukteśvara, there would appear to be such an one by some other author, but who could it be? The Bhaktavijaya was completed in 1762.

5. Mahipati, born 1715 died 1790, completed his Bhaktalilāmṛita in 1774. It is a full account of Eknāth from his birth to his death. It is not an independent account, but is a reproduction of Keśavasvāmi's account only in Mahipati's own words. When placed side by side, this dependence on Keśav's account is clearly evident, not only in the details of the stories, told in the same order, but in parallelisms of words and phrases. There can be no doubt that when writing the Bhaktalilāmṛita Mahipati had before his eyes a copy of Keśavasvāmi's Eknāth charitra. That Eknāth had not fogotten that he wrote an Eknāth charitra in his Bhaktavijaya, twelve years previously, is also evident, because certain portions from the Bhaktavijaya are bodily copied in his Bhaktalilāmṛita (Compare Bh. Lil. 20, 79-87 with Bh. Vij. 46, 24-33). It would seem as though when Mahipati wrote his account of Eknāth in his Bhaktalīlāmṛita, he felt that Keśavasvami's

complete account of Eknāth, was a better authority than the one he possessed when he wrote the short and incomplete account in his Bhaktavijaya. He, therefore, completely discarded his former authority and closely followed Keśava.

6. Bhimasvāmi Shirgavkar wrote a Bhaktalīlāmṛita in 1797, in which is included a Life of Eknāth. It is rather apparent that when he wrote this he had before him the Bhaktavijaya of Mahipati not the Bhaktalilāmṛita. He includes, however, many stories not told by Mahipati in either of his works. These additional stories would seem to have come to him through oral tradition, in circulation among the followers of Eknāth, for at the close of his Eknāth account he says, "I have in my slight knowledge sung the life of Eknāthsvāmi. I have heard the stories from the lips of the saints, and only those have I written in my devotion to him." Some of the stories in Mahipati's Bhaktavijaya differ in very important matters from those told in his Bhaktalilāmrita, and when these are compared with Bhimasvāmi's account, it is clear that Bhimasvāmi follows the Bhaktavijaya account, rather than the Bhaktalilāmrita version of the same story. While Bhimasvāmi's account may not seem to have much value, nevertheless it preserves traditional stories current in 1779, and cannot be entirely neglected in a study of Eknāth's life. It may be that those same stories may yet be found in some now unknown manuscript, in some collection at present unavailable.

7. Eknāth's name and fame have made a deep impression on the religious teachers of Mahārāshṭra, and many of the poets, though in brief words, sing his praise.

Among those previous to Mahipati, who thus honoured Eknāth in their writings, may be mentioned, Uddhavachidghana, Raṅganāth, Śivarāmasvāmi, Rāmavallabhadās, Siddhachaitanya, Mukund, Jayarāmasuta, Uddhavasuta, Khaṇderāya, Mukteśvara, Dāsopant, Tukārām, Niḷobā, Krishṇadayārṇava, Śridhar, Devadās, Ekeshvarāvadhuta, Amritarāya, Ātmārām Rāmdasi, and Moropant, the latter in his well known Sanmaṇimālā. None of these admiring poets add, however, to our knowledge of the life of Eknāth. They do, however, emphasize the strong influence that Eknāth left behind him. It appears from the life of Tukārām that he owed much of his inspiration, and his ideas to the great Eknāth.

The Relation of these Original Sources to One another.

The problem of determining the written source or sources from which Mukṭeśvara, Keśava and Mahipati, in his Bhaktavijaya, obtained their information, can only be stated in the form of a theory, which future discoveries may confirm or disaffirm. My present belief is that after the death of Eknāth in 1609, oral tradition preserved the stories of his life until about 1640, when some one, or several, reduced those stories to writing. One collection of traditions, which I shall call, Tradition A, was reduced to writing somewhere about 1640. From this written account Mukṭeśvara drew his Śri Khaṇdyā story, unless it may prove true that he himself was the author, who first reduced to writing the traditions of his distinguished grandfather Eknāth. From this same source Keśavasvāmī drew his account sometime before 1684. Keśavasvāmi's account was almost slavishly followed by Mahipati in his Bhaktalilāmrita completed in 1774.

Another collection of traditions, which I shall call, Tradition B, was also reduced to writing and became the authority from which Mahipati drew his information, when writing his Bhaktavijaya, completed in 1762, later followed by Bhimasvāmi. This unknown hypothetical writer may however, be identical with the one who reduced Tradition A to writing, possibly Mukteśvara himself, and in that case the difference in the two lines of accounts would have to be explained on the principle of selection, two differing streams from one source. A double authorship seems, however, the more probable; for the writing of the lives of the saints was at that period a frequent undertaking by the poet-saints of Mahārāshṭra. If this relationship of the original sources to one another should seem to some to be too hypothetical, and lacking sufficient evidence, I trust that at any rate it will be a stimulous to a more thorough study of the subject than I have been able to give it, and that some scholar will more accurately settle the problem of their relationship. In the meanwhile my own conception of their relationship is that as described above, which may be graphically represented as follows.

EKNĀTH Varying Oral Traditions Tradition A
Tradition B Unknown Redactor of Tradition A
About 1640 Unknown Redactor of Tradition B
About 1640 Mukteśvara, c. 1649 One chapter Śrī
Khaṇḍyākhyāna Keśavasvāmi, Eknāthcharitra, c. 1684
Mahipati's Bhaktavijaya c. 1762
Bhimasvāmi Shirgāvkar Bhaktalilāmṛita c. 1797
Mahipati's Bhaktalilāmṛita c. 1774.

Dates of Eknāth's Birth and Death.

The whole subject of the dates of the Mahārāshṭra poet-saints needs more research work, and more scientific handling than it has yet received. I do not propose to weary the reader with a discussion of the subject here. It is sufficient to say that Mr. Pāngārkar, in his Eknāth charitra gives the birth of Eknāth as in 1528, and his death in 1599. In this he depends on an inscription over the building containing the *samādhi* of Eknāth, the verse being, he says by Keśava (died about 1684). Also on a verse by Krishṇadayārṇava, (born 1696), which he found at Paiṭhaṇ in an old *bad;* a collection of poetry in manuscript. Rāghava also gives the same date for the death of Eknāth, 1599. The distance between the death of Eknāth and these poets, cited as authorities is considerable, and their evidence is not altogether convincing. Mr. Bhāve in his Mahārāshṭra Sārasvata, (First Edition, Page 113, note,) accepts Mr. Pāngārkar's opinion, and decided for 1599, as against the commonly held date of 1609. In his Second Edition, however, Mr. Bhave (page 245 note) accepts, without question, 1609 as the date of Eknāth's death. His birth he places in 1648. As I do not think Mr. Pāngarkar's evidence is conclusive, I shall follow for convenience sake the commonly accepted dates, 1548 for the birth, and 1609 for the death of Eknāth.

EKNĀTH'S LIFE.

As the story of Eknāth's life, told in the Bhaktalilāmrita, is practically all we know of him, the translation which follows this makes a resumé of his life unnecessary. It is well, however, to remember the law that governs tradition. A man makes a certain impression on his generation. The stories of his life are handed down from mouth to mouth. They may in time vary from the actual facts of his life, but that variation will be in the line of the impression that man made. Whether the stories told and handed down about Eknāth are the exact truth, it matters little, compared with the undisputed fact of the great and noble impression which Eknāth made on his generation. It is interesting also to observe that the literary works of Eknāth show him to be a man of the highest ethical standard, besides being a man of intense religious devotion. And this impression from his actual works corresponds, one might say, exactly with the impression gained from the stories, tradition has handed down.

Putting together, then, the impression made upon one by the reading of Eknāth's works, and the impression made by the traditional stories of his life, it is evident that he was a man of very high and noble character, with high ideals of life. Of necessity his birth, his education, his environment, his intellectual beliefs, his forms of worship, his Brāhmaṇhood, his caste ideas, all made themselves felt in the outer manifestations of his life. But it is not to these outer manifestations to which we should especially look, but to the spirit behind them, which shines out with marvellous purity. No one can read the life of Eknāth without receiving an inspiration for a higher and better life.

EKNĀTH'S FAMILY LINE.

The first ancestor of Eknāth was Bhānudās, his great grandfather. Presumably he was born at Paiṭhaṇ. The interesting story of his life is found in the Bhaktavijaya, told by Mahipati. Viṭṭhalkavi, Keśava-svāmi, and Mahipati in the Bhaktalīlāmṛita, tell the story of his bringing back to Paṇḍharpur the idol of Viṭṭhal, that had been taken away by the king of Vidyānagara. Bhimasvāmi Shirgāvkar covers practically the same ground as the Bhaktavijaya. It is however, to the Bhaktavijaya of Mahipati that we owe the fuller story of Bhānudās, though, nothing is told of his death. (See the translation of the Bhaktavijaya account by Justin E. Abbott in the Poet-Saints of Mahārāshtra Series, No. 1, on Bhānudās, and the Introduction to his life.)

His story in brief is an early inclination to the religious life. Family necessities made him yield to pressure from friends, and he became a petty cloth merchant. He insisted on telling the truth in his selling of goods, he was the world's first merchant to adopt the system of fixed prices, and he deserves to be remembered and honored as the father of that system. He prospered, but his heart was not on worldly goods. He gave up his merchant life, and devoted it entirely to the religious life. The story that has, however, made him especially famous is his bringing back of the idol of Viṭṭhal from Vidyānagara. On the authority of Eknāth himself (Eknāthi Bhāgavata 1,33) Bhāṇudās lived until the birth of his grandson, whom he named Surya, and then died.

Chakrapāṇi, son of Bhānudās and grandfather to Eknāth, together with his good wife, had the sorrow of losing their son Surya after the birth of Eknāth. To them therefore fell the care of Eknāth, whom they dearly loved during his infancy and boyhood. These loving grand parents recognized Eknāth's inclination to serious things, and provided accordingly for his religious and intellectual training. They provided a paṇdit to teach him Sanskrit. and were proud of his attainments. It was a great blow to them to have Eknāth suddenly disappear, without taking leave of them. (See Bh. Lil. 13, 62 and 15, 8-54). They knew not what had become of the boy, nor where he had gone. When at last they recognized their lost Eknāth in the youthful ascetic, their joy was great. Again they cared for him and had the joy of bringing about his marriage to a very helpful wife. They lived to an old age, with the happiness of seeing their beloved grandson honored and loved. Such is the story told by Keśavasvāmi and repeated in the Bhaktalīlāmrita.

Surya, also called Suryanārāyaṇa, and his wife Rukmiṇi were the parents of Eknāth. The Bhaktavijaya differs in its story of the childhood of Eknāth, from that told in the Bhaktalilāmrita. In the Bhaktavijaya it is the parents who brought up their son, mourned over his loss, and rejoiced at finding him again. Bhimasvāmi following the Bhaktavijaya also narrates the same version of the story of Eknāth's parental relations. (See Bhraktavijaya 45, 10-19; 45, 68, 69). The fact that Mahipati in his Bhaktalīlāmṛita follows so closely the story, as told by Keśavasvāmi, and discards many particulars, he, twelve years before, related in his Bhaktavijaya, it may perhaps be temporarily accepted as evidence that to Mahipati Keśava svāmi was a better authority for the details of Eknāth's life. We may, therefore, with Mahipati think of Eknāth as having been brought up by his grandparents after the death of his parents.

EKNĀTH'S BIRTHPLACE.

Paithan, called in ancient times by its Sanskrit title, Pratishṭhāna, was Eknāth's birthplace, the scene of his life's career, and the place of his death. Pratishṭhāna has had a long and distinguished history. It is mentioned by Ptolemy, the Greek geographer. It has figured as the capital of the Śālivāhana dynasty. It was long an important industrial centre for cotten and silk goods. It is still well known for the skill of her weavers. (Those who may wish to acquaint themselves with discussions connected with the very ancient history of Paiṭhaṇ, may consult *the Early History of the Deccan* by the late Sir Rāmkrishṇa Gopāl Bhāndārkar, Bombay Gazetteer Vol. 1 Part 11, The *Journal of the Bombay Branch of the Royal Asiatic Society Vol. VIII page 239*, and the *Indian Antiquary* Vol. XX pp. 240-248).

Paithan, or Pratishṭhānā, is situated on the left bank of the Godāvari. This river is often called the Gaṅgā. It is in the Hyderabad State, about 56 miles easterly of Ahmednagar. A good motor road extends from Ahmednagar to Paithan. A good motor road extends also from Paiṭhaṇ to Daulatābād, some 40 miles to the north the old Devagiri, where Eknāth's *Guru*, Janārdan, lived, and where Eknāth spent the early years of his discipleship with his beloved *Guru*. Eknāth's house and *mandir* are still there, renewed, however, and his *samādhi* by the river side. The annual pilgrimage to Paiṭhaṇ, in honor of Eknāth takes place on the sixth of the month of *Phalgun* (February and March) *Vadya*.

GLOSSARY OF MARATHI WORDS USED IN THE TRANSLATIONS AND OF WORDS WHOSE TRANSLATION PRESENTS DIFFICULTIES.

It might have been possible to have used fewer Marāthi words in these translations but where there is no English word that exactly expresses the Marāthi word, or where it requires a whole English phrase to express the meaning of a simple Marāthi word, it has seemed to me better to keep the Marāthi word, so familiar to India, and let the English reader learn its meaning by its context, or by the following glossary. English literature is already enriched by many Marāthi words. I see no reason why it should not still further enrich itself.

There are certain words, that are untranslatable except by a long explanation; others, where even the English word conveys only a part of the Marāthi meaning. I have translated these words and expressions as best I could, but it seems worth while to include some of these words, in a glossary in order that the reader, familiar with both languages, may understand why I have used and the special English word or words, sometimes in opposition to Dictionary authorities, even Molesworth. Usage has to be considered, as well as etymological meaning. The glossary will furnish the examples that have suggested the above remarks. I have used Molesworth's definitions freely, as carrying authority.

A

Abhang. "A particular metrical composition in praise of the Deity." It is the popular meter of the poet-saints in their hymns of praise; the *abhangs* of Eknāth, the *abhangs* of Tukārām etc.

Abheda-bhakta. A *bhakta* who has the conception of no-difference (*abheda*) between the *paramātmā* and the individual ātmā. Abheda-bhakti is the worship of God in harmony with the conception of the identity of the *paramātmā* and the soul (*ātmā*) of the worshipper.

Āchārya. Head of a religious order or sect.

Adhelā. A copper coin worth half a pice.

Agnihotri. The priest who maintains the Sacrificial fire.

Anushṭhāna. "Performance of certain ceremonies and works in propitiation of a god."

Ārati. " The ceremony of (waving around an idol, guru etc.,) a platter containing a burning lamp. 2 The platter and lamp waved." 3 The piece of poetry chanted on the occasion of the ceremony of waving expressing praise or worship.

Aśrama. 1. The abode of saints and rishis. 2. The word is also applied to four conditions of living, the *Brahmacharya,* or the period of chaste youth, and study; The *grahastha,* the householder in his married and secular life; The *vānaprastha,* who as age comes on passes his worldly cares over to others, and goes into the forest for meditation, and the fourth the *Sannyāsi*, who entirely abandons all worldly cares, delights and passions, and is wholly absorbed in contemplation or the worship of God. These four *āśramas* are considered the ideal life for a Brāhmaṇ.

Ātmā. The soul, the soul of the universe, the human soul, the vivifying principle, the self, the ego. For clearness the soul of the universe is spoken of as *parama* (supreme) *ātmā,* to distinguish it from the individual *ātmā,* the two, however, in Vedāntic philosophy being identical. Brahma, or the *Parama-ātmā,* partially defined as *satchidānanda* (Existence, intelligence, joy) is the sole existing substance. The universe, as it appears in animate and inanimate forms, with their special names, is but the form in which the *ātmā,* the *paramātmā,* or *Brahma* manifests itself. The human soul, or *ātmā,* is, therefore, only a form in which the *paramātmā* appears. The "great sentence" *aham-bramhāsmi,* I am Brahma, is the conscious acceptance of the philosophic postulate of the oneness of the soul of the universe with the individual soul.

Avatāra. Etymologically it means "one who has descended." A divine *avatāra* is the coming down to earth of such a divine being, as for example, Vishṇu in the form of Krishṇa, or Rāma. In Indian mythology, as well as in all popular conceptions, these *avatārs* are for the sake of combating some evil condition or conditions in this world, or, "to save the world from its sin and misery."

Human *avatārs* are also recognized (*mānava avatāra*), that is, a good man who has died, reappears later in some other good man, to carry on, or to complete, the work of the former. Eknāth is spoken of as an *avatār* of Dnyānadeva, and Tukārām as an avatāra of Nāmadeva. Or Eknāth, for example, is spoken of as an *avatār* of God, making him, therefore, both divine and human.

Bachnāg. Poisonous root of the Gloriosa Superba.

B

Bhajan. Adoration or worship. 2 Repeating the names of God as an act of worship. 3 A hymn, or verses sung in the worship of God.

Bhakta. "A worshipper, votary, or follower of; one devoted or attached to." While the above definition is etymologically correct, in usage, by the poet-saints, there is connected with it a moral idea. A *bhakta* implies a really pious man. A hypocrite is not a *bhakta,* though technically and outwardly he might appear to be one. 2. A special religious class devoted to the religious life.

As the different manifestation of God, and the various *avatārs* appeal differently to different minds, there is a personal choice as well as the traditional, or family choice of the special manifestation of God. There is thtrefore, a *Vishnubhakta,* a *Sivabhakta,* a *Haribhakta,* a *Rāmbhakta,* a *Viṭṭhal bhakta,* and so forth.

Bhakti. Literally, worship or adoration. It is the attitude of the *bhakta* towards God. It always implies a moral idea of sincerity and purity of worship, accompanied with love. Again and again the poet-saints affirm that there can be no *bhakti* without sincerity and love. *Bhakti* is, therefore, more than mere worship, which can be so easily a mere outward form. *Bhakti* must be the true feeling of the heart, of reverence, and love of God, whether expressed in outer forms of worship, or in the mental worship (*Mānas pujā*)

Bhaktimārga. Bhakti-mārga, the way of *Bhakti.* Three ways are recognized for the deliverance of man from the succession of births and deaths, with their sins and sorrows, and with their good deeds and joys, as well. The *Dnyānamārga* (The Way of Knowledge) holds the highest place in the minds of philosophers, because, when by true Knowledge Ignorance disappears, all causes of sin and sorrow disappear. The *Karmamārga* or Way of Works is recognized by the poet-saints as a way, but a very hard way, and a very dangerous way. In the case of both, of the above ways the danger is pride, and with pride comes a fall. The safe way, the sure way, the easy way, for all high or low, is the *bhakti-mārga,* in which a man throws himself on the mercy of God, *bhakti* on man's part, and mercy, forgiveness, and salvation, on God's part. With *bhakti* sincere, and the consequent gift from God of *moksha* (salvation, deliverance), a return to this earth is avoided, and there is eternal life in the presence of God. Because it is a sure and easy way for all, the poet-saints give the *Bhakti-mārga* the highest preference. Although, the word etymologically does not imply it, the usage of the poet-saints in strongest terms emphasizes the moral side of *Bhakti,* not only sincerity in *Bhakti,* but a pure ethical life is essential to the very idea of *Bhakti.* Eknāth's writings are especially emphatic on this importance of internal and external moral purity.

Brahma. The One substance of which all existing things consist. *Brahma* is the substance of which all things exist. Existing things have forms and names (*nāma* and *rupa*). That they exist and have *forms* and *names* is as real as is the real substance *Brahma.* To consider these forms however, as different from *Brahma,* making a duality, is due to *ignorance,* that Ignorance personified being called *māyā.* (which see.)

Brahmachāri. A Brāhmaṇa who observes the strictest chastity for a time or for life from a religious motive.

C

Chakōr. A bird that is said to subsist on moonbeams, This idea is very frequently used in poetic figures and illustrations.

Chātaka. A bird said to drink only from the clouds, hence always eager for the rain. The idea is very frequently used in poetic figures and illustrations.

Chūl. A fireplace. In its simplicity it may be three stones so arranged as to have the fire between them, and the pot or pan resting on them, or a semicircular erection of earth to contain the fire in its cavity, and support the cooking vessel on its rim.

D

Darśaṇa. Literally, sight, seeing, looking. In the religious usage of the word there is, however, much more than the physical sight, seeing or looking. There is an implication of respect, reverence and worship. There is no English word corresponding with this use of *darśana.*

Dasarā. A festival commemorating the period of the year when the Marāthā Kings started out on their campaigns.

Dhotar. The garment worn by men, consisting of a long piece of cloth wound around the body, tucked in front at the waist and also behind taking the place of the European trousers.

Divāli. The annual festival of lights.

Dnyāna. 1 Knowledge in general. 2 Knowledge of a specific and religious kind.—that which is derived from meditation and the study of philosophy; which teaches man the divine origin and nature of his immaterial portion, and the unreality of corporal enjoyments, sufferings and experiences, and the illusoriness of the external and objective universe; and which sanctifying him during life from earthly attachments and fleshly affections, accomplishes for him after death emancipation from individual existence and reunion with the universal spirit. In some parts of India the word is pronounced *gyāna.*

Dnyānamārga. The Way of knowledge. (See Dnyāna).

G

Gāyatri. A scared verse from the Vedas, repeated by Brāhmaṇs at their morning and evening devotions.

Ghatika. A period of twenty-four minutes.

Ghāṭ. 1 A mountainous range dividing countries. 2 A pass or difficult passage over a hill. 3 quay, wharf, stairs, landing place (on banks of rivers or tanks). Hence applied by washermen, tanners, dyers, Brāhmaṇs, etc., to their respective places of resort.

Ghi. Clarified butter, also known as *tūp.* The butter is melted, thus removing the water that may be in it, and then preserved in jars.

Guṇā. 1 A quality, attribute, affection, or property whether of matter or mind; a power, faculty, excellence, virtue; a property inherent or an affection supervenient in the most comprehensive sense. 2 The constitution of created things, as comprised in three *guṇas; satva* (existence truth, goodness, brightness etc.) *raja* (energy, passion, action etc.,) *tama* (evil) darkness, ignorance etc.) All created things are a mixture of the three, *Satvaguṇa, rajoguṇa,* and *tamoguṇa,* and therefore, are spoken of as *Saguṇa* (possessing these *guṇas*), and Brahma, the *paramātmā* is *nirguṇa* (unpossessed by these qualities). In God, in good men, in good things the *satva* predominates. In evil men or spirits or demons the *tama* predominates. The *rajoguṇa* is in all as the activity of either the good or the evil, or both. In God all is *satva,* because it is the *satva* that is in activity (rajoguṇa). In man there is a mixture of the *satva* and *tama,* and the activity (rajoguṇa) makes man a mixture of good and evil, sometimes the good predominating, sometimes the evil.

Guru. A religious teacher; one who instructs in the Śāstras.

H

Harbarā. A vetch, gram. Cicer arientinum.

J

Japa. The repeating of *mantras* or the names of God. A rosary may be used so as to know the number of times the *mantra* or names have been used. As this outer form requires an inner reality, *japa* stands also for meditation, for worship, for prayer, indeed for the true spiritual life of a man. The correlative of *japa* is *tapa* (which see). *Tapa,* literally religious austerity, is also extended in meaning to comprise the outer religious life of a man. *Japa,* his inner religious life and *tapa* his outer religious life.

Jiva, Śiva. When Jiva and Śiva are thus used together Jiva stands for the individual ātmā, and Śiva for the Universal ātmā.

Jondhaḷā. A cereal plant or its grain. Hulcus sorghum.

K

Kaḍabā. The stalks with their leaves of the *jondhaḷā,* or *jvāri,* Hulcus sorghum, used for fodder.

Kākiṇi. A weight of shells equal to 20 cowries.

Kaliyuga. The present, fourth age of the world, the evil age. Its duration is considered to be 432,000 years, after which the world is to be destroyed. The present year A.D. 1926 corresponds with the *Kaliyuga* 5027. The initial year is 3101 B.C. The four *yugas* are the *Kritayuga, Tretāyuga, Dvāpārayuga* and the *Kaliyuga.* The four *yugas* together make a *Mahāyuga* (Great *yuga,* 4,320,000 years. It is this evil *kaliyuga* that has necessitated the frequent *avatārs* to check evil and to save mankind from its effects.

Karma. 1 An act or a deed. 2 Religious action, as sacrifice, ablution etc., 3 Destiny; destiny being only the allotment, to be enjoyed or suffered in the present life of the fruit of good and evil actions performed in former lives. 4 Deed or action. As all actions through the laws of cause and effect determine the actions in the next life. Karma is equivalent also to fate.

Karmamārga. The law of works; the road to heaven through observance of rites and ceremonies and performance of virtuous deeds. (See Dnyānamārga, Way of Knowledge, and Bhaktimārga, Way of Devotion). "The way of deeds". One of the three ways of Deliveranc :—Dnyānamārga, Karmamārga, and Bhaktimārga.

Kāvaḍ. A bamboo lath provided with slings at each end in order to contain baskets, jars etc. and carried on the shoulder. Used for carrying water, vegetables etc.

Kavaḍi. A cawrie. A shell used in making small change.

Kirtan. Celebrating the praises of a god with music and singing. Reciting the names of the deity. In practice, however, it is a religious service of song. The leader has a topic which he delivers in song. He is accompanied with a chorus leader, and musical instruments. Following their leader the audience may break out in ecstatic repetitions of the names of God, or of the lines of a chorus.

Kshetra. A sacred spot, a sacred city, a place of pilgrimage; also the human form.

M

Mahant. 1. The chief or head of an order of Gosavis, Bairagis etc., a religious superior. 2 Applied to the head or leading man among paṇḍits, devotees etc.

Mandap. An open temporary structure, made with *bamboo* or other poles, with cloth roof and sides, erected for festal occasions, for marriages, *kirtans* etc.

Mana. Mind. According to Western psychology the mind is the soul itself viewed as thinking or imagining. Mana, however, is regarded as an organ (indriya) of thinking and imagining and not a part of the pure Ātmā (Soul).

Māyā. This word is usually translated " Illusion," but this is not a satisfactory translation. Vedantic philosophy postulates that there is but one substance, called *Brahma,* or *paramātmā,* or ātmā. This substance appears in the form of the universe, and to the various *forms* there are *names* (nāma-rupa). These forms are temporary and changeable, and with the change of form the name disappears. It is due to Ignorance that these forms are supposed to be distinct from the One Substance. The reality of these forms is not denied, but that they are distinct from the One substance is denied. That they are distinct *i.e.*, that there is a duality, is the particular form of illusion which is indicated by the word *Māyā.* In usage Māyā becomes personified as the cause of the Ignorance (*adnyāna*) which sees duality where is unity. One of the stock illustrations is that of gold in the form of various ornaments, each with its own name. That the gold appears in the form of various ornaments is not denied, but that those ornamental forms are permanent and distinct from the gold is denied. The ornaments can be melted; they disappear as ornaments, but the gold remains unchanged. To think the ornaments were distinct from the gold would be through Ignorance (adnyāna), and the cause of the ignorance, by a sort of personification is *māyā.*

Moḍi. Is the cursive writing of the Marāthi. The old Aśoka alphabet of the inscriptions, 250 B.C., gradually developed in time into the *Devanāgari,* used in transcribing Sanskrit literature, as also Marāthi literature. In business writing however, haste being important, and the pen being lifted from the paper as little as possible, it led to a change in the form of the *Devanāgari* letters, which to the casual observer seem a different character, but which can be most easily traced back to the *Devanāgari origin.* The tradition that Moḍi was brought from the south, or that it was the invention of Hemachandra in the 13th century, may be due to the character of the southern cursive writing, and it could well be that Hemachandra adopted it as the form for official documents. There is no doubt, however, that the *Modi* has developed from the *Devanāgari* simply by rapid writing, with the lifting of the pen from the paper as little as possible.

Mukti. Exemption of the spirit from further migration and the reabsorption of it into its source, the divine monad, Brahma, the substratum and substance of universal being. This deliverance from births and deaths, must be understood to include in the idea the deliverance from the sins and sorrows, even from the good deeds and joys of life, for each life is made up of these. The four forms of *mukti* are *sāyujyatā, salokatā, samipatā* and *sarupatā,* (see sāyujyatā).

N

Namaskāra. Worship, obeisance, reverential or respectful address or salutation. It is performed by joining the palms, inclining the head and pronouncing the word *namaskāra.* A *sāshtāṅga namaskār* is the prostration on the ground, so that eight parts (*ashta*) of the body touch the ground, and is the most profound method of showing reverence to God or man.

Nirguṇa. *Nir-guṇa,* Literally without a quality. *Brahma,* or *ātmā, paramātmā* the one substance which appears to us as the universe, cannot be described in human words. It is indescribable (*avāchya.*) While the one substance cannot be described the forms in which it appears can be described, and their qualities determined. The forms with their names are, therefore, *saguṇa*, (Sa-guṇa) with quality. God, as a personal being, creator of the special form, in which the universe appears, is recognized as one of the forms in which the One eternal substance appears. God, therefore, is *saguṇa,* that is, he has qualities which can be described in human understandable words. *Brahma* is *nirguṇa;* God (*iśvara*) is *saguṇa.* The gods, all *avatārs,* idols, and the visions of God, are all *saguṇa* manifestations of the *Nirguṇ Brahma,* or *nirguṇa ātmā.* The *saguṇa iśvara,* being but the one of the many forms in which the *nirguṇa iśvara* appears, are, of course, to be identified as the golden bracelet is identified with the gold of which it consists. The poet-saints therefore in their hymns of praise, their invocations, their worship, and their prayers, make no distinction. They are addressed as well to the *nirguṇa* God as to the *saguṇa God.* This identity of the *saguṇa* and the *nirguṇa* is often asserted very definitely.

Nivṛitti. Cessation from worldly concerns and engagements; also Absorption into Brahma.

O

Ovi. A stanza of a particular metre of Marāthi verse.

P

Pada. A variety of metrical compositions, used in hymns or anthems. Very many of the poet-saints have written in this metre. (See the Padasangraha in the Kāvyasangraha Series for examples).

Pāduka. An impression of a foot on stone, worshipped as the trace of some god or guru.

Pāp. Sin in the abstract, or an evil deed. It is the exact negative correlative of the word *puṇya,* goodness or holiness in the abstract, or a good or holy deed. That *pāp* and *puṇya,* evil and good deeds must receive a future reward of suffering or happiness is a part of Hindu philosophy, but this idea does not belong to the words themselves. Molesworth's Marāthi English Dictionary of 1831, founded on the Marāthi-Marāthi Dictionary of 1829, rightly defines these words. I differ absolutely from the Notes on these words in Molesworth's Second Edition of 1857, and from its definition of the word *puṇya* as "merit," a meaning it never has had in Sanskrit, or in the whole course of Marāthi literature, until influenced by Molesworth's second edition. See further discussion under *puṇya.*

Pānsupāri. A roll of the Piper-betel leaf with Areca nut, cloves, lime etc. (See Viḍā).

Pradakshiṇā. Circumabulation of an object, keeping the right side towards it These objects may be idols, sacred trees, the *tulsi* plant, a temple, even a sacred city. Keeping the object to the left would imply irreverence.

Prahar. An eighth part of the day of 24 hours. A *prahar* is therefore a period of three hours. The *prahars* begin at sunrise, at six, hence *Donprahar* (two-praharas) is noon.

Prakriti. In philosophy *prakriti* and *purusha* are words that denote the material and the immaterial universe. *Prakriti* (Nature, matter phenomenon) conceived as female, and *Purusha* (male, the soul, life, activity) by their union makes the whole universe, an anthropomorphic expression of the idea expressed in English as " matter and mind."

Prākrit. In the usage of the Marāthā poet-saints the *Prākrit* language means the Marāthi language. As distinguished from the Sanskrit (the polished language), it means the common vernacular of the people. As may be seen from the lives of the poet-saints and their works, they had to encounter a certain amount of opposition against their Marāthi, or *Prākrit* versions of the sacred Sanskrit texts. (See Eknāth's life, Bhaktalilāmrita Chapter 21).

Prārabdha. Deeds in former births determined the course of one's life in the birth previous to this. Deeds in the previous life have determined the course of one's present life. Deeds in the present life will determine the life in the next birth. This is the law of prārabdha.

Prasād. 1 Favor, graciousness, propitiousness. 2 Any thing (a fruit, flower, rice etc.) given by an idol, a guru, a saint, as a blessing or a mark of favor." 3 Food etc. presented to an idol or a holy person to be distributed, thus honored, among worshippers etc. 4

The sweetmeats and fruit distributed among the audience at the conclusion of a *kathā, kirtan*, or puraṇic reading.

Puṇya. Goodness or holiness in the abstract, or a good or holy deed. Its negative is *pāp*, or sin in the abstract, or an evil deed. In the definition of this word as also in the definition of the word pāp I differ absolutely from Molesworth's Marāthi and English Dictionary, second edition of 1857. In a note it says, "The word bears not the feeblest implication of holiness, godliness or purity of spirit." On the contrary it implies all three. And by its using the definition of "merit" (not found in the edition of 1831) an idea foreign to the word has since then been attached to this noble word. "Merit," meaning a future reward of a good deed, is no part of the meaning of the word *Puṇya*, which is simply goodness or holiness in the abstract or a holy or good deed. The idea of merit belongs to Indian philosophy, but not to the word *puṇya*. Every *puṇya* will have its reward in the future, as will every pāp, but this idea is not in the word itself.

The first edition of Molesworth of 1831, founded on the paṇḍit's Marāthi-Marāthi edition of 1829 has the correct definition. See also Monier-Williams Sanskrit dictionary under *puṇya* and *pāp*. The word puṇya, twice used in the Ṛigveda, many times used in the Upanishads, and Bhagavadgitā, and all through old Marāthi literature, is the exact negative of pāp. It, in no single instance, means "merit" as implying a future reward.

Puranpoḷi. A wheaten cake with stuffing of coarse sugar, pea flour etc.

Purāṇa. A particular class of Hindu sacred literature, generally regarded as eighteen in number. They deal with stories of the creation of the world, its destruction, its renewal, of gods, goddesses, and heroes. The eighteen are Brahma, Padma, Vishṇu, Śiva, Liṅga, Garuḍa, Nārada, Bhāgavata, Agni, Skanda, Bhavishya, Brahmavaivarta, Mārkaṇḍeya, Vāmana, Varāha, Matsya, Kūrma and Vāyu, but there are other lists of 18, slightly varying from this. Of the Purāṇs the Bhāgavata, giving the life and teachings of Krishṇa, has had the greatest influence on the thought and life of the Marāthā poet-saints.

Purāṇik. " A Brāhmaṇ well read in the Purāṇs. A public expounder of them." On account of the vast extent of Sanskrit literature those who expound the sacred books have to specialize. There are those who make a speciality of expounding some Purāṇ and are known as Purāṇiks.

Purusha. See Prakriti.

S

Sadguru. Literally a true, or good guru (see Guru). While primarily the word applies to human teachers, or gurus, the poet-saints even applied it to god, for a sadguru is regarded as a manifestation of God. The Marāthā Poet-saints frequently refer to the high moral qualities, the sincerity, the unselfishness, the unhypocritical spirit, that marks a *sadguru*, as distinguished from a false guru.

Sādhana. The means employed to obtain deliverance from births and deaths and all that life implies in its sins and sorrows and even joys.

Saguṇa. See Nirguṇa.

Santa. A saint, practically synonymous with *sādhu* (which see). He is one who has lost worldly desires and devotes himself to the worship of God. But whatever he may appear outwardly, no one is a *santa* without purity of heart and life. The appellation *Kavi-santa,* or poet-saints, designate those saints who were poets. The Marāthā poet-saints begin with Dnyāneśvara, about A.D. 1290, so far as their works are known, and continue to the present day.

Sansāra. 1 The world, mundane existence, human life, man's mortal state. 2 The affairs of life; worldly business; the vocations and engagements, the cares and troubles of secularity.

Sannyāsi. One who has cast off all worldly possessions, and carnal or natural affections, an ascetic. The poet-saints distinguish between the hypocritical, formal *Sannyāsi,* who outwardly appears only to have given up all, and the true and sincere *sannyāsi,* whose giving up of the world is genuine.

Satchidānanda. Existence-intelligence-joy. Although *Brahma,* or the *paramātmā* cannot be described in human words (avāchya), yet because, it is believed to *exist,* to be that which takes the form of *intelligent beings,* and to express itself in beings feeling *joy*—*Brahma* being the substrate of these—this definition of Brahma is very frequently employed. It should be noted that these three words, *existence, intelligence* and *joy* are not adjectives, but nouns. They do not connote that *Brahma exists,* is *intelligent* and *happy,* but that the One substance, *Brahma* in taking form, appears in the form of existing things, in the form of intelligent beings, and those possessing joy and goodness.

Sādhu. A holy man; a saint or sage; one of subdued passions and of contemplative habits. The poet-saints give the word a moral emphasis, hence a *sādhu* is a man of pure character, one truly devoted to God, a spiritually minded man; a good man. A man can appear hypocritically a *sādhu,* and not be a *sādhu,* for a *sādhu* must be pure in heart and life. The wandering professional *sādhu,* called such, may or may not be sincere, but he is not considered a true *sādhu* without purity of heart and life.

Sāshtānga-namaskāra. See Namaskāra.

Sayujyatā. The fourth of the four states in which *mukti* (final deliverance) is distinguished, *viz.,* absorption into the essence of Brahma. The four are *Sayujyatā* (absorption into the essence of Brahma;) *Salokatā* (residence in the heaven of a particular deity); *Samipatā* (Nearness to the Deity); and *Sarupatā* (Bearing the likeness of God).

Sāvadhāna. Literally "attention," "heed." At the moment of marriage, the priests in solemn tone repeat the words "*Sāvadhānam, sāvadhānam*" and at that moment the curtain between the bride and bridegroom is removed, and the marriage is complete.

Siddhi. "A supernatural power or faculty supposed to be acquirable through the performance of certain magical, mystical, or alchemical rites or processes. Eight are enumerated, *viz., aṇimā, mahimā, garimā, laghimā, prāpti, prakāmya, ishitva,* and *vaśitva.*" The powers or *siddhis* are personified as female beings, or siddhis, who come and serve those who by their austerities or otherwise gain those powers.

Śrāddha. A kind of funeral rite or ceremony in honor of the departed spirits of dead relatives, observed with great strictness at various fixed periods, especial honor being given to paternal and maternal ancestors.

Śudra. The fourth grand division of the Hindu body; also an individual of it. The four grand divisions are *Brāhmaṇa,* (the priestly caste); *Kshatriya,* (the warrior, military, governing class); *Vaiśya* (agricultural and mercantile class) and *Śudra* (the servile class, whose duty is to serve the upper three). The *atiśudra,* also called *anāmik, antyaja,* are those still lower than the śudra, and outside of the four grand divisions. Hence they are *aspriśya* (Untouchable) or *anāmika* Unmentionable).

Śānti. Peace. Unruffled mind.

Śloka. A verse, a stanza, a quantity of four lines. A particular metre; praise. In the Marāthi commentaries the *Śloka* commented on is the Sanskrit text.

Śruti. The Vedas severally or collectively. The word is from the Sanskrit, meaning "hearing."

Skandha. A section of a book, a book, a chapter.

Stotra. 1 Praise, panegyric, eulogium. 2 A book or writing in celebration of the praises; also a hymn.

Svāmi. A master or lord, the master or lord of, also the proprietor or owner of. Applied to the Deity, a god, a king, or prince, a spiritual preceptor, a husband, a holy personage, a learned Brāhmaṇ, a *Gosavi*, *Sannyāsi* etc. It is used also as a title, as Keśava-svāmi.

T

Tapa. Religious austerity, pious mortification of the body. It is especially connected with the *yoga* system, and the *yogis* carry it to its extreme limit. But it also has less austere usage, meaning the duties of life, the special duties of Brāhmaṇs, Kashatriyas, Vaiśyas and Śudras. It is, therefore, the correlative of *Japā*. *Japā* signifying the inner spiritual life, and *tapa* the outer religious life. (See Japa).

Tilak. The spot or line made with coloured earths or unguents upon the forehead. It is considered either as an ornament or as a sectarial distinction.

Tirtha. 1 A holy or sacred place, any place of pilgrimage, but especially particular spots along the course of sacred streams or in the vicinity of sacred springs. 2 A holy stream, or water brought from one. Water in which a Brāhmaṇ, sannyāsi etc., has dipped his foot, which has been poured over an idol; holy water.'

Tulsi. A plant venerated by the Hindus, Holy Basil, Ocymum sanctum. It is usually grown in an earthen altar before the door of the house, or in the garden behind the house. Its leaf is used in offerings, in garlands, and its stalks also have sacred uses. Those worshipping the plant go around it, keeping it to the right (pradakshiṇā) with palm to palm, repeating a *mantra,* or prayer.

U

Upāsanā. Worship or religious service.

V

Viḍā. A roll of the leaf of Piper-betel with Areca-nut, cloves, lime etc. It is usually chewed after a meal. It is distributed to an audience after a *kirtan,* or any public assembly, and is the final act. It is believed to be a digestive, and also as purifying the mouth. It is generally called *pan-supāri* (leaf supāri nut). Many have the habit of chewing it constantly.

Videhi. Literally, one without a body (vi-deha). In usage however, it implies a temporary or permanent absorption of the mind in a way to make one unconscious of the possession of a body, as when one is intensely listening to a *kirtan,* he is for the time being a *videhi.* Or when through a life of constant contemplation of the *ātmā,* or of God, the ascetic or devotee loses all thought of his body, of cold or heat, hunger or thirst, desires or passions, he is a *videhi.* A man is a *videhi* when the spiritual completely dominates the physical.

Vairāgi. An ascetic or devotee; one who has subdued his worldly desires and passions. The word is also applied to a class of religious mendicants. The word is also pronounced *bairāgi.* The poet-saints distinguish between the true and the hypocritical *vairāgi.*

Vairāgya. 1 Absence of worldly desire or passion. 2 Popularly, Renunciation of all sensuous delight or gratification.

W

Wādā. 1 A stately or large edifice, a mansion or palace. 2 A division of a town, a quarter, a ward, as Brahmaṇwāḍā, Mahārwāḍā."

Wādā. 1 An enclosed piece of meadow-field, or garden ground; an enclosuere. 2 A cluster of huts of agriculturists, a hamlet.

Y

Yama. The god who rules over the spirits of the dead.

Yoga. Spiritual or abstract devotion; union with Brahma through abstract meditation, or contemplation; also the practice or exercise of this sort of worship.

Yogabhrashṭa. One who was interrupted in his preceding birth during the performance of *Yoga* (abstract meditation upon *Brahma*).* As an example, a pious outcaste, devoted to Eknāth, is called a *Yogabhrashta.* In the Autobiography of Bahiṇābāi, a calf, because of its peculiar pious actions, is called a *yogabhrashṭa.* Indeed any pious person can be described as a *yogabhrashṭa,* as one whose pious life in a former birth was accidentally interrupted and has now a further opportunity.

Yogi. 1 A performer of the abstract meditation called *yoga.* 2 An ascetic or devotee in general. Popularly a *yogi* is supposed to be able to gain extraordinary powers through his practice of *yoga,* called *siddhis* (which see), and the ash-covered *yogi* is able to instil much fear in the minds of the ignorant. The poet-saints, of course, distinguish between the hypocritical *yogi* and the true *yogi* whose heart and life must be pure.

Yojana. A measure of distance equal to four *Kos* roughly about eight miles.